THE LAST OF THE APACHES

Uruguay's most notorious bank assault and the

end of the Cassidy legacy in South America

THE LAST OF THE APACHES

Richard Dean Young

Uruguay's most notorious bank assault and the
end of the Cassidy legacy in South America

The Last of the Apaches

ISBN-13: 978-1511886468
ISBN-10: 1511886463
(CreateSpace Assigned)

DEDICATION

This book is dedicated to my loving and patient wife Beverly Joan who encouraged me to keep going during the many years this project took as it bumped along its way, reminiscent of certain red Model T Ford.

Special thanks to friends in Uruguay and Argentina who opened their lives and hearts to recount the effects and memories of an unpleasant period that, in some cases, changed forever the course of their personal history.

And to those librarians, researchers and others who so kindly, in the best *espíritu uruguayo*, guided me through the books, documents and old newspapers that were necessary to put together a story that was distressingly clear back in the days of WWI, but has since mostly faded from memory.

A very special thanks to the management and staff of the *El Telégrafo* Newspaper in Paysandú, and the *La Prensa* Newspaper of Salto, who opened their archives for my perusal.

Also to the *Liga Salteña de Fútbol* which graciously allowed me to see and photograph the original founding documents of the Salto Soccer League. Argentina and Uruguay

Butch Cassidy's activities centered in Patagonia, principally in or near the Cholila Valley in Chubut Province.

The Tin Can Gang, which formed twelve years later, was active in Buenos Aires, Montevideo and especially in the Uruguay River cities of Paysandú and Salto.

https://maps.google.com.ar

Map: "Atlas Geográfico de la República Argentina," Garnier, Paris, 1881

Map: "Encyclopedia Britannica", 9th Edition, 1899

https://maps.google.com.uy

The band of *Apaches* or the *Tin Can Gang*, as we will also call them, crossed over from Argentina to Uruguay in September of 1917. They based their activities in the river city of *Paysandú*, and attempted to carry out their heist in the other major river city of *Salto*. They were eventually captured south of the *Dayman River* on the *Hervidero* Ranch.

Contents

GLOSSARY xiii

INTRODUCTION 17

CHAPTER ONE: APACHES DOWN SOUTH 21

CHAPTER TWO: SMOKING COLTS 41

CHAPTER THREE: FALLEN HERO 55

CHAPTER FOUR: THE CASSIDY LEGACY 87

CHAPTER FIVE: TRES COMPINCHES................ 105

CHAPTER SIX: "ONCE IN THE DANCE..." 167

CHAPTER SEVEN: STEAL ON WHEELS 179

CHAPTER EIGHT: MARK OF HONOR 213

CHAPTER NINE: SHOOTOUT AT DAYMAN 219

CHAPTER TEN: THE BOILER AND THE CANS 249

CHAPTER ELEVEN: THE NOT SO *OK* CORRAL ... 269

CHAPTER TWELVE: GOODBYE COMPAÑERO 287

CHAPTER THIRTEEN: THE PHANTOM OF THE
REPAIR SHOP.. 299

CHAPTER FOURTEEN: THE SINS OF THE
CRIMINALS 313

ABOUT THE AUTHOR 327

GLOSSARY

Spanish terms used in this book and their meanings

Note: these are meanings from Uruguayan and Southern Cone everyday usage; they may not exactly fit other Latin American usages.

Americano - American, a person or thing of American origin, in North America this is usually used of US citizens, but in the rest of Latin America they also consider themselves "americanos". In this book I have used the North American meaning of this word, under protest from my friends in the rest of the "Americas".

antiguo - old, antique

apellido - last name

bandolero - bandit

barrio - neighborhood

cometido - commitment, task

compadre - buddy, godfather

compañero - partner, companion, associate

compinche - crony, sidekick, chum

conflicto - conflict, strife

Cono Sur - Southern Cone; the geographical area, resembling a cone, which is comprised of Argentina, Chile and Uruguay

desesperado - desperate - usually used of desperate criminals *In the Old West of the United States this Spanish term was shortened in English to "desperado"

desplumar - remove feathers

edificio - building

Estancia - ranch

fxtranjero - foreigner

frigorífico - meat packing plant

fuerza - strength

gordo - well fed, a bit round

grueso - thick

gringo - a foreigner, usually referring to Europeans like the Italians but also referring to North Americans of European descent

grito - to yell, call out

hervidero - boiler

jefe - chief, boss

malestar - anger, discontent, this word also has a health-related use as in a physical discomfort

nada - nothing

negociante - businessman

nombre - name

pandilla - gang, mob

Pandilla Salvaje - Wild Bunch

peon - pawn, laborer, roustabout

Policía Fronteriza - Frontier Police

Pulpería - tavern and country store

prendimiento - project, plan, scheme (a rioplatense term, not used like this in other parts of Latin America)

río - river

Rio de la Plata - River Platte - literally "River of Silver" - the large river that separates Uruguay and Argentina, really more of a river "mouth" as it is made up of the confluence of several large rivers, Río Paraná and Río Uruguay, as well as several smaller rivers out of Argentina's hinterland

Rioplatense - of or pertaining to the countries or cultures of the countries that share the Río de la Plata

Salteño - native of the Uruguayan District of Salto, or pertaining to Salto

sanatorio - hospital

simpatía - sympathy

sinverguenza - shameless person, a real idiot

talabartería - saddlery

ternura - tenderness

traición - treason

trámites - procedures, paper work, red tape

Uruguayo - Uruguayan, of or pertaining to Uruguay

Yanqui - Yankee - used for all North Americans from the USA without reference to zone, and especially for southerners

INTRODUCTION

Crouched in some of the most miserable, thorny underbrush ever naturally appearing on God's normally good earth, were three *desesperados* from whom fear emanated almost as palpably as the smell of their sweat; it had been two days of running and hiding under the best cover possible, and that vegetation happened to include some of the most uncomfortable and impassable thickets one might ever choose to enter. They had managed to move west about ten miles, right up to the banks of the Uruguay River, hoping to swim back over to the Argentine side. With hundreds of officers beating the brush along the river, they then moved some nine miles to the south, zigzagging back and forth on the ranch looking for cover and trying to avoid the authorities. Now open farmland laid in front of them both west towards the River and east towards the north-south Salto-Paysandú railroad.

The river might just give them a chance to cross over under the cover of darkness; to somehow escape the narrowing net that had been thrown around them by 350 police and army troops, and even patrol boats moving up and down the big river. All their pursuers were primed to shoot, because these three wannabe robbers had just killed the most popular sports hero in north Uruguay.

They had just barely escaped at the crossing of the Dayman River with only the clothes on their backs, a collection of weapons and some canned food in their small backpacks. Even drinkable water was hard to find, because approaching the banks of the smaller Dayman River risked a run-in with their pursuers, and stopping at any of the several streams that crisscrossed the large ranch would bring them out in the open.

They had done everything possible to avoid detection, they had moved at night and holed up during the day. But the uncanny ability of the troops, who were literally beating the bushes as they followed their trail, seemed almost mystical. Not one of this gang of three paid a thought to the fact that each time they ate they had simply left the tin cans on the ground after their furtive meal.

Few today would pay attention to the odd tin can lying along the path, but back in 1917 those cans stood out like sign posts, pointing the way for the ever encroaching officers who had determined to bring these *sinvergüenzas* to justice, dead or alive.

At least one in this gang may have been associated with Butch Cassidy's Wild Bunch in Patagonia, southern Argentina. Much careful planning preceded the heist, this was the *Cassidy* legacy. But it went horribly awry because of the reaction of a muscular, fast-moving British sportsman who happened to be the Bank Manager.

The trail of cans was getting shorter while all of the Uruguayan press was curiously referring to this gang as "*Apaches*". We will also refer to this sad crew as the *Tin Can Gang*.

The three "Apaches" captured on the Hervidero Ranch

CHAPTER ONE: APACHES DOWN SOUTH

"The criminal is the creative artist; the detective only the critic."
G. K. Chesterton

Upon entering the office of the *El Telégrafo* Newspaper in Paysandú I announced to the two receptionists behind the counter, "I'm looking for Apaches." After explaining to the surprised newspaper staff just who were the Apaches I was seeking, the newspaper's editor gave me free access (1) to the archived copies of the actual newspapers printed back in 1917 when a gang of American and Mexican bank robbers crossed over from Argentina to Uruguay with the intention of robbing one of the richest banks along the river that separates the two countries.

@Richard Dean Young

They made the river city of Paysandú their center of operations for the detailed planning that was needed to pull off the heist without major snafus. Such planning was always a mark of Butch Cassidy and his sidekicks; Butch was known for his careful preparations, striking his targets from a prudent distance, and he was especially careful that these strikes would be far from where he would be holed up or living.

Frank Lewis, not his real name which remains a mystery, the apparent leader of this gang of Apaches, may have been with Butch Cassidy in Patagonia, Argentina some 12 years earlier. We will analyze this possible connection in later chapters. We have only a few hints of Lewis's wanderings and activities between the time Cassidy and the Sundance Kid left Argentina in 1906 and the attempted robbery of the Bank of London in Salto, Uruguay in October of 1917. But those years were likely spent in Argentina itself, and the assault in Salto was indeed the first and only incursion of North American outlaws into Argentina's smaller neighbor to the east.

Headlines in La Prensa on the capture of the "Apaches"

"The celebrated apaches of the red car, now in prison"

Now, where did they get the idea that North American crooks were Apaches? The same lore from the Old West that kept many North Americans entertained through the newspapers, books and magazines of the late 19th and early 20th centuries was followed assiduously down south by highly literate societies in both Argentina and Uruguay, so everyone would know who were the real Apaches up north.

The President of Argentina, Figueroa Alcorta, attends La Rural in 1910

Each year, in the early part of the 20th century, a troupe of American cowboys arrived in Buenos Aires for *La Rural*, the largest fair and rodeo show of South America. Argentina's wealth came from its interior ranches and especially from its cattle and meat packing plants, thus La Rural was an event attended especially by the high society of Buenos Aires. It was discovered that several of the cowboys who performed with the American troupes were actually hunted criminals from much further north who decided that performing in South America was preferable to a jail stay back home. (2)

Les Apaches Parisiens

While the connection between Argentina and the American Old West, and a group of its outlaws who transferred south, has been well documented, the *Apache* terminology, that came to distinguish this new breed of bandoleer's, has a completely different provenance, or, at least, a more circuitous route from its true origin to its application in South America.

Some of the Paris "Apaches" who compared their daring and strength to that of the famous American tribe.

The fame of the Apache tribe was well known in South America, but the use of the tribal name *Apache* to distinguish modern bank robbers, gang members and a whole variety thugs did not arrive in South America along a direct line. Rather the youth gang culture of Paris literally passed on this moniker to the South American criminal element.

In the early 20th century the young street thugs and hooligans of Paris decided to name themselves after the famous Apache tribe of recent American lore. Not only did they use this indigenous tribal name to distinguish their criminal societies; two of their more notorious leaders took the names of Cochise and Geronimo.

The Fighting Apaches

ENCORE LES RÔDEURS !
Rencontre d'Apaches et d'agents de police sur la place de la Bastille

Batalla entre apaches y gendarmes en los Campos Eliseos. Le Petit Journal Ilustreo 14/08/1904.
Image 2 of 14

CLOSE ✖

An all-out battle between d'Apaches and the Paris Police in the Campos Eliseos. Image published in Le Petit Journal Ilustree, August 14, 1904

    The Paris gangs, like those of New York, had violent clashes with the Paris police and were the scourge of the French middle class. They preferred using a wicked looking weapon that became known as the *Apache Revolver*; a pinfire pepperbox contraption, mounted with both brass knuckles and a knife blade.

    It is no secret that Argentina and Uruguay looked to France as their model of culture, architecture and all other aspects of the finer side of life. At the same time the criminal element in both Argentina and Uruguay, as well as the press, began to use this "Parisian" underworld title, evidently with no conscious thought of just who were the real Apaches. Buenos Aires and Montevideo even produced tangos about their *Apaches* who were running from the law, and Europeans produced films where the Paris Apaches were central figures. (3)

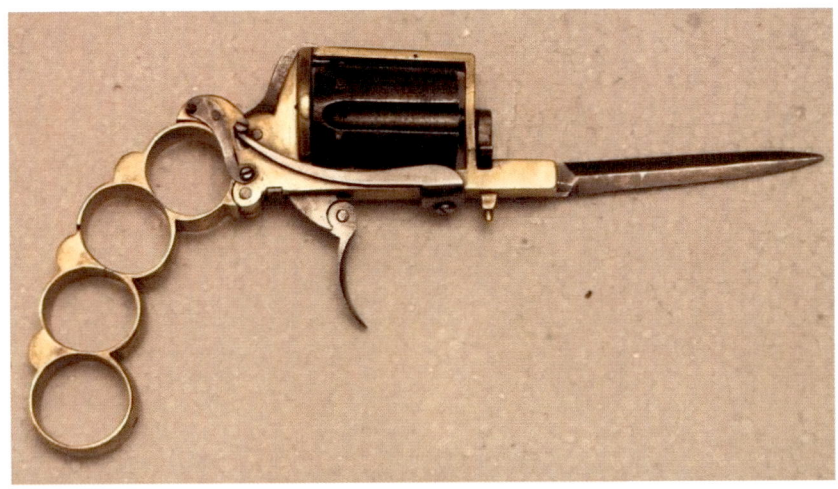

The Apache Revolver; *many like this were manufactured in Belgium by L. Dolne. Photograph from the collection of a friend in Belgium*

Some studies state that it was the Parisian press itself that gave these youth gangs the Apache name, similar to what appears to have followed in the Southern Cone of South America where the press indeed had a major part in applying this tribal name to the criminal element. However in Paris, where the youth gang leaders enthusiastically named themselves after Apache chiefs, it is obvious that the adoption of these American Indian titles was much more than a simple invention of the press. (4)

Apache Uruguayo

Dedicado al distinguido señor don Enrique Piqué.

Tango Criollo

(1er. Premio en el concurso verificado por el Casino de Montevideo)

F. Baldomir

Apaches in Music
A tango composed by Francisco Baldomir highlighting the criminal element in Montevideo

The First World War in Europe brought to an end the phenomena of the Paris Apaches. The military authorities gleefully inducted almost all of these kids into the French Army and sent them to the front. The Apache title basically disappears from France after the War's devastating impact as well the social tumult and cultural change that placed all of France into a new, grimly altered world.

But in South America, where the war was basically *news*, no such changes took place. So the use of the Apache designation continued on as before right through the 1920's.

During this period the *apache* tangos were composed. However in the next several decades this name took an increasingly diminished role as part of the language of delinquency in both Argentina and Uruguay.

By contrast the identification of North American outlaws as Apaches disappears much sooner because the presence of *yanqui* outlaws was severely reduced by arrests, imprisonments and death. This decline in number as well as fame of the American bad guy happened during the same WWI years that saw the disappearance of the Paris Apaches. As far as we know the last reference in the Southern Cone press to North American *desesperado Apaches* was to this very gang and its infamous assault in Uruguay.

Fort Apache

Even today the Apache symbol is linked to the toughest, most dangerous neighborhood on the outskirts of Buenos Aires. A series of drab monoblock buildings were raised in the 1960's, supposedly to resolve the problems of another earlier rough and miserable barrio. But today Fuerte Apache continues to be the fiercest and most intractable area of gangs, crime and hopelessness in all of the huge metropolitan area of Greater Buenos Aires. The famous Argentine Juventus player, Carlos Tévez, grew up in this hellhole and remembers shots outside his family's windows and terror of going out at night. The letters FA in Buenos Aires stand for the brutal side of life, whether it is taken by a singing group, by a gang or sewn onto a T-shirt to give it some true grit.

Nothing of the Apache about him...

When our gang of two Americans and one Mexican made their daring raid on the unsuspecting Bank in Salto, the newspapers spontaneously called them "Apaches", as they would have done concerning any local or foreign criminal association. One reference that appeared right after the capture of the gang, which stands out as exceptionally humorous to us, came from a Salto paper which, when identifying Pablo Martinez, the rural and poorly educated Mexican, literally said of him, *"he has nothing of the Apache about him."* (5)

The contradiction arises from just who were the real Apaches, because, of the three captured gang members, only Martinez would look to us at all like a real Apache, and if he had Indian blood, which was likely, he could well have had a distant link to that tribe. But for the reporters of that day, mostly of European background, and operating in their own cultural setting, this Mexican just didn't look like someone from the common criminal element to which they were accustomed. This would be like saying that a particular criminal today in New York or Chicago had none of the *Mafia* about him.

The Wild Bunch Down South

"Mr. & Mrs. Place" at the Cassidy-Sundance Ranch in Cholila, Chubut, Southern Argentina

Apart from the criminal handles imported from France, there was a whole string of "imported" North American outlaws who arrived and carried out a series of famous robberies and shootouts in Argentina in the early 20th century. Some of the most famous hits were perpetrated by members of Butch Cassidy's gang. Cassidy and the Sundance Kid mostly kept their names clean and attempted to establish themselves as honorable ranchers in Patagonia, with land and animals purchased thanks to their proceeds from up north. But some of their sidekicks were not as careful, and these entered into the ignoble chronicles of robbers, murderers and otherwise unsavory *Apaches* of the Southern Cone of South America.

Many have written about the stay of Butch Cassidy and the Sundance Kid, alias James Ryan and Harry Place, in Argentina, and in those accounts we find some of their *compadres* who didn't make the same studied attempt to steer clear of trouble, either close to or far from home.

One of the best studies of these men and their exploits in Southern Argentina was written by Santa Fe author and journalist Osvaldo Aguirre, titled, *"La Pandilla Salvaje - Butch Cassidy en la Patagonia."* (6)

We will not recount the Cassidy story in Argentina other than to point out the link to a Frank Lewis who lived in the southern Argentine Province of Santa Cruz, and the appearance of another Frank Lewis 12 years later in Uruguay.

The Cassidy-Sundance cabins in Cholila, today in disrepair

The real Frank Lewis was a rancher who had been born in Tierra del Fuego to British parents from the Falkland Islands. Indeed, he was the first person of European origins to be born in Tierra del Fuego. He and his brother William entered the lore of the southern lands when in the winter of 1894 they moved 1500 sheep over 150 miles from *Cabeza del Mar* on the Strait of Magellan up to their new ranch at *Cañadón del Toro* to the west of the Port of *San Julián* in Santa Cruz Province. This area, like almost all of Patagonia at that time, was open range, a detail that also attracted Cassidy and Associates.

Cholila, Chubut, Argentina
Underlying image from Google Earth, 2006

In 1905 Frank Lewis actually met three members of the Cassidy gang twice. These same North Americans, on the February 14, 1905, robbed the Bank of London and *Tarapacá*, an institution funded with British capital, in Rio Gallegos on the far southern Atlantic shore of Argentina's Patagonia. Supposedly the two robbers were Butch and the Sundance Kid; the true identity of the two men is disputed, but in any case it was either Butch and Sundance or two of their crew.

New York Herald Article - US Outlaws in Argentina
*Chuckles upon seeing the above spelling of Desesperados,
also a right-handed outlaw with his holster on backwards.*

The best scholarship, by Aguirre, points to the well-planned heist as fitting quite well into Cassidy's penchant for planning, his pattern of ingratiating himself with local sources of information, and especially in the almost comic play-out of the robbery that takes the whole town by surprise.

Before the heist Frank Lewis first met this group along the *Río Gallegos* and evidently spent a few days with them, because he recounted that every morning they would chase their horses into the river and swim them across and back. When Frank asked why they were doing this, they answered that one day they might have to cross the same river in a hurry. (7)

Later, after the robbery, Frank again met up with the same three gang members when they were heading north along the *Río Chico* at a place known as *Cerro Conche*. (8) Frank then went to Puerto Santa Cruz to inform the authorities of his two encounters with the outlaws, but evidently his report was not taken that seriously.

In Uruguay there has long been a view that the later Salto Bank assault was somehow connected with Cassidy's Wild Bunch. We will later detail our investigations into what appears to be a somewhat tenuous but tantalizing connection. And many questions still need to be answered both concerning the real identity of the gang that appears in Uruguay in 1917 and the previous activities of the Cassidy bunch further south.

Several of Cassidy's Wild Bunch had appeared with him even earlier than the Bank heist in Rio Gallegos. These outlaws were found together further north in Patagonia, in Chubut Province, where the two *businessmen* along with Etta Place had set up their ranch in *Cholila* up against the Andes mountain range. All, like Cassidy and the Sundance Kid, took false names because of their records in the United States. And some were caught locally in different acts of skullduggery; these therefore disappeared from Cassidy's loose band at one time or another. Two of the names that appeared under these circumstances were Grice, no first name given, and Emil Hood.

Some even surmised that Harvey Logan, Kid Curry, was with Cassidy in Argentina, and there were disputed reports of his actions there as well as his simultaneously verified death in the US.

La Rural, Buenos Aires, 1946

Parade of *Los Toros at La Rural*, Buenos Aires

In this study we will ask: could the *Uruguayan* Frank Lewis be one of these players who earlier accompanied the Wild Bunch in Chubut Province in northern Patagonia, and then moved about a 1000 miles southeast to the coastal area of southern Patagonia, perhaps stayed there some years and finally ended up in La Plata and Buenos Aires?

Moving that far inside Argentina would not seem at all daunting for a criminal who had already moved at least 7000 miles south from the USA to be able to breathe easier. Whether the two gang members who ingratiated themselves with the Rio Gallegos community only to later rob their bank were really Cassidy and Sundance Kid, or if they were two others whose names appear with the gang further north, it is, for our study, more important to note that the real Frank Lewis' testimony mentions three North Americans, not two.

It is now known that at least one of the Cassidy associates, who got in trouble further north in Chubut Province, never showed up there again. Would he or another of Cassidy's associates be the third rider that Lewis met those two times? Would this third man have then decided to borrow Frank Lewis' name? We will try to tie together some of these strings as we move along with the story.

Ricardo Perkins, Manuel Sánchez and Robert Evans

Three outlaws on a beach near Río Gallegos in 1908. Perkins and Evans were both connected earlier with Butch Cassidy in Chubut Province

Another, perhaps more plausible, explanation for the appearance of a second Frank Lewis connected to American outlaw elements is that he was one of the rodeo show crowd that moved south to avoid criminal prosecution in the US. His choice of the name of Frank Lewis could then have been a coincidence or have something to do with names or associations he worked out from his North American past. That he was linked to, and later sought out by, an American criminal gang is unmistakably established by the investigations that followed the Salto assault.

Photographs and Identities

We are left with quite grainy newspaper photographs of the gang that was captured in Uruguay on October 19, 1917. None of the photographs we have gives a clear likeness of any known Wild Bunch member. This is twelve years later and appearances can change in that period of time, at least partially. At the same time, there are no surviving photographs of several of Cassidy's Argentine sidekicks. Also, the best photos from Uruguay seem to have been taken right after the attempted robbery when the two American outlaws were roughed up some by the police, and even more by a mob when they arrived at the police station; so their photos not only show them without shoes, a precaution against flight, but also with their hair wildly messed up. We'll see later that a policeman's sword did some of the messing. Along with their Mexican sidekick they do look like a ragtag crew after the arrest - actually, for us, they may have come a bit closer to our image of real Apaches.

References: Chapter I

1. For this quick and open access to the newspaper's archives it helped that I am a Baptist Pastor, because Hugo Batista, author and appreciated contributor of weekly columns for the newspaper in this historic city on the Uruguay River, was the local Baptist Pastor... a somewhat 1unusual phenomena in Uruguay - not that he was a Baptist Pastor, rather that a Baptist Pastor wrote for an important regional paper.

2. Osvaldo Aguirre, "La Pandilla Salvaje - Butch Cassidy en la Patagonia," Grupo Editorial Norma, Buenos Aires, 2004), p. 210

3. A famous 1915 silent film, *Les Vampires*, re-released in 2005 in DVD, is not only unique for being one of the longest films ever made, 7 hours, but because it highlighted the Apache gangs of Paris. A 1927 French/German Film with Ruth Weyher, directed by Nikolai Mahkoff, was titled *Die Apachen von Paris* - "Apaches of Paris", it tells the story of an attempt to reform the youth gangs of Paris during the War years.

4. *"During the Belle Époque, Paris journalists revived the custom of calling gangs after Indian tribes, designating youth gangs collectively as Apaches. Reports concerning these youths mixed myth with reality. Supposedly, they numbered 20-30,000 altogether in the Paris metropolitan area, but in fact they were divided into a number of neighborhood gangs, each with its own territory.... Fearful citizens associated Apaches with robbery, and in 1910 there was a lively debate in the press as to whether or not flogging should be reinstituted... All Apaches vanished into the army in 1914."*

Pieter Spierenburg, "A History of Murder: Personal Violence in Europe from the Middle Ages to the Present," Polity Press, Cambridge, 2008, p. 173

5. "El Asalto al Banco, Nuevas Declaraciones...," *La Prensa*, Salto, October 21, p. 1, col. 2

6. Osvaldo Aguirre, op. cit.

7. Robert and Katharine Barrett, "A Yankee in Patagonia," Houghton Mifflin Company, Boston and New York, 1931, p. 250

8. Osvaldo Topcic, "Rio Gallegos, 1905, ¿Butch Cassidy Cabecilla del Robo? Asalto al Banco de Tarapaca," *Todo es Historia*, No. 276, June 1990, Buenos Aires, pp. 59-60

CHAPTER TWO: SMOKING COLTS

"GOD CREATED MAN
COL. COLT MADE THEM EQUAL."
~ Engraved on the slide of a Colt .45 ACP ~

A 1911 Colt Semi-Auto Pistol, similar to the one used to kill the bank manager.

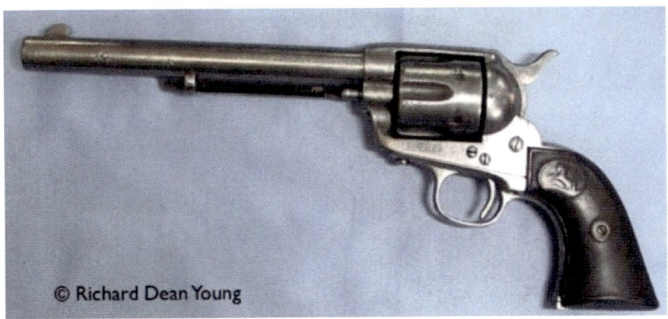

© Richard Dean Young

The actual Colt Frontier .44-40 used in the Dayman shootout.

The third time I was offered the "original" Colt Peacemaker that supposedly killed the Bank Manager in Salto, Uruguay in 1917, I was starting to paint mental images of a sensational bank robber armed with two large Colts rammed into holsters as well as another stuck in his belt, and perhaps a short-barreled Colt in the top of his boot. That image might have been accurate for pirates of an earlier century... without repeating arms, of course, but I did realize that a few purveyors of antique wares in Montevideo were trying to increase their old weapons' values by linking them to the most famous bank heist in Uruguay's history. Up to that point I was not aware of this attempted robbery and murder, and I certainly had no idea that the purported leader of the band may have been one of Butch Cassidy's sidekicks who, along with Cassidy and several others, moved to South America in the early 1900's, when the law and the Pinkertons complicated the possibility of them exercising their chosen profession in the USA's shrinking Old West.

An Unusual "Antiques Runner"

About 10 years back this seminary professor and pastor in South America, with an earlier stint in South Asia where his three children were born, began an export business that doesn't quite fit the image of an almost pacifist man of the cloth. My younger brother, Dave, in Oregon, had gone to Vietnam as a US Army armorer, and later was the gunsmith for the Oregon State Police. Signing up as a gunsmith for Vietnam was Dave's way to avoid having to carry and shoot a rifle - only to find out that the armorer is needed where the fighting is the heaviest, so he ended up having to do more than a *few repairs.* (1)

In any case, I had seen that there were a variety of antiques from the 19th and early 20th centuries in both Argentina and Uruguay, and along with collecting a few odd items that interested me, I began collecting some antique guns. I talked Dave into receiving a few shipments, and soon we had a lively antique gun business going. I have always been fascinated by history, and studying the background and provenance of these old firearms has been both a hobby and a way to pay for some our mission projects in South America. Our younger daughter, who worked with us in Montevideo for over ten years, laughs and says her dad is a "gun-runner". I correct her and others saying that, no, I am an "antiques-runner". Legally these old guns are no longer considered firearms, neither in Uruguay nor in the US, where the gun laws are quite similar.

The Realini's - A Salteña Family with a Story to Tell

The continuing offer of this special Colt Peacemaker sparked my Wild South interest, so I began to do some investigation as well as to eventually make several trips to the NW section of Uruguay where the 1917 drama had played out. And it was the fortuitous contact with a particular antique dealer in Montevideo that actually got me headed in the right direction in my investigations. Mr. Eduardo Realini grew up in Salto, owned a classic hotel in downtown Salto for many years, and always loved collecting antiques. One day he decided, with his wife and son, to move to the bigger city and start their own antique business. Mr. Realini's late wife, Graciela Curbelo White, happened to be the granddaughter of the murdered Bank Manager's best friend. On October 17, 1917 her grandfather John White, a British businessman in Salto, headed the funeral procession for George MacFarlane, the unfortunate manager of the Bank of London branch.

Eduardo Realini at home with some of his varied personal collection

Surrounded by hundreds of antiques in the Realini shop - in cases, on shelves, hanging from the walls and a few attached to the ceiling - the amiable talks with Mr. and Mrs. Realini and their son, Eduardo, gave me a sense of the magnitude of these happenings for the city of Salto and for many local families back during the First World War.

All the contemporary newspapers in which I eventually searched for information on the Salto holdup were filled with the stories and news from Europe about the then-raging First World War. Most of Uruguay's population were immigrants from Europe; Spain, Italy, Great Britain, France, Germany... and many still had relatives directly impacted by the war. For that reason the Bank of London holdup seldom moved the war in Europe from the front pages. But the news for the society in Salto itself was definitely more earth shaking than the Great War going on halfway around the world.

Headlines from the Great War

An example of the daily headlines that brought the European War close during the same year of the bank holdup in Salto. Here a photograph of a German Submarine that took refuge in Spain.

Because of the Realini family link to George MacFarlane, the murdered bank manager, they had been studying this happening for some years. Eduardo, the son, had done his own investigations, especially in the city of Salto, and gave me copies of newspaper articles and other leads into the specifics of this event. And Eduardo Jr. has especially been my sounding board for many of the discoveries I have made and personal conjectures concerning the events that transpired in 1917. Growing up among antiques and dealing with them for many years now has turned Eduardo into an accomplished historian, something that often happens with professionals in the antiques trade.

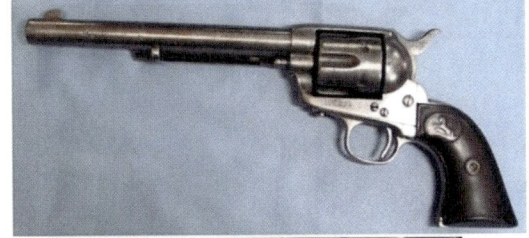

Three views of the Dayman Colt Frontier

SPECIFICS OF THE COLT:

Model Frontier

Serial #154388

Caliber: .44-40

Manufactured in 1894

TEXT OF THE NOTE FOUND IN THE BARREL OF THIS
COLT:

"This revolver was used the fatal day of October 16, 1917, in
the assault on the Bank of London and Rio de la Plata in
Salto (perpetrated by the Mexican Pablo Martínez and the
North Americans Frank Lewis and John Atkins) with which
one of the outlaws "Frank Lewis" killed with one shot
through the back the manager of said bank, Mr. George
MacFarlane." (2)

An Intriguing Colt

A quite fascinating aspect of these investigations was
the identity of the actual Colt revolver thought to have been
used to shoot Mr. MacFarlane. A local gun dealer told me his
story of years back having purchased from a widow a Colt
revolver chambered for the .44-40 Winchester cartridge, a
normal transaction for a gun dealer with an interest in
historic firearms. When he was checking out his purchase he
noticed that something was stuck in the barrel - he extracted
a rolled-up note that said simply that the revolver had been
used to kill the manager of the Bank of London in Salto.

He then told me of the many attempts he made to
certify the validity of the note. The gun very possibly was
used in the robbery and perhaps for the murder, and it
looked like one that would be carried by a desperate outlaw,
roughed up from long use, different grips on each side with
breaks and nicks. But he was unable to discover any clear
link to the Salto incident. So he finally decided to sell the
revolver in a local auction, something he now regrets. My
other friends, the Realini's, happened to be at the auction
that day, and knowing nothing about the note which had
been returned to the barrel, they bought the gun simply
because it was a Colt.

While we now know that it was not a Colt revolver that was used to kill the Bank Manager, the circumstances do point to this particular Colt being one of the actual pieces used in the holdup and subsequent shoot-outs. In Uruguay, back in those days, the arms and evidence taken after a capture like this were not always turned over to either the higher authorities or to the courts, and were almost never stored as evidence. In fact there was a tradition that a confiscated firearm should be given to the arresting policeman who had endangered his life while carrying out his duty.

The "Seagull's" Revolver

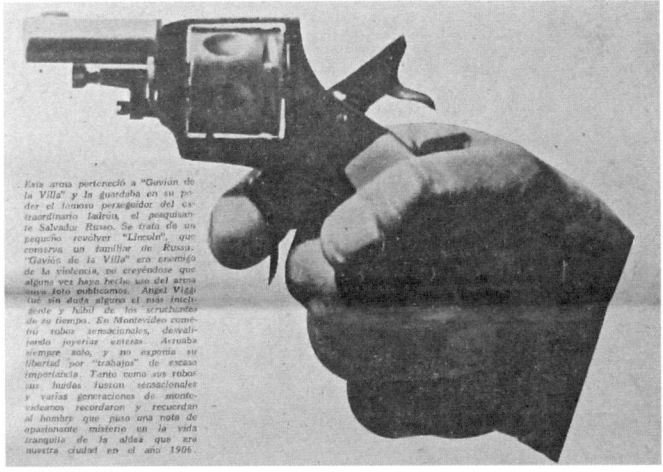

The Seagull's tiny revolver

The revolver belonging to "El Gavión" - confiscated and kept by Inspector Russo who finally arrested this jewelry store thief in Montevideo, Uruguay, December, 1906.

I have in my own collection a small Belgian revolver that has a documentary link back through a Montevideo family to the investigative officer who finally captured the most famous jewelry store thief in South America; the burglar was an Italian known as the *El Gavión* - the seagull.

47

He was famous for working alone. No incidents are known of his actually using his small .320 pistol, and he was even more notorious for *flying* free from jails, entrapments and other near misses.

The investigating and arresting officer of *El Gavión* in Montevideo, Salvador Russo, was known in the early 20th century for capturing several important thieves, and a few years back his family finally put up for sale their historic firearm. (3)

The Real Murder Weapon

The actual firearm that was used to kill the manager of the Bank of London in Salto was a 1911 Colt semi-automatic pistol chambered for the .45 ACP cartridges. This pistol was handed over when the three outlaws were arrested and returned to Salto. Both the Salto *La Prensa* newspaper and *El Telégrafo* of Paysandú report on October 18th, citing the findings of the autopsy done on Mr. MacFarlane, that the bullet that killed the Bank manager had entered from his right side, passed through the right lung, through the heart and then lodged in his left lung. The bullet itself was recovered from MacFarlane's body during the autopsy, and was identified as a copper-jacketed projectile that had been fired by a *Browning* pistol; the 1911 .45 ACP "Browning" Colt. (4) Later it was established that it had been the Mexican member of the gang, Pablo Martínez, who fired the fatal shot. (5)

The *Tribuna Salteña's* list of captured arms does not include MacFarlane's own revolver, which was taken by the thieves. But the bank manager's firearm was mentioned in several other newspaper accounts among the items found on the three Apaches when they were captured. MacFarlane's gun was a fancy nickeled revolver with mother-of-pearl grips. Also not listed were any left-over Colt .45 ACP cartridges, but an ammo clip for the Colt .45 was left behind at the Bank after the assault.

If there were any .45 Colt cartridges left they were most likely "requisitioned" for personal use by officers at the time of the arrest, although there is good reason to believe that much of the gang's ammunition was used up in the two gun battles that followed the bank hit. The arresting officers, who took the Colt .44 revolver and perhaps a few other captured items, did turn in some .32 caliber cartridges as well as the Remington rifle cartridges which were unique new bullets for Uruguay and could not be used in any of the more popular rifles and carbines then in service. They had to turn in the new Remington carbines because of the attention they drew after multiple public mentions of their use in newspaper articles. The Colt .45 semi-auto pistol could not be "requisitioned" because it was the real murder weapon. But several items were taken for personal use or even for later official use.

Because they were carbines, the Remington's were often referred to as "Winchester's" before the actual capture. The Winchester Carbine, usually chambered for the .44-40 cartridge, was in use all over the Southern Cone and was the best known firearm in South America.

No information was ever given as to the make or chambering of MacFarlane's revolver, but we assume it is item "k" on the published list and was either a British Bulldog type revolver chambered for the .38 S&W cartridge or a Smith & Wesson top-break revolver because these were widely sold in a configuration with pearl grips and a nickeled finish. But the fact that they mention an "imitation" Smith & Wesson revolver, "d" on the list, makes it improbable that they would have trouble recognizing a real Smith & Wesson, had one been captured. In the early 20th century there were a great variety of handguns chambered for the .38 S&W, but in Uruguay the three main types in use were the British Webley Revolver, the Smith & Wesson and an assortment of British and Belgian Bulldog revolvers.

The List of Captured Weapons, Ammunition, etc. from *Tribuna Salteña*

    a. 2 Remington Carbines repeaters (6)

    b. 1 Colt Revolver, caliber 38

    c. 1 Colt Pistol "repeater"

    d. 1 Revolver, Imitation Smith & Wesson

    e. 2 belts with holsters

    f. 1 belt without a holster

    g. 1 jar of vasoline for the firearms

    h. 49 Remington cartridges

    i. 16 revolver cartridges, cal. 32

    j. 1 Revolver, caliber 32

    k. 1 Revolver caliber 38

    l. 1 blue hat with the brim destroyed by a gunshot (7).

The other item not included on any of the lists is the .44-40 Colt revolver, but there is reference, as we will see later, of a policeman being wounded by a .44 revolver cartridge in one of the shootouts the Apaches had with law officers.

By our modern investigative standards there were quite a few lapses in the procedures and reports made by the arresting officers. But we have to remember the date, and more importantly, the fact that Uruguay had never ever experienced a bank holdup. And this one turned out to be even more tragic and spectacular than many of the previous assaults that even banks in Argentina had experienced in the two preceding decades.

References: Chapter 2

1. I avoided the draft because I was in Canada as a student of divinity, which gave me the 4-D classification on my draft card. 4-D is the only classification that can never be called for duty; it applies to Ministers, students of divinity and lunatics - literally.

2. *"Este revolver fué utilisado [sic] el fatídico 16 de octubre de 1917, en el asalto al Banco de Londres y Río de la Plata de Salto, (Perpetrado por el mejicano Pablo Martínez y los norteamericanos Frank Lewis y John Atkins) con el cuál uno de los forajidos "Frank Lewis"* mató de un disparo por la espalda al gerente de dicho banco el Sr: George Macfarlane"*

Transcribed from the note found in the barrel of the Colt Frontier Revolver belonging to Mr. Eduardo Realini, Montevideo, Uruguay. *Because the newspapers first reported that Lewis had fired the fatal shot, and because the court did not later identify the author of the crime, many in Uruguay and even in Salto continued to believe that Frank Lewis was the person who pulled the trigger.

3. Arnoldo del Campo, "El Gavión de la Villa," *Revista Mundial*, Año VIII, Nº 154, September 1947, Montevideo, pp. 6-8,

4. "Una Banda de Apaches...La Autopsia y el Sepelio," *La Prensa*, Paysandú, October 17, 1917, p. 1, col. 5

5. "El Asalto al Banco," *La Prensa*, Salto, October 21, 1917, p. 1, col. 2

6. Repeater is mentioned concerning the two carbines and the Colt 1911 Semi-auto pistol; in Spanish this can mean a *semi-auto repeater* as in the Colt pistol, or *repeater* can refer to one of several different rifles with either semi-auto systems or lever actions, like Winchesters, as well as pump action rifles. Several reports mention the "modern" rifles

that the gang carried. The two long guns taken from the prisoners were Remington Model 14 Pump Carbines, in production between 1912 and 1936, and almost certainly chambered for the .35 Remington* cartridge. The .35 Remington would not be a match, at least in effective range, for the 7x57 Mauser cartridges which were used in the rifles carried by the Police and Military of Uruguay, but the .35 was a very good short-range cartridge with a tremendous knock-down punch at up to 150 yards.

*A newspaper photograph shows two later model Remington 14-1/2 Carbines. These were represented as the two long guns used by the outlaws in the Dayman River shootout. It also shows the cartridges as .44-40 Winchester rounds. The problem with this is that all the reports of the ammunition later captured say that the rifle rounds were "Remington". The .44-40 was a Winchester cartridge, not a Remington cartridge. The Remington Model 14 Carbine could be chambered for four "new" Remington cartridges, all of almost equal stopping power as the .35 Remington round. These were the .25, .30, .32 and .35 Remington cartridges. We only know of the .35 Remington cartridge being imported to Uruguay.

7. *"Los objetos que llevaban los Apaches:*

En poder de los apaches se encontraban los siguientes objetos:

2 carabinas Remington de repetición

1 revolver Colt calibre 38

1 pistola Colt de repetición

1 revolver imitación Smith

2 cintos con cananas

1 cinto sin canana

1 pomo vaselina para armas

49 balas Remington

16 balas revolver 32

21 balas revolver 38

1 gorra azul con visera destruido por balazo"

"El asalto al banco de Londres...Los objetos que llevaban los apaches," Tribuna Salteña, Salto, October 19, 1917, p.4, column 3

Note: The *Tribuna* article does not include many secondary items that other newspapers did list, like clothing, shaving supplies, a mirror, etc., nor does it include a very important checkbook belonging to Mr. Atkins.

CHAPTER THREE: FALLEN HERO

Manifestación de "simpatía" frente á la Jefatura del Salto

"Some Actions are even baser than the people who commit them."
Joaquim Maria Machado de Assis

When the captured gang was returned to Salto from the Ranch south of the Dayman River where they were corralled after two and a half days of massive search, all of the newspapers of Salto and Paysandú noted the large crowds that gathered in front of the police station. The crowd was infuriated and literally tried to lynch the three thugs who had killed one of their most beloved sports heroes. The newspaper's photo above gives this title to the scene: "Manifestation of *Sympathy* in Front of the Police Headquarters in Salto." (1) While there was true sympathy for the fallen bank manager, the word *"simpatíá"* used for the manifestation itself is a remarkably mild euphemism for the real feelings that were expressed during those hours of shock and horror. The only book ever written that mentions this incident, *"Salto de Ayer y Hoy"* by Eduardo Taborda, published in 1947, includes a chapter about the Salto assault. Taborda writes that when two of the criminals were about to be introduced into the police station by the main door,

"...the crowd rose up and tried to lynch them, which was energetically avoided by the authorities, using the butts of their Mausers." (2)

A newspaper article from Salto tells of at least two irate individuals who approached with loaded revolvers trying to get a clear line of fire, especially at Frank Lewis, who had initially been identified as the assassin.

"The public, forming a circle around the car, brutally punished the delinquents, amid shouts and insults, while from a short distance two men, whose names are unknown, were pointing their revolvers to end the life of Atkins, Lewis and Martínez. In order to control the situation, the Chief of Police and other policemen grappled with the public to prevent the prisoners being torn away." (3)

Three cars transporting the prisoners to the Salto police headquarters had arrived at about 11 a.m. on Thursday, the 18th of October, the same day of the early morning capture of the bandits. One of the cars, with only Atkins aboard, was wisely taken around to the back of the police station, but the two cars in which Lewis and Martínez were being transported approached the front entrance, right where the huge crowd was gathered. It was here, squarely in front of the main entrance to the police headquarters that Lewis especially got roughed up badly by the "sympathetic" crowd.

"La Jefatura" - Police Headquarters, Salto

The Police Headquarters in Salto, Uruguay, where the three "Apaches" were returned after their capture

A reporter for the Salto *Tribuna* Newspaper had accompanied the photographer who captured the pictures of the crowd in front of the Headquarters, and he commented later that Lewis' head had fallen onto the hood of the car. It would have taken some exceptional physical violence to throw a man out of the front passenger seat of a Ford Model T and slam him directly onto the hood. Lewis had his hands tied behind his back, so defending himself had been impossible. The same reporter, who had been close enough to notice such details, wrote that the Police Chief, Bernardo Gómez, standing up on the side of the car behind, which was carrying Martínez, used an unloaded Mauser rifle to part the crowd so the two cars could enter the Headquarters' inner patio. (4)

Some papers simply reported the public reaction giving details of the especially angry rough-up, but others did lament the lack of police readiness for such a lynching crowd, and some actually pointed out the illegality of allowing such treatment.

"And that is how we saw with disgust that they landed punches, they slapped and spat on their faces, their hair was pulled. The prisoners received here their first tortures, which the police could well have avoided." (5)

And the abuse didn't stop there, one of the Salto newspapers, in two different articles, deplored the situation that reigned in the jail itself for several hours after the prisoners were delivered to the police headquarters. People moved in and out at will, talked with the prisoners and even threatened them. (6) The action of several young men, who showed up at the jail to threaten the prisoners, comes across like the furious ravings of a modern gang of soccer hooligans:

"It is claimed that some young men were in the prisoners' cells threatening them saying that there would be a rapid judgement and warning two of the bandits that the next morning they would be shot in the public square." (7)

George Lovell MacFarlane

Just who was this George MacFarlane who generated so much sympathy? George Lovell MacFarlane was born in 1880 to a Scottish family in Middlesex, England, a community which is now part of greater London. When he was 11 years old he moved with his family to Santa Fe Province in Argentina. His dad was one of thousands of British citizens who came to the Southern Cone of South America in the last decades of the 19th century.

George MacFarlane c1912

Pampa Beef and British Investment

The beef produced on the Pampas of Argentina has no rival anywhere in the world. Back in the late 16th century a few head of cattle got away from the first Spanish colonizers of Buenos Aires; after some years they caught one or two of the beasts and couldn't believe the tenderness and taste of the meat. Down through the geological ages the glaciations of the Andes Mountains and deposits of loess on the humid pampas have produced the deepest topsoil known on earth. In Iowa, North America's best beef producing region, the topsoil at times reaches six to eight feet; compared to the six to *eight* inches that most of us live with elsewhere. On the pampas of Argentina the topsoil easily descends to thirty feet. That produces a prairie grass with prodigious amounts of nutrients. Cattle that eat this grass are not sent to a feed lot to prepare the meat for sale - it is ready to eat right off the hoof. There are European and especially British restaurants and hotel chains that only use Argentine beef.

It was the growing beef industry, and especially the top-rate beef products that drew the interest of British companies and investment towards the end of the 19th century.

Many today are unaware that the largest group of expatriate British subjects in the world at the end of the 19th

59

century was not found in India; rather it was residing in Buenos Aires. While Argentina, Chile and Uruguay were not part of the British Empire; they certainly formed part of the British business empire of that period. The British especially invested in the beef industry of the Southern Cone; they built many of the meat packing plants, and they both built and operated the railways in both Argentina and Uruguay. They also put in dams, roads and whatever else was needed to help establish the businesses as well as the infrastructures of these countries.

An enlightening study on development showed how in the late 19th and early 20th centuries the British put the capital earned from their far-flung empire primarily into four overseas countries that were stable, progressive and sympathetic to British interests; these were the United States, Canada, Australia and *Argentina*. (8) In a large sense it was British money that made these countries strong economic centers. Uruguay was also part of that picture, but as a small country it was not included in the study.

Swift Meat Packing Plant Montevideo

American-Uruguayan Meat Packing Plant 1907

The one country on this list that eventually rejected the British influence and money, for nationalistic reasons, was Argentina - this corresponded essentially with the first

60

military take-overs in the 1930's, the later nationalization of the railroads by Juan Peron, and an anti-imperialistic notion rooted more in emotion than in real-world economics and solid growth.

Argentina has never regained its early 20th century standing as the 7th richest nation in the world, while, for obvious reasons, it does keep its standing as the 8th largest country in the world in terms of land mass.

In 2011 the country that did take 7th place in GDP worldwide was, ironically, Great Britain. And Great Britain's old investment targets have done pretty well; the US is #1, Canada is #11 and Australia is #12, while the educated, resource-rich, but mismanaged country of Argentina has slipped down to #26; behind Iran and Norway. Uruguay took a similar nationalistic route to that of Argentina, although the results were not as drastic.

Belgrano Athletic Club

George, front left, in a photograph of the Belgrano Athletic Club upon winning the Tie Cup in 1900

The Soccer Connection

Besides their business acumen, financial investments and some limited British cultural influence on the Southern Cone countries, the British also imported their favorite sport.

In the early 1890's the MacFarlane family moved to Buenos Aires, where in 1896 they formed one of the first soccer clubs in Argentina: Belgrano Athletic Club. The photo here shows young George who played with this club in Argentina. He and his family went on to exercise an important role in the introduction of this *British* sport to the Southern Cone.

George and Daisy in Uruguay

In June of 1907, after a time in England, George MacFarlane married Daisy MacVicar, and in July set sail with his new wife to take on a job with the Bank of London branch in Montevideo, Uruguay. After George Robert, their first son, was born in Montevideo in March of 1908, the MacFarlane's were assigned to Salto, where George became the accountant of the Salto Branch. Between 1908 and his death in 1917, four more children arrived in the MacFarlane home. During most of this time they resided at N° 98 Rivera Street.

Then in March of 1917 George MacFarlane replaced Theodore Rudolf Bourse as manager of the Bank of London in Salto. (9) It was at this time that the MacFarlane family moved into the official residence reserved for the bank manager. This house was right next to the Bank of London which itself was located in the financial center of the city at N° 43 Sarandi Street.

The MacFarlanes had resided in this house only seven months when George was murdered. Since George MacFarlane had moved to the Southern Cone with his family at the young age of eleven he became what we call today a "third culture kid." He learned Spanish early in life, and evidently learned it well. He was able to take in the culture and ways of the Italian and Spanish immigrants to both

Argentina and Uruguay in an informal, natural way. We later find George mixing easily in both the Anglo-Uruguayan circles as well as in the unique Latin world of Uruguay's intellectual and business society - a society that was soon to become the most educated in the world. Even today literacy in Uruguay is higher than in the USA.

MacFarlane and the Salto Soccer League

George MacFarlane had become the most loved sports figure in Salto precisely because of his dedication to the youth of that city and the introduction of soccer into its sports culture. From the time he arrived in north Uruguay, George began teaching, along with two other British businessmen, Frederick Dickinson and George Armstrong, the *British* game of soccer. Among the personal comments made by these friends concerning George we discovered that he had a nickname, at least among his British friends; they affectionately called him "Mac." (10)

On June 14, 1911 George MacFarlane became the founding President of the new *Liga Salteña de Fútbol* - Salto Soccer League. Not only did MacFarlane teach the game of soccer, he was also the first referee for the games of the Salto Soccer League.

Salto's River Port

The beach that can just barely be seen behind the dock was where we think MacFarlane, Dickinson and others taught the youth of Salto the game of soccer.

There was a working class barrio just to the north of city along the Uruguay River. From that neighborhood many workers walked each day to the large meat packing plant, *Frigorífico La Caballada*, further south along the river. On a low spot next to the river, somewhere between the working class neighborhood and the meat packing plant, close to where the city of Salto itself now reaches the river today, historian Alberto Equiluz tells of George and his friends teaching the young *Salteños*, many just coming off their shifts and others about to show up for work, how to play soccer. (11)

Uniforms, Soccer Balls and Dedication

MacFarlane and his friends did not merely train and organize several teams, they put up their own funds and commitment to the end of establishing soccer in the region, this by importing from England the uniforms, soccer balls and other items necessary to get started one of Uruguay's most lively regional soccer leagues.

```
ACTA DE FUNDACION DE LA "LIGA SALTEÑA DE FUTBOL".-

ACTA No.1, DEL 14 DE JULIO DE 1911.-

PRIMER PRESIDENTE: Jorge L. Macfarlane.-PRIMER SECRETARIO: Flo-
rencio Martínez.-
Otros integrantes del Primer Consejo: José L. Gomensoro; Dr.As-
drúbal Delgado; Federico Dickinson, Adolfo A. Fernández; Jorge
Armstrong.-
Clubes fundadores: "Uruguay F.C" y "Club Juventud Salteña".-
```

Spanish summary of the founding document - Salto Soccer League

MINUTES OF THE FOUNDING OF THE "SALTO SOCCER LEAGUE"

RECORD Nº 1, ON JULY 14, 1911.

FIRST PRESIDENT: Jorge L. Macfarlane. - FIRST SECRETARY: Florencio Martínez.

Other Constituents of the First Council: José L. Gomensoro; Dr. Asdrúbal Delgado; Frederico Dickinson, Adolfo A. Fernández; Jorge Armstrong.

Club's founders: "Uruguay F.C" [Uruguay Football Club] and "Salto Youth Club".

From all accounts MacFarlane himself was an athletic person who not only trained the new players, and acted as the first referee in their games, but he himself continued to participate in the game of soccer, just as he had done in his younger years. George also played tennis and was active in the rowing club. MacFarlane was a muscular, athletic young man who was also known as an all-around British gentleman.

"George MacFarlane had appeared in sporting events on both sides of the River Plate. He was a great soccer player, and took part in important championships." (12)

"Mr. MacFarlane was a gentleman who knew how to balance his serious obligations as a banker with an intense love of sports. He came here several times, asking in the name of those from Paysandú that he be the referee in the interdepartmental games with those from Salto." (13)

Salteño Soccer Players

Today two top soccer strikers, Edinson Cavani and Luis Suarez, are well-known Salteño players. Edinson is a direct product of the Salto Soccer Junior League while Luis Suarez moved with his family to Montevideo when he was six years old, although he evidently had already played soccer in Salto because his parents immediately looked for a team with which he could play after the move. These two have played with the European teams of Naples and Liverpool, and in

2013 Cavani was transferred to the Paris club Saint-Germain. And these are just two of a long line of top-rate Salteño players who have helped their teams to victory both in and out of Uruguay.

Salto - Richard Young and Alberto J. Eguiluz

Alberto Eguiluz, Salteño journalist, who introduced me to the MacFarlane sporting history and the beginnings of the local soccer league. Alberto has written about many aspects of Salto's history, including the series, "Crónicas de un Salto Desconocido." - "Chronicles of an Unknown Salto".

The most famous Uruguayan soccer player was a poor Afro-Uruguayan kid, José Leandro Andrade, who was born in the *La Cachimba* neighborhood of Salto on November 22, 1901. His family moved to Montevideo when he was quite young, so while he was not a direct product of the Salto Soccer League, José did become the most famous *Salteño* player ever. Known as the first Black soccer player in the world, José was one of the first superheroes of world soccer. Even before the first Soccer World Cup held in Uruguay in 1930, he was already famous in Europe where the French named him *Le Merveille Noire* - the Black Wonder. Like Pelé later, José as a midfielder was a virtuoso with the ball, and he led several European and South American teams to

66

victory. He was already the hero of the 1924 and 1928 Olympic Championships in Europe, when in 1930 he led the Uruguayan team to victory in the first World Cup. Few now know that José Leandro not only played the violin but was also an expert tango dancer. He became the soccer idol of the youth in his own country, but died partially blind and in poverty in 1957 at the age of 56. (14)

José Andrade - first super star of soccer

José Leandro Andrade stands third from right in the top row - he led the Uruguay selection to victory in the first Soccer World Cup in 1930.

Fading Memories

Besides being the founder and President of the Salto Soccer League, George MacFarlane was treasurer of both the Salto Lawn Tennis Club and the Larrañaga Theater Society. (15)

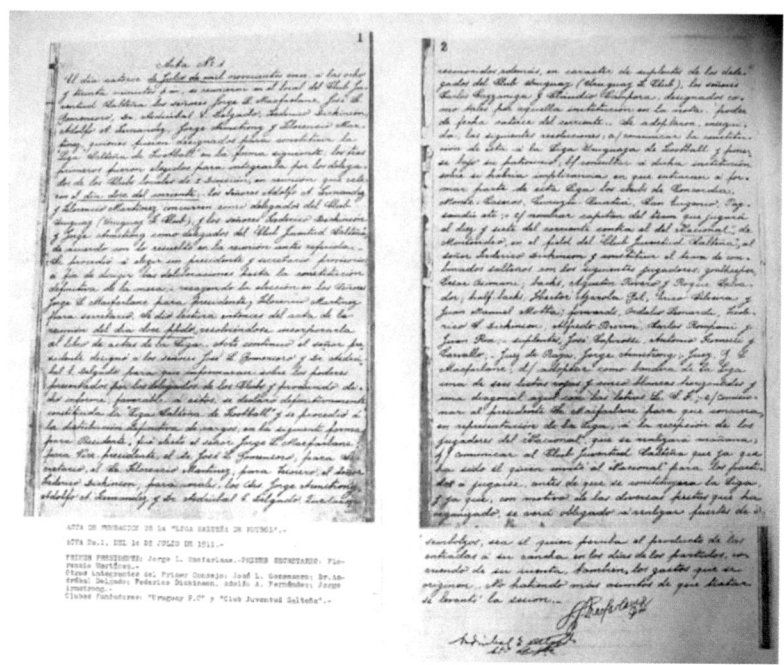

Liga Salteña de Fútbol - Julio de 1911

The founding document of the Salto Soccer League

But as time went on the memory of MacFarlane's contribution to Salto's sporting and civic life was eventually forgotten. Years later when funds were raised to build a large soccer stadium in Salto, it carried the name of his colleague Dickinson, not that of MacFarlane.

When Eduardo Taborda put together his radio programs and the later book, *Salto, Yesterday and Today*, almost three decades had passed since MacFarlane's contribution to the sporting and civic life of Salto, this followed by his sudden, tragic death, as well as that of his wife. But not all was forgotten; Taborda could say of George and his family:

*"Today at the distance of 28 years in time, we know [the following information] concerning the rest of the family MacFarlane, **of such noble and high prestige in our city...**" (16)*

And Taborda goes on to recount the little that was then known of the life of the five children who left Salto as orphans.

George Lovel MacFarlane, 1908

One-Way Trek to the Hospital

We will later see the details of the actual assault on the Bank of London that fateful Tuesday of October 16th, almost 100 years back, when George MacFarlane was brutally murdered. After he was shot directly through the side of his chest while trying to subdue one of the bank robbers, he fell to the floor gravely wounded. He had taken a slug from a Colt 1911 semi-automatic pistol. Several medical doctors were called immediately to attend to MacFarlane at the bank residence.

Among these were Doctors Cuenca, Lamas, Laffranchi, Pablo Muñoa, Maldini, Bessio and Olarreaga. (17) Soon after the time of the shooting, from approximately 2:00 p.m., these professionals attended to MacFarlane's wound, and later in the afternoon the decision was made to move him to the closest hospital, *Sanatorio Salto*. Although all of the medical personnel were of the same opinion that the internal bleeding was too great to hope for saving his life, they still decided to try a surgical intervention.

At 5:45 an improvised stretcher was arranged and MacFarlane was taken the seven blocks east along Uruguay street *"llevada a pulso,"* taken at a slow or firm pace. The *El Diario* newspaper of Paysandú gives greater detail concerning the transportation of MacFarlane to the hospital. This newspaper reports that he was hand-carried on a stretcher all the way to the hospital. This would explain the slow pace mentioned in the other news articles.

"Mr. McFarlane was anesthetized and taken on a stretcher down the street Sarandí, Dayman and then Uruguay, to the building of the Salto Hospital. A huge crowd followed the individuals and doctors who were   escorting Mr. Macfarlane." (18)

The Surgeon Dr. Pablo J. Muñoa was given the task of doing the delicate operation. It was sometime after 7:30 when they actually had MacFarlane on the operating table. Muñoa was ready to make the first incision when the other attending physician, Dr. Cuenca, took MacFarlane's pulse and motioned for Dr. Muñoa to stop - he felt that MacFarlane was slipping away. Indeed, at 7:50 PM George MacFarlane quit fighting for his life:

"....being at 7:50 that the distinguished gentleman died, sealing in martyrdom a life of honesty and work." (19)

JORGE L. MACFARLANE

Q. E. P. D.

FALLECIO AYER· 16 DE OCTUBRE DE 1917

La Comisión Directiva del «Salto Lawn Tennis Club» invita á sus asociados para el entierro del que fué su Tesorero don Jorge L. Macfarlane, que tendrá lugar hoy á las 5 de la tarde

Casa mortuoria: Sarandí N.o 43

La Comisión.

Salto, Octubre 17 de 1917.

JORGE L. MACFARLANE

Q. E. P. D.

FALLECIÓ AYER 16 DE OCTUBRE DE 1917

La Comisión Directiva de la Sociedad Teatro Larrañaga invita á los accionistas de esta institución, para concurrir al entierro del que fué su Tesorero, señor Jorge L. Macfarlane, que tendrá lugar hoy á las cinco de la tarde

Casa mortuoria: Sarandí N.o 43

Por la Comisión,

El secretario.

Única invitación.

Two funeral notices the day following George MacFarlane's death. *The first by the "Salto Lawn Tennis Club" and the second by the "Larrañaga Theater Society."*

On reading a copy of the actual death certificate of George MacFarlane, issued the day after his death, we find the curious information that his death was certified to have happened at 5:00 p.m. on the previous day, instead of 7:50 as was witnessed by several physicians. And even odder is the address given for his death, not the hospital, nor even his own residence, rather that of the Bank of London: "N° 43 Sarandí!"

The Wake and the Funeral

During the evening of Tuesday, October 16th, there was a wake at the MacFarlane residence. Friends and acquaintances stopped by to express their condolences, and many made reference as to how Daisy MacFarlane held herself as a true Englishwoman. Then at midnight, she surprised everyone by asking that they leave her alone with the body of her deceased husband. Wakes in South America almost always last the full night, and usually with many mourners. The last picture these guests held in their mind was of Daisy leaning over the casket contemplating the remains of her husband of ten years and the father of their five children.

Salto, Uruguay Street

Calle Uruguay, the street up which George MacFarlane was taken on the improvised "ambulance" to the Salto Hospital

The next day when the funeral was held at the British Cemetery, to the southwest of the main part of town, Daisy did not attend. The graveside service was announced for 5:00 p.m. on Wednesday - just 24 hours after MacFarlane had been taken to the Hospital. In the funeral procession, which included several cars, there appeared the same taxi that the Apaches had "borrowed" for use in the assault. The papers speak of the large group that attended the funeral service, but it is the name of the orator that surprises us and gives us another view of George MacFarlane. We know that MacFarlane was involved in several clubs and even cultural societies, but a special friend was the one who:

"Pronounced a beautiful speech in name of several cultural organizations, giving an expressive and worthy tribute to the deceased." (20)

The person who gave this talk was a well-known writer, educator, artist and literary critic for whom are named many schools in Uruguay today; José Pereira Rodríguez. So we discover that among the personal friends of MacFarlane are not only those of the sporting and business world of Salto, but also renowned artists and thinkers who have contributed to Uruguay's educational and cultural richness.

As we write these lines about George MacFarlane we really do sense that we are only scratching the surface of a multifaceted person who had become an integral part of Salto's society. Two paragraphs from the first page of the Salto *Diario Nuevo* newspaper express the deep shock as well as the sincere respect that the city of Salto afforded to this young man:

"The death of the knightly MacFarlane caused the deepest impression in the heart of Salto's society, where the deceased had attracted immense sympathy for his affable and generous character. Still young and illustrated, he occupied a high place in the most distinguished levels of Salto's society, where he was able to assert the prestige of his social intercourse that tested the metal of his fine education." (21)

A longer anonymous eulogy was published in the *Salto Tribuna* Newspaper the day after MacFarlane's death. Within the quite flowery style of Spanish writing, one can still capture the deep emotion and heartfelt appreciation expressed by a friend who, while admiring MacFarlane's selfless contribution to the Salto society, lamented deeply, as

73

did many, his untimely passing. The full text of the eulogy, in both Spanish and English, is quoted in the footnotes at the end of this chapter. (22)

MacFarlane's family in Argentina was notified of his death by telegraph the day after his passing. His father at that time was on a trip to England, but his mother and brothers were found in Buenos Aires, living near the *Miramonte* train station. One of George's brothers, who worked for City Bank in Buenos Aires, made attempts to travel to Salto, but a regional train strike kept him from traveling immediately. (23)

Double Tragedy

The further story of Daisy MacFarlane adds even greater sadness to the cruel murder of her husband. Daisy made a tremendous effort to hold herself up during the first three days after the assault and the death of her husband. When the three criminals were brought back to Salto she actually asked to be able to go see them in the local prison. She was accompanied by George Armstrong, one of MacFarlane's associates in the founding of the Salto Soccer League, and a Mr. Jones. (24) The Police themselves were astonished that she would ask for this encounter, and comments in the newspapers expressed surprise as to why the victim would even think of having to confront those who had done her so much personal damage.

Larrañaga Theater, Salto

After seeing the locked-up outlaws, Daisy told the police that the night before the assault she had seen the same three men in a function at the theater house known as *Au Trinón* which was located next to the bank. She had called her husband's attention to the three who had been talking together and looking "insistently" at George. Daisy said that after the function the same three men were on the sidewalk facing the bank, looking across and talking among themselves. We have testimonies from others that only Martínez was seen in Salto the night before the attempted robbery, but that doesn't rule out the possibility that all three were in downtown Salto that same night.

The only known photo of Daisy MacFarlane

The next day, Saturday October 20th, the day after asking to see the gang members at the police headquarters, Daisy fell into a deep depression; the great effort she was putting into surviving her horrendous loss, and that of her young family, finally came to an end.

A newspaper ad for the Salto Hospital, where both George and Daisy MacFarlane were taken in 1917

Daisy was admitted to the *Sanatorio Salto*, where she progressively lost all will to live. Without the knowledge that we have today concerning mental illness, both the medical establishment, where Daisy was under the care of Dr. Muñoa, and the press, found themselves at a loss regarding the roots of her condition. And the day after she was sent to Montevideo to see if others could elicit some kind of response, a note in the social section of the *Prensa* newspaper made this comment, wondering if the British temperament had something to do with her malaise:

"Bewildered, and without the intellectual guidance of her brain, she fell into several incoherent acts that some attribute to that somewhat eccentric nature of the Saxon race." (25)

This glaringly contrasts with an earlier comment on Daisy's Saxon heritage when she was seen as holding up splendidly, and this from the same newspaper...

"At all times this lady has shown exemplary fortitude, typical of the Saxon race, which has caused admiration in our social world." (26)

One-Way Trip to Montevideo

On December 5th, three days after being sent to Montevideo, and 50 days after the death of her husband, Daisy MacFarlane also passed away. Five small children were left without both parents. We will see later that relatives in Argentina took in the five children, and that the sad saga of pain and death did not end in Uruguay.

The absolute mental collapse of Daisy MacFarlane can be understood better from a later perspective, where both psychological and medical experts have studied the phenomena of the loss of will to live that has ended in death for some. There are examples, especially among older couples, cases where after a difficult life or the rigors of failing health, one of the partners dies and the other that remains seems to give up and follow quite quickly. But for this to happen in a younger couple seems unexpected.

We have to understand something of the larger context of the immigrant experience to begin to comprehend what happened to Daisy, which, of course, will never be totally understandable to us because we cannot go back and get to know her personally, nor can we converse with those who surrounded her and especially with those who treated her in those last days of her life.

Daisy was a young English girl who happened to marry a cross-culture kid from halfway around the world. While the opportunity of moving to the Southern Cone might have seemed like an adventure, the immigrant experience always takes a certain toll. One has to learn a new culture and a new language, bring a family into the world in a setting that is completely foreign and unknown, all the while learning and adapting to this new world without the support of close family and long-time friends.

For us, the fact that Daisy stayed sane and functional up to this point might be the miracle; but the incremental buildup of frustrations, unmet expectations, the feelings of loss as well as the lack of cultural anchors could well have already been taking their toll on this young woman. If this sad tragedy had not struck, she may well have survived and even thrived in this new world, but, at the very least, we can start to understand why she lost her will to live.

"There are crimes that are truly uncomely. With crimes, whatever they may be, the more blood, the more horror there is, the more imposing they are, the more picturesque, so to speak, but there are crimes that are shameful, disgraceful, all horror aside, so to speak, even far too ungracious..." – Fyodor Dostoyevsky. Demons

References: Chapter 3

1. "Manifestación de 'Simpatía' frente a la Jefatura de Salto," *El Telégrafo, Salto*, October 19, p. 1

2. *"...el pueblo se amotinó e intentó lincharlos, lo que fué evitado enérgicamente con las culatas de los mauser, por las autoridades."*

Eduardo S. Taborda, "Salto de Ayer y Hoy," Salto, 1947, p. 86, - transcribed radio programs

3. *"El público formando un círculo junto al automóvil, castigaba brutalmente, en medio de gritos e insultos, a los delincuentes mientras a corta distancia dos hombres, cuyos nombres se desconocen, apuntaban con sus revolveres para concluir la vida de Atkins*, Lewis y Martínez. Fue necesario, para dominar la situación, que el jefe político y otros funcionarios de policía lucharan con el público para evitar que los presos, les fueran arrebatados."* *Atkins was actually in the third car and did not face the crowd

"El asalto al Banco de Londres," El Pueblo Indignado," *La Prensa*, October 24, p. 1, col. 5

4. "El Asalto al Banco de Londres...Nuevas fotografías, La intentona del pueblo," *Tribuna Salteña*, Salto, October 19, p. 4, col. 2

5. *"Y es así como hemos visto con repugnancia que se les propinaron golpes de puños, se les abofeteó y escupió el rostro, se le tironeó del cabello. Los prisioneros sufrieron aquí las primeras torturas, que muy bien pudo evitar la policía."*

"Lindezas Policiales," *La Prensa*, October 21, p. 1, col. 1

6. ibid., "Lindezas policiales," *La Prensa*, October 21, p. 1, cols. 1-2,

7. *"Se afirma que unos jóvenes estuvieron en la celdas de los presos simulando formar un rápido proceso y adirtiéndolse a dos de los bandidos que a la mañana siguiente serían fusilados e la plaza."*

"Señores Jueces." *La Prensa*, Salto, October 20, p. 1, col. 1

8. Lawrence E Harrison, "Underdevelopment is a State of Mind: the Latin American Case," Center for International Affairs, Harvard University, 1985

9. Some have reported that MacFarlane went to Salto to be the manager of this branch of the Bank of London, but that would have been unlikely because of his young age and lack of experience in 1908 when he arrived in the northern Uruguay city. We also checked the records of the Anglican Church in Salto, and besides the reports of the births, for example, of the MacFarlane children who arrived in Salto, and of MacFarlane's burial on the 17th of October the day after his death, we also found a reference to a marriage, on January 15, 1912, of Theodore Rudolf Bourse - MacFarlane's boss - to Sara Juana Herrera, whose father, Nicolás Herrera was a bank manager. Bourse, at the time of his marriage, is listed in these records also as a *bank manager*. Later we

found a reference in *La Prensa* to George MacFarlane being promoted to the manager position in March of 1917.

"Una Banda de Apaches...El Gerente Señor MacFarlane, su Fallecimiento," *La Prensa*, Salto, October 17, p. 1, col. 5

10. "El Asalto al Banco...Telegramas de pésame," *Tribuna Salteña*, October 19, *op. cit.*, p. 4, column 1

11. Alberto J. Eguiluz, interviews in Salto, May 2009

12. *"Jorge MacFarlane había figurado mucho en los (word not legible) sportivos de ambas orillas del Plata. Fue un gran jugador de football, que tomó parte en grandes campeonatos."*

"Ecos del asalto al Banco, Datos sobre MacFarlane," *Tribuna Salteña*, Salto, October 20, 1917, op. cit., p. 4, col. 2

Note: we find it interesting that, writing in Spanish, they use the English term *football*, not *fútbol*, as the word is used universally today in all Spanish-speaking countries.

13. *"Era el señor Macfarlane un gentleman que sabía alternar sus graves obligaciones de banquero con una intensa afición a los deportes. Aquí vino diversas veces, reclamando por los propios sanduceros para que fuera juez en la luchas deportivas interdepartamentales con los salteños."*

"La indiada en el Salto, Muerte del Señor Macfarlane," *El Telégrafo*, Paysandú, October 17, p. 2, col. 4

14. "El Pelé de Uruguay que murió pobre y abandonado," *Clarín*, Buenos Aires, September 30, 2010

15. *La Prensa*, October 17, op. cit., p. 2

16. *"Hoy a la distancia de 28 años, en el tiempo, sabemos que el resto de la familia Macfarlane de tan noble y alto*

prestigio en nuestra ciudad, lo siguiente..." bold letters in English translation are mine.

Taborda, op. cit., p. 88,

17. "Una banda de apaches.. El Gerente Señor MacFarlane, su Fallecimiento," *La Prensa*, October 17, op. cit., p. 1, col 4

18. *"El Señor Mcfarlane fue antestesiado y conducido en unas parihuelas por la calle Sarandí, Dayman y luego Uruguay, hasta el local del Sanatorio Salto. Un enorme gentío seguía a las personas y médicos que iban escoltando al señor Macfarlane."*

"La indiada en el Salto, El señor MacFarlane," *El Diario*, Paysandú, October 19, 1917, p. 1, col. 4

19. *"siendo a las 7.50 fallecía el distinguido caballero que selló con el martirio una vida de honestidad y de labor."*

"Una banda de apaches...El gerente, Sr. Mac Farlane, su fallecimeinto," *La Prensa*, October 17, op. cit., p. 1, col 5

20. José Pereira Rodriguez *"pronunció un hermoso discurso, en nombre de varios centros sociales, haciendo un expresivo y merecido elogio del extinto."*

"Ecos del suceso de martes, Sepelio del Señor MacFarlane," *La Prensa*, October 18, p. 1, col. 3

21. *"El fallecimiento del caballero Macfarlane causó la más honda impresión en el seno de la sociedad salteña, donde el extinto se había captado inmensas simpatías por su carácter afable y generoso. Joven aún e ilustrado, ocupaba un lugar de preferencia en la más distinguida sociedad del Salto, donde su persona supo imponer los prestigios de su trato social que puso a prueba el grado de su delicada educación."*

"Los apaches en el Salto, Don Jorge Macfarlane," *Diario Nuevo*, Salto, October 17, 1917, p. 1, col. 4

22. "Anoche en nuestra ciudad

La gravedad de la herida que recibiera en la tarde de ayer el gerente del Banco de Londres señor Jorge L. Macfarlane, en las circunstancias de que damos cuenta en otro lugar, tuvo anoche a las veinte horas su fatal desenlace, en el Sanatorio Salto, a donde había sido trasladado el herido para practicársele la extracción del proyectil.

La noticia del fallecimiento del Sr. Macfarlane circuló rápidamente por todas partes, arrancando de todos los labios palabras de condenación para los bárbaros criminales y de protesta por la prematura desaparición de un culto y distinguido caballero, lleno de juventud y de esperanza, vinculado por múltiples motivos a la sociedad salteña, en cuyo seno militaba como uno de sus miembros más prestigiosos por sus dotes caballerescos y su amplio espíritu de iniciativa, dispuesto siempre a practicar el bien, ya se tratara de una obra de beneficencia o ya de realizar una idea suya o ajena que encarnara una manifestación de progreso para esta ciudad que él consideraba como la de su nacimiento por las arraigadas vinculaciones que lo ligaban a ella.

Hombre de ambientes amplios era absoluto ajeno de toda manifestación de egoísmo.

El que estas líneas escribe estaba lejos de pensar en que tan cercano se hallaba el fin de este hombre simpático a todos cuando, en conversación personal, momentos antes de la reciente asamblea americanista del Ateneo, oyó de labios del malogrado muerto frases de elogio, de gratitud y de cariño para esta ciudad, a propósito de la alta misión de cultura física y social que aquí realizan las nuevas instituciones de Remeros y de Tennis, centros, especialmente el ultimo, que han ganado los prestigios de que gozan gracias a la actividad y amplio criterio de Macfarlane.

Es un dignísimo representante de Inglaterra que muere defendiendo la enorme responsabilidad de su cargo.

El señor Macfarlane vino a Salto hace diez años a ocupar la contaduría del Banco de Londres, sucediendo en la gerencia del señor Bourse cuando este, hace pocos meses, renunció el cargo para radicarse en Buenos Aires.

Trátese de un hombre de gran porvenir que arranca a la vida, al hogar y a la sociedad cuando en cada una de esas entidades más necesaria era su presencia y su colaboración.

Si grande es en la sociedad el dolor que produce su muerte, es inmensamente mayor, sin duda alguna, en el seno de su hogar, en el corazón de su esposa y de sus cinco hijitos que la mano trágica de un apache viste de rigoroso luto.

Nosotros que supimos de la virtudes del caballero que acaba de caer para quien 'se hizo la noche en la mitad del día' podemos atestiguar de la inmensa significación de esta pérdida que ha provocado en todos los corazones un verdadero sacudimiento.

Sobre la tumba de Jorge L. Macfarlane, tempranamente abierta, deshojarán su muchos amigos la eternas siempre vivas del recuerdo."

"Jorge L. Macfarlane," Tribuna Salteña, Salto, October 17, 1917 - p. 2, col. 4

Full English translation of this eulogy:

"Last night in our city

The severity of the wound received yesterday afternoon by the manager of the Bank of London, Mr. George L. MacFarlane, in circumstances that we have reported elsewhere, at eight o'clock last night, in the Salto Hospital, where the wounded had been transferred to attend to the extraction of the projectile, had its fatal outcome.

The news of the death of Mr. MacFarlane quickly circulated everywhere, drawing from everyone's lips words of condemnation towards the barbaric criminals and protest of the untimely demise of a cultured and distinguished gentleman, full of youth and hope, bound by multiple links to Salto's society, within which he was active as one of its most prestigious members, for his chivalrous gifts and his generous spirit of initiative, always ready to do good, whether it concerned a work a charity or bringing to fruition an idea of his own or of others that embodied a manifestation of progress for this city, which he regarded as his own, because of the deeply rooted ties that bound him to her.

He was a man with spacious horizons, who was an absolute stranger to any manifestation of selfishness.

He who writes these lines could not have imagined that the end was so close for this man who was friendly to all, when, in personal conversation, just before the recent American Assembly of the Athenian Society, he heard from the lips of the unfortunate one, who has now passed, words of praise, of gratitude and of affection for this city, because of the important mission of physical and social culture that the new institutions of Rowing and Tennis are realizing, societies, especially the latter, which have won the prestige they have enjoyed, thanks to the activity and broad criteria or Mr. MacFarlane.

He is a worthy representative of England who died defending the enormous responsibility of his office.

Mr. MacFarlane came to Salto ten years ago to occupy the accounting position of the Bank of London, succeeding Mr. Bourse in its management when, a few months ago, Bourse resigned the office to move to Buenos Aires.

84

We are speaking of a man who had a great future before him, who has been torn from life, home and society, when in each of these entities his presence and collaboration was most needed.

If for society at large his death has produced sorrow, it is vastly greater, certainly within his home, in the heart of his wife and his five little children that the tragic hand of an Apache has dressed with mourning.

We who knew the virtues of this gentleman who has just fallen, who turned 'the night into full day,' can attest to the immense significance of this loss, which has caused in all our hearts a true shaking.

Over the grave of Jorge L. Macfarlane, opened early, his friends will keep the eternal memories alive forever."

23. "Cómo se Efectuó la Captura...Ante los Victimarios," *El Telégrafo*, October 18, op. cit., p. 2, col. 4

24. "El asalto al Banco de Londres, La viuda de Macfarlane," *Tribuna Salteña*, Paysandú, October 19, op. cit., p. 4, col. 3

ibid.,"Cómo se Efectuó la Captura...Ante los Victimarios," *El Telégrafo*, Paysandú, October 19, p. 2, col. 4

25. "*Desconcertada, sin la guía intelectual de su cerebro, se produjo en ella algunos actos incoherentes que algunos atribuían a esa naturaleza un tanto exéntrica de la raza sajona...*"

"Sociales," *La Prensa*, December 2

26. "*Aquella señora ha demostrado en todo momento una ejemplar entereza de ánimo, propia de la raza sajona, que ha causado admiración en nuestro mundo social.*"

"Los célebres apaches del auto rojo, La Viuda del Sr. MacFarlane," *La Prensa*, October 19. *op cit*., p. 2, col. 2

CHAPTER FOUR: THE CASSIDY LEGACY

"Criminal: a person with predatory instincts who has not sufficient capital to form a corporation." - Howard Scott

The entrance to the city of Paysandú, from its port on the Uruguay River, has hardly changed in the almost 100 years since the Tin Can Gang crossed over from Argentina to Uruguay.

The Tin Can Gang in one aspect did carry on the Cassidy legacy; this in its planning of the heist in Salto. The gang, which at the least was composed of three members: Frank Lewis, John Atkins and Pablo Martínez, arrived in Uruguay on September 21, 1917, by traveling up the Uruguay River from the port of Gualeguaychú in the *Entre Ríos* Province of Argentina, to the city of Paysandú in the country of Uruguay.

There were one or two other players or associates who remained in the background, and while one appears to have been an actual member of the band the other may have simply been a source of information or this same member by another name. Alfredo Mecuel, identified by Martínez as another Mexican, assisted the group from Montevideo, and a shadowy character named Alfred McWiden, Mecuel by another name as we shall see, was also found in Montevideo backing the gang in several ways. But the main events and actions leading up to the assault on the Bank of London in Salto were carried on in that northern region, from the city of Paysandú and in the area around Salto itself. (1)

Thriving River Cities

Paysandú and Salto were lively ports in the early 20th century. The first passenger steamers arrived at these ports on the Uruguay River in 1907, and from then on regular steamer passenger service was available for the major Uruguayan river cities from Salto in the north, to Paysandú, then on to Fray Bentos further south, and finally Gualeguaychú, Argentina. Some of the steamers would continue further to either Buenos Aires or Montevideo.

Historical "Exodus of the Oriental People" *at Salto in December 1811, crossing at the lower set of rapids.*

While the land route between Salto and Paysandú totaled 75 miles, the river route was only 57 nautical miles.

River ships and freighters could go no further north than Salto. This was because of the *"salto"* or "leap"; a natural stretch of rocky falls and rapids that could be transited at flood tide, but only by a well powered steam ship. Today a large dam, Salto Grande, crosses the river at the upper, larger set of falls, and provides electricity for both Argentina and Uruguay.

The "Big Leap"

"Salto Grande" - the larger set of falls where today stands a huge dam across the Uruguay River

The famous cattle business of both Argentina and Uruguay had attracted the investment of significant British funds as well as British companies, and the local banks were literally *moving* the ample proceeds of what would become part of the greatest economic boom ever experienced in South America.

Shopping for Banks

From all accounts of the later events in Salto, it is manifest that the Apaches had originally settled on robbing one of the banks in Salto itself. They were not simply in

Uruguay looking around to see what opportunities might present themselves, although they did present themselves as doing just that to the presiding Judge. As we have mentioned, their arrival and stay in Paysandú followed the Cassidy tradition of planning and striking from a distance. The group might cause some stir as foreigners in one town or location, but it would only be later, when their plans were carried out, that the link would be made between the hold-up and their sojourn in the distant locality where the preparations were made, in this case Paysandú.

First river steam ships

The Guarany, one of two identical steamers made in Great Britain that visited all ports on the Uruguay River.

While they stayed in Paysandú, moving out frequently to further check out the situation in Salto and set up their strike, no one there was alarmed, nor did any warning bells go off. There is no record of the Paysandú Police investigating or even observing this group, something that did happen in Salto, even then without major suspicions being raised. Frank Lewis introduced himself as a rancher or land agent looking to purchase property in Uruguay, and at the same time he said he was trying to find work for his two friends, Atkins and Martínez.

What appeared to be a sincere request for work for his two friends in a local utility company was in reality a chance to look over the office set-up, and one night during their stay in Paysandú the business was robbed of 5,000 pesos. Suspicion fell on this group only after the Salto disaster, but no link was ever made between this robbery and the Tin Can Gang.

If the locals had taken time to observe the three, they would not have noticed anything unusual about what seemed just another group of foreign business folk looking to invest in Uruguay's growing trade and especially its cattle business. The presence of a talkative Mexican *peón* type character would raise no eyebrows, because the two Americans were apparently not that fluent in Spanish, so a working-class helper would seem quite natural tagging along with two *negociante*s. Because of Frank Lewis' possible longer stay in the Southern Cone it turned out that he actually spoke Spanish, but Martinez almost always appeared translating for the two North Americans. However Lewis' fluency in Spanish, infrequently used, could be one of the reasons that he was seen as leader of the group. In most conversations it would be Lewis who would speak using Martínez as the translator, this was logical, because, as we will show later, Lewis himself spoke excellent Spanish while Atkins spoke practically none at all. By acting as the main spokesman for the group Lewis could keep a short leash on the talkative Mexican, something that Atkins would not be able to do. It was this role taken by Lewis that led to many thinking that he was the actual leader of the group.

The Base in Paysandú

The *pandilla* arrived from Argentina on September 21, 1917, and immediately checked into the finest Hotel in downtown Paysandú, the *Hotel Central*, located on the main plaza next to the Roman Catholic Cathedral. (2)

@Richard Dean Young

Headquarters in Paysandú

The old Hotel Central in Paysandú where the Tin Can Gang set up shop upon arriving in Uruguay.

Today the same building is a residence for the Roman Catholic Church. John Atkins, who was the true leader of the gang, and who bankrolled the project, paid for three days of stay for the trio, and later on the 24th paid for another seven days.

The day after arriving in Paysandú the group took a river Steamer to Salto. After that, several incursions were made into the Salto region, 75 miles north. But the planning, the purchase of animals, the gathering of supplies and other preparations were, for the most, part done in Paysandú.

Paysandú Port Today

A later type of riverboat, diesel powered, that carried on a lively trade back and forth from Argentina as well as up and down the River.

In those days the road connections were passable, but they were dirt or gravel roads used by horses, carts and a just few of the new automobiles. Most transportation between the two cities was done by river steamer or by train; and both offered daily passenger options back and forth. The rails followed the land road north to Salto, on a route that paralleled the road, but often ran several miles closer to the river. Regional railroad strikes that hit both Argentina and Uruguay right when the gang made its move to consummate the robbery in Salto, may or may not have been taken into account by the gang, but there is no doubt that the strikes made it harder for the authorities to respond.

Hotel Scanavino

On the morning of September 22, the three men checked into the Hotel Scanavino in downtown Salto. Edmund Scanavino, the owner, personally attended to the three travelers. The next day a person who was lodged in the same hotel received a letter from a friend in Paysandú telling of robberies that had been committed there in two hotels - neither the one that this group used. An Italian had been arrested but two other thieves got away. Since the robberies were perpetrated in public residences, the friend was sending a warning to Salto saying that his friend should be on his guard.

These robberies had nothing to do with our three gang members, but the person who received the letter was staying at the same hotel, and he showed the letter to Mr. Scanavino. At this point the hotel owner questioned the group about their names and their purpose for being in Salto. Today one cannot check into any hotel in Argentina nor Uruguay without immediately providing their name, documentation, home address, and so forth. It sounds as if back then the payment for the room was all that was required.

Pablo Martínez spoke for the group and identified himself by this name, later it was discovered that he was also Pablo García. He presented his associates as Frank Lewis and John Atkins. He indicated that his nationality was Mexican and that the two others were North Americans. He also said that they had arrived from Paysandú, which increased the concern of the hotel owner, who then reported to the Police that he possibly had suspicious folk lodged in his hotel. That evening a Deputy Hernandez showed up at the hotel and the following conversation was heard between him and Martínez:

> *"I would especially like to know if you came from Paysandú?"*
>
> *"Yes, sir, we came from Paysandú."* -
>
> *"Are you looking for work?"*
>
> *"That's the truth,"*
>
> *"What work would you prefer?"*
>
> *"My associates are cattle buyers."*
>
> *"And you?"*
>
> *"I'm their interpreter."* (3)

The Deputy didn't find anything particularly suspicious about the three, but the next morning the Police also asked an American to talk with the three. This unnamed American, in fact, had several conversations with them during their time in Salto, without reporting anything unusual about the visitors.

A photograph from 1890 when the London Bank building was under construction. *The tall door to the right under the overhang was where all customers and employees would enter the building. It is also the door through which passed the three Apaches in 1917. Sometime before 1917 this facade and columns were removed from the front of the building.*

Photograph from a special collection of the Museum of the National Library, Montevideo and used with permission

Casing the Bank of London

During their stay in Salto the pandilla was seen entering two banks, *El Banco de la República*, the national bank, and *El Banco de Londres*. They saw that movement in the Banco de la Republica was quite intense, so they concentrated their attention on the Bank of London. When they entered this Bank, Atkins and Lewis went straight to the section for money transfers, from there they could see all of the office set-up inside and at least partially into the rear parts of the bank.

With Martínez translating, the two asked a bank employee, either a Mr. *Espinelli* or *Minelli*, first about how to make a transfer to New York, and then about the cost of sending a sum of US$500. While Minelli was making the calculations the Americans were talking in English among themselves. Four days after this visit to the Bank of London the three returned to Paysandú on a river steamer, and Atkins went on to Buenos Aires to retrieve the funds he had deposited there.

Odd Job

Between the days of October 2nd and October 5th Frank Lewis was absent from Paysandú. Lewis said that he had also traveled to Buenos Aires on the 2nd. Several investigators pointed out that there was no steamer scheduled that day for Buenos Aires. Instead there was a train running to Salto. While it was never proven, it seems likely that Lewis made the trip back to Salto to rob the jewelry store of a Mr. Maglio. (4)

Horses, Saddles and Equipment

On the 10th of October the group was found in Paysandú using a Mr. Bottino's car to pick up items from two different saddleries, *La Talabartería Origo* and that of *Ferrero*. (5) They also attended the *Feria Ganadera*, the livestock auction of Paysandú, where with 100 pesos they purchased "three strong horses." (6) Two other newspaper accounts go into more detail concerning the purchase of the horses; these relate that they continued in Mr. Bottino's car to the dairy of a Mr. Dessimoz near the livestock auction grounds, and there they dismissed the car because individuals were waiting for them with several horses. It is most likely that Mr. Dessimoz offered the horses at the auction itself, but that the deal was completed and the horses delivered at his dairy. (7)

One newspaper account from Paysandú adds that the three, after purchasing the horses, went to the business of *César Perrero & Hijo*, where they purchased implements for three horses - we assume saddles, halters, stirrups, etc. - and paid 66 pesos for these items. They also purchased from Mr. Perrero two revolvers. Later on, when they were riding in the Dayman area, Martinez tried out one of these guns, a copy of the Smith & Wesson revolver. There is no mention of the origin of this copy, most likely Spanish, but it could have been one of two revolvers the later confiscated chambered for either the .32 or .38 cartridges.

Passenger Steam Ship "Rivadavia"

The first passenger steam ship to arrive from Buenos Aires at a port on the Uruguay River. Built in England in 1894, it made its first stop at the port of Concepción, Argentina, on February 1, 1907.

Martinez was aware that these imitation guns were not of the best quality. He later mentions that he used an imitation Smith & Wesson in the assault. We know that he killed the bank manager with the Colt semi-auto pistol, not with a revolver. We will show from testimony at the scene of the crime that he retrieved the Colt pistol from the floor before firing the fatal shot. We will also see that later, when the bandits confronted the Paysandú police on the Hervidero Ranch, that Atkins once again had the Colt pistol, and Martinez gave up a .38 Colt revolver when he surrendered. Most of the firearms seemed to have stayed with each of the actors in the various scenes, as is common in most criminal gangs because of ownership, preference or reliability, but Martínez evidently used different revolvers at different times. (8)

Coincidental Skullduggery

All of the later investigations and newspaper accounts of the time the Apaches were in Paysandú preparing for their strike further north mention several unsolved robberies in Paysandú itself, such as that of a jewelry store, and of the utility company. While no one could later pin any of these actions on the Tin Can Gang, the coincidence is more than striking.

A Low-Crime Nation

It is important to underline that Uruguay was, and is, the absolute safest country in all of the Americas. In fact, the attempted robbery of the Bank of London in Salto was the very first incident of an assault on a bank in Uruguay's history. Not until the mid-twentieth century did Uruguay begin to catch up with the rest of Latin America in terms of bank heists, holdups and other such criminal activity. And this did not then come from home grown criminals, rather it coincided on the one hand with the arrival of continental gangs after the Spanish Civil War, and on the other with the later appearance of gangs from Argentina, which, after crossing the *Rio de la Plata*, immediately went after several Uruguayan Banks which they, of course, considered soft targets.

Safe City

On the first road trip my wife and I made to Montevideo in 1989 from our home, at that time in Tucumán, northwest Argentina, when we arrived in Montevideo we found out that our hotel, right in the middle of a built-up part of the city, had no parking garage. When I asked the concierge about this, he answered, "Don't worry, your car is safe on the street - if anyone bothers it, it will most certainly be an Argentine." While showing some bias against Uruguay's large neighbor to the southwest, this statement did carry a grain of truth. Today one does not leave his car on the street at night in Montevideo without a state-of-the-art alarm system. But statistically Montevideo continues to be the safest major city from Alaska to Tierra del Fuego. (9)

It was this peace and sense of civic safety that was rudely ripped apart in this first major bank assault in Uruguay's history, and this in the even more peaceful northern city of Salto.

Misreading the Opposition

One of the challenges that didn't seem to faze these detail *bandoleros* was the personnel at the Bank of London. If you had asked them earlier what would happen if the Bank manager were to resist, they would have responded that they were more than ready to deal with him. Not in their remotest dreams would they have thought of a *bank manager* as the most popular guy in town, and they surely would have held the opinion that bank administrators were a bit soft and nicely plump around the middle from sitting in their oak swivel chairs all day long. There is no way that they could have been prepared to run up against one of the fittest athletes in Uruguay.

Grabbed from Behind

I had a "MacFarlane" experience a few years back in Montevideo, although I lived through mine. I often went to a large street market on weekends in a *barrio* close to downtown. There one can often find antiques and trinkets from the 19th century or earlier. The *Tristán Narvaja* market, named for a street where many antique shops are located, actually stretches over multiple city blocks. If one has patience, walking through this sprawling display with items on tables, on cloths placed on the ground or cages piles up, and hundreds of tarps hung for shade... one can find everything from car parts to fresh fruit to live birds. Along with the wondrously varied market items are mixed in a certain number of pickpockets and minor thieves. The dangers are not as great as in some Latin American countries. I have never heard, for example, of someone losing their finger along with a gold ring. Usually they do the quick hand-in-pocket routine once they have established where the spending money is kept. Since I am rather large, and carry a bit of weight in some sections, these small-time thugs usually leave me alone.

But one day two guys snuck up behind me, one grabbed me from behind, in a similar way to which Atkins, as we will see, tried to subdue the bank manager to keep him from using his gun. The other would-be thief, the hand-in-pocket kid, was quite tall and skinny. I never managed to get a good look at the guy who ended up somewhere in the air above my back when I let out a banshee yell and shook him off. Both were reaching for real estate as quickly as their spindly legs would allow, they had no idea that this old man, who was slowly walking down the street checking out different wares, still had enough *fuerza* to best two skinny kids!

Of course, there is always the "rest of the story," as Paul Harvey used to say; the pickpocket member of the tag team managed to extract a handful of minor bills from one of my pockets, but they all fell to the ground, and he only got away with a small coin purse. A lady came up and started picking up some of the bills, lamenting all the while about the thieves plaguing the market, then another young man picked up several peso bills, but when he handed them to me he suddenly grabbed the largest with his index finger and thumb and said, "This one's mine." In my daze, and anger and stupor, I let him take it. Only later did I realize that I got conned! There is no way that someone is going to get down and pick up someone else's strewn-about money with one of their own bills already held by thumb and forefinger!

I'm sure that my pickpocket tag-team was confident in their methodology and experience, what they did not count on was an old duffer still having some strength and spirit left in him. Just so the Apache team; they were overconfident in their strategy and planning, quite simply they had never experienced going up against an all-around sportsman, and one who had even thought through what would be his reaction should his bank ever get held up.

References: Chapter 4

1. "Una banda de apaches operando en el Salto," *La Prensa*, Salto, October 17, 1917,

2. "El Asalto al Banco...Los delinquentes en Paysandú," *La Prensa*, October 20, op. cit., p. 1, col. 2

"Ecos del asalto...La Estadía en Paysandú...," *Tribuna Salteña*, October 21, op. cit., p. 1

3. *"Tendría especial interés en saber... si ustedes vienen de Paysandú.*

> Sí, señor, de Paysandú venimos. -
>
> ¿En busca de trabajo?
>
> Es verdad. -
>
> Qué trabajo prefieren?
>
> Mis compañeros son compradores de ganado. -
>
> ¿Y usted?
>
> Yo soy intérprete. -"

"El Asalto al Banco...Las sospechas se desvanecen," *La Prensa*, Salto, October 24, p. 1, col. 3

4. "La indiada en el Salto, Las coincidencias," *El Diario*, Paysandú, October 17, p. 1, col. 5

5. ibid.,"La indiada en el Salto, Los delinquentes han estado en Paysandú," *El Diario*, October 17, p. 1, col. 4

"Ecos de…La Estadía..," *Tribuna Salteña*, October 21, op. cit., p. 1, col. 5

6. ibid., "La Indiada en el Salto - Los delincuentes…," *El Diario*, October 17, p. 1, col. 4

Rios Silva, "El Asalto al Banco de Londres, Siguen los viajes," *Tribuna Salteña*, November 4, 1917, p. 5, col. 3

*Three horses for only 100 pesos was a bargain basement price compared with the value of horses in the US. During the War the Uruguayan peso had appreciated significantly over the dollar and by 1918 it took 78 pesos to buy US $100. So the amount paid for the horses was close to US $128, but even that was less than half of what the same animals would have cost in the USA. While the value of horses did fall in the US during the war, their average value by 1913-1915 was in the range of $150 to $180 US dollars. After the war the price of horses fell precipitously in the US from the economic fallout of the war itself and the increase in the use of automobiles. By 1920 hundreds of thousands of US horses were being sent to the slaughterhouses.

United States Congress, House Committee on Appropriations, "Army Appropriation Bill, 1915", Government Printing Office, Washington, 1913, p. 404

7. "Ecos de.La Estadía..," *Tribuna Salteña*, October 21, op. cit., p. 1, col. 5

8. "Los asaltantes del Banco de Londres, Los autores en Paysandú," *El Paysandú*, Paysandú, October 18, 1917, p. 2, col. 5

"Los asaltantes del Banco de Londres, Con Pablo García," *El Paysandú*, October 24, p. 1, col. 4

9. For years the city of Montevideo, Uruguay has appeared on the EIU - *The Economist Intelligence Unit* - livability rating list as one of the most livable cities in the world, in fact it always rates along with Buenos Aires and Santiago as one of the three most desirable cities in all of Latin America. In 2012 Buenos Aires made the top 10 in the world, and Montevideo was right behind.

The real input data that puts Montevideo at the top of this list every year does not have to do with its outstanding night life, theaters, etc., which Montevideo does have, but rather with the exceptionally low rate of crime. Uruguay has also become a destination for retiring Europeans and North Americans; the culture, the peaceful setting and favorable laws concerning the transfer of retirement funds have highlighted this unique country.

http://en.mercopress.com/2011/09?p=42 (6th article down the page)

CHAPTER FIVE: TRES COMPINCHES

**"To have once been a criminal is no disgrace.
To remain a criminal is the disgrace"
Malcolm X**

En marcha hacia el Salto, en involuntario regreso

**John Atkins, recently arrested, is led handcuffed to
his encounter with the Salto authorities**

While the story of the attempted robbery and murder in Salto has to do mainly with three cronies, *compinches*; Frank Lewis, John Atkins and Pablo Martínez, all the records and later investigations show that there were others, or *another*, involved, and these others were never brought to justice.

Mecuel and McWiden

The other Mexican supposedly involved in the attempted heist was Alfredo Mecuel, an alias, who had made a trip to Salto to check out the Bank of London and later reported to Atkins that it was lightly guarded. Other accounts relate that Mecuel had actually worked in Salto for some time at a utility company, and had taken advantage of his time in Salto to check out the Bank of London.

What is quite revealing is the search we ran on internet to see if a surname *Mecuel* would show up connected with Mexico. With any normal, or even abnormal, last name one will get thousands of hits, or at least a few hundred - but with this one... absolutely none. It is not a Spanish surname, rather it is an invention of Martínez who, when asked about the gang's associate in Montevideo, made up the *apellido* on the fly. It is quite easy to work this out; the group together decided, probably on their run through the countryside before getting caught, that if apprehended they would use the name "McWiden" for their associate, who was almost surely the elusive Sam Brown we will meet in a moment. McWiden is the associate's name given to the judge by both Lewis and Atkins.

Martínez, who did speak English, but not like a native, could not get the English *Mc* sound through his lips, and the English *w* is also a tongue twister for Spanish speakers, usually replaced by *a u* or even a *b*. So it was simply easier for Martínez to invent a surname similar to the unpronounceable McWiden. Saying that this newly invented *Mecuel* was Mexican would also help to throw off the scent from their American friend and cohort. Again and again the journalists covering the testimony of the three Apaches comment on how Martínez loved to talk and also loved to make up things on the run.

We never found a reference to any of the investigators questioning a surname like *Mecuel* - they certainly did wonder if it was just another alias, but they did not ask whether such a last name might or might not even exist. Uruguay is a nation of immigrants from all over Europe; there are last names from Spain, including unpronounceable Basque names, as well as surnames from Italy, Britain,

Hungary, Germany and every other small space that has its own language and culture. So it didn't even occur to the investigators or to the journalists that such a surname did not exist anywhere in the world. (1)

According to later testimony of Martínez, he and Atkins traveled by steamer from Buenos Aires to Montevideo during the first days of September. This is when they made contact with the Mecuel character as *well* as with a Mr. Alfred McWiden. Martínez and Atkins agreed that it was on this visit to Montevideo that they put together the plot to hold up the bank in Salto. And, of course, their encounter with Mecuel was totally by "chance." Martínez went into great length when talking about Mecuel and his ideas for the holdup, and when asked why Mecuel didn't accompany them to Salto, Martínez said that "he drank too much". (2) Atkins then gave the same excuse concerning the elusive Mr. McWiden. The penchant for alcohol by this parallel figure with three surnames was actually confirmed by a banker in Buenos Aires in a letter we shall see shortly.

John Atkins, of course, referred to this elusive character as McWiden; the elastic Mr. Alfred McWiden. Since the testimony was often confusing and contradictory, and since at least once they referred to Mecuel as an American and not as a Mexican, it is much more than probable that these two personages were one and the same person.

The Judge was so convinced of *McWiden's* involvement in the plot that he asked the National Investigative Police in Montevideo to send an officer to Salto for consultations. A Police officer named Francisco Rousserie did then arrive in Salto, and an order for the arrest of McWiden was immediately issued. Since nothing came of the order, it is most likely that McWiden or Mecuel or Brown... had already removed himself from the scene, especially since the debacle of the operation was now national news. He could not but have been sufficiently concerned for his continued liberty and quickly made the decision to travel to regions beyond. (3) In the letter from the banker in Buenos Aires on the 30th of October, 1917, the banker locates John Brown/McWiden in Buenos Aires at that date because Brown himself responds to the Banker's request for information about King-Atkins *after* the mayor of Salto solicits the names and details of anyone connected with the account.

Buenos Aires, Argentina

In the early 20th century Buenos Aires was the main banking, shipping and business center of South America.

Anne Meadows writes of the earlier testimony of Daniel Gibbons' son, Albert, concerning crimes committed by members of the Cassidy gang in Patagonia. Gibbons Sr. had covered for Cassidy in quite a few incidents in Chubut. The younger Gibbons later testified that at the Place.and Ryan house, Sundance and Cassidy' ranch, he had met a certain American named MacQuirk, who stayed there a few days and said he was then traveling to Bolivia. While it may simply be a coincidence to mention the previous MacQuirk with relationship to the mysterious McWiden of Montevideo, it is revealing when we hear Ann go on to say:

"There was no shortage, however, of Mc's and Mac's knocking around; Pedro McCraig was said to have known Butch in southern Chile; J. MacVeigh or MacVey was said to have ridden with Butch and Sundance in Bolivia; and Mr. MacVeagh, a reputed alias for a mysterious Mr. Grogan, who was said to have been a 'Hole in the Wall' fugitive in Bolivia." (4)

Jim King and Sam Brown

The other two names that appear linked to Atkins; Jim King and Sam Brown, this time from Buenos Aires, are both connected with the bank account from which Atkins withdrew the money with which the raid was funded. The mayor of the Salto District, (5) upon the discovery of a checkbook in Atkins' possession, wrote to the American Bank in Buenos Aires requesting information about the person(s) associated with the account number found in the checkbook. The Assistant Manager wrote back identifying both King and Brown as the two who had links to the bank account. The first name, King, is quite clearly Atkins himself, since that was the name on the account. King or Atkins then traveled to Buenos Aires, and on the 29th of September retired all of the funds. The second name, Sam Brown, also most certainly an alias, as are King, Atkins and McWiden, corresponds to a younger man "some 25 years of age" who, like King, said that he was traveling to Paraguay. We are including below the complete text of the letter from the American Bank in Buenos Aires. The letter is a bit awkward in its composition, almost sounding like an abbreviated telegram at times, in fact the second paragraph is a direct quote of a telegram sent to the Mayor earlier on the same day the letter was written.

"Buenos Aires, October 30, 1917
Mr. Don Bernardo Gómez, Mayor
Salto, Uruguay

Dear Sir,

We received your telegram today in which you asked us to inform you concerning the name which corresponds to the checkbook numbered 881 to 890, to which message we responded on today's date, as follows:
'The checkbook belongs to Jim King, gaucho, light brown hair. He arrived from North America last April, he left for Paraguay in mid September, it is said along with a

Mexican Indian named Gonzalez or Garcia, 21 years old, very talkative.

Details in letter.'

Jim King came to this country in the month of April this year, and the 17th of the same month he came to the Bank to deal with us about a certain remittance of one Sam Brown, both American gauchos.

Said Sam Brown now informs us that he was with Jim King in the States of Texas and California, U.S., also in the city La Paz, Baja California, Mexico. The second is a man about 25 years old, almost red hair, with little culture. He is a very quiet man, but according to reports we have obtained here, he appears to get drunk too often. Mr. Brown did not know any member of the King's family, if he has any, nor could he tell us the place of his birth. We are told that during the time he stayed in Argentina, before leaving for Paraguay, he was not involved in any kind of work, and when he left he was accompanied by a Mexican Indian, about 21 years old, with a peasant's face, (6) and quite a charlatan named Gonzalez.

Having referred to our records, we have ascertained that Jim King came by the Bank on the 29th of September, asked for the balance of the credit in his account and withdrew that with his own check; so that the date of his departure was rather at the end of that month and not in the middle, as we reported in our telegram. While closing his account he informed us that it was his intention to go to Montevideo.

Permit us to include with the present a specimen of the signature of Jim King, as well as a copy of the status of his account with us, according to which you will be able to ascertain that the account is closed.

With no other motive, for the time being, we you send our sincere greetings." (7)

A real Gaucho

The information given by both King and Brown that they were traveling to Paraguay was an attempt on their part to keep their true destination a secret, at least at first, because later, when King retired the funds and closed the account, he did mention that he was heading for Montevideo. Today many in North America confuse Paraguay with Uruguay because of their similar sounding names, and from a somewhat challenged knowledge of geography. One is a landlocked country with a large Indian population, the other is a "European" island on the coast of South America. Uruguay is the only country in the Americas that no longer has any Native American population. While the names of these two countries can be confused from far away, anyone traveling in South America would find it impossible to geographically or culturally mistake one for the other.

It is certain that Sam Brown of Buenos Aires was the same mysterious Alfred McWiden who then appears in Montevideo during rest of the gang's sojourn in northwestern Uruguay. (8) There is not a shred of doubt that Jim King is our John Atkins of dubious fame in the Salto holdup. The gang members active in Paysandú and Salto commented more than once that their elusive partner, McWiden, Sam Brown of Buenos Aires, did not come along because of a problem with drink. And, as we have seen, even the bank manager in Buenos Aires confirmed Sam Brown's drinking problem.

The Uruguayan Wild Bunch

But we need to look closely at the three principal characters. Because they were caught and sent to jail in Uruguay we do have a body of certain and also not-so-certain knowledge concerning the three *Apaches* who attempted to rob the bank in Salto. Theirs was an association put together *along the way* and doesn't have the feel of a well-organized band that already had a series of assaults under its belt.

Even the earlier association of Butch Cassidy and the Sundance Kid, along with others who are listed as part of their Wild Bunch in the US as well as in Argentina, while anchored by these two, was constantly experiencing an ebb and flow as a steady stream of different criminals and sidekicks entered and left the gang for different holdups as well as for different reasons.

To us it is apparent that this Uruguayan *Pandilla Salvaje* was put together specifically for the purpose of the Salto heist. Sponsors or "investors" back in the US may well have existed, because Atkins arrived in the Southern Cone with ample funding for carrying out this new gang's plans.

However we have never caught a hint that such investors existed for the group, although it is possible. And by the same measure it is conceivable that John Atkins/King and Sam Brown were funding this project with their own honestly, or ill-gotten gains. How these two, along with Martinez, got aimed at South America, and especially at Uruguay, is a standing mystery.

We assume that both Atkins/King and Brown/McWiden had criminal pasts up north, this because of their actions and manners once they arrived in the southern lands and by their dogged insistence on carrying through with both the preparations and the actual strike on the Bank in Salto. And even more telling, as will be seen, was that John Atkins was consistently concerned to cover up his identity and would not let his face be seen clearly for any of the first photographs taken of the Apaches.

Almost certainly the Uruguayan officials sent inquiries north, most likely through the US Embassy in Montevideo, asking corresponding police sources if they had any information on the outlaws from the US. They would have reported the same aliases that we now know, and would have received back the same paucity of information we have of this gang's North American origins and activities.

Pablo Martínez

"He is a talkative and cynical guy, there is nothing of the apache about him other than his appearance, because just hearing him talk he degenerates into a charlatan." (9)

Pablo Martínez or García, the roustabout and translator of the gang, while under oath in Salto, declared that he had recently left Chihuahua, Mexico on the second of May of the same year as these happenings. He testified that he had traveled on a steamer from Panama to Valparaiso, Chile, and from there he arrived in Buenos Aires. He claimed to have then met John Atkins by chance in Buenos Aires a month or two before the Salto adventure. The testimonies of both Martínez and Atkins are contradictory, especially in that their association was found to have begun more than a year earlier.

Martínez claimed that he ridden with Pancho Villa, (10) and added that he had served in Pancho Villa's firing squad during the years of 1912 to 1915. Since he declared that he was now 20 years old, he would have started out as an official firing squad member at the tender age of 15, (11) although one newspaper, El Diario, reports his age as 25. Several journalists who interviewed Martínez commented that he was a quite talkative and somewhat vulgar fellow, direct quotes may be printable, but they can also be disgusting, and that he showed a tendency to embellish his career as well as to lie through his teeth. His surname was originally given as Garcia - this when he arrived in South America, at least, but that could also be an alias. Nevertheless almost all newspaper articles and even court documents refer to him by the surname Martínez, which he gave at the time of the heist.

The physical description of Martínez was of a mixed-blood Mexican, with dark hair and eyes, well built but thin. He had blue tattoos on both forearms; on the left was the figure of a woman with the initials below: J.P.H. He said this was one of his girlfriends in the US, from whom he could have learned some of his English. On his right arm was the drawing of a scimitar. (12) Martínez, in conversations with reporters, never showed any sympathy towards MacFarlane nor signs of remorse, perhaps he *had* served with that firing squad.

When asked about the horses that were left at a crossing of the Dayman River for the later escape (it had been noted that they were shooed on top of new hoofs and that would probably cause the horses some pain) he answered that he reluctantly did that but only because Atkins had given him a direct order. The reporters noted that when dealing with animals Martinez did show some signs of *ternura*, tenderness, but he showed none for the Bank manager whose life he had taken.

All Martínez would say about killing MacFarlane was that he was defending his partner, Atkins:

"If you bring along a dog, and it gets in trouble, aren't you going to defend it?" (13)

John Atkins

"Atkins gives the impression that he is a sincere person. His manner of relating inspires no doubt in this respect. Moreover it seems that the state of his health is severe, some thought to have him transferred to the Hospital." (14)

John Atkins/Jim King is the most shadowy figure of the known trio. While trying to distance himself from the Mexican, one discovers that his wanderings actually happen to exactly parallel those of Martínez; possibly from Chihuahua, but at least from Baja California, to Panama to Valparaíso to Buenos Aires. What becomes clearer in the cross examinations is that the two had been associated together for more than a year, and they certainly arrived in South America with the intention of carrying out important thefts.

In his testimony Atkins declared that he was son of Samuel Atkins and "Josefa" William of Texas. His mother's first name may have been translated into Spanish by the court scribe or simply misunderstood, but since "Atkins" was an alias, this testimony is suspect from the get-go. (15) John Atkins gives his age as 26. From the first photos it is hard to ascertain even his approximate age, but 26 seems to us as rather young. A photograph taken a year later at the sentencing, shows Atkins with a clearly receding hairline, something possible at age 26, but it makes him appear more like a more mature 40-year-old.

Compared to the other two he is the least fit physically; he is sometimes called *"gordo"* in the newspapers, which would not mean extremely heavy, more like *well fed*. Atkins could not give testimony immediately after the arrest because he was unwell from the ordeal he had been through in the escape and the days on the run. Not only did the police swordplay give him some painful bumps about the head, he had been the least fit for handling the rigors of the chase through the outback. All testimony of both Lewis and Martínez indicates that Atkins never lifted a hand to do any physical work; rather he consistently paid for others to handle matters that required a strong back or even the slightest effort.

Later records show that Atkins passed away in prison in Montevideo in 1927, after suffering from pneumonia. If we go by his given age that would make Atkins only 36 years old at the time of his death. Either he *was* a quite sickly fellow, or he had lied about his age and was moving along towards those middle years when many did succumb to various illnesses back in those days. According to Eduardo Taborda *both* Atkins and Lewis were later appreciated for their work as mechanics maintaining the vehicles of the prison system in Montevideo. Atkins learned this skill from Lewis, and obviously he had the strength be involved in some physical labor while in prison.

Wellingtons and Wool

Atkins was described as tall and heavy, they also used the term *"grueso,"* for which we would say something like *thick*. He had small blue eyes, blond hair cut against the grain and standing up. He used underwear that was combined with wool, we are not given the important detail with which other cloth the wool was combined. When he was caught, he was wearing yellow boots with a double sole. Several journalists were intrigued by these odd yellow boots; we assume these were common Wellingtons or what we simply called "rubber boots" when I was a kid. They also reported that Atkins had a stronger "Yankee" accent than that of Lewis. (16) In South American parlance that makes Atkins more of a Southerner than Lewis, perhaps the Texas origin was truthful.

We up north have our stereotypes of how people are in Latin America; for example, many of us think that all of Latin America is an extension of Mexico. Very often when Uruguayans or Argentines speak English and live or travel in the US, they are mistaken for Europeans; frequently people cannot believe they are from South America because they don't talk like Mexicans. The people in the Southern Cone also have their own stereotypes of just who North Americans

are. I, for one, do not speak English, or Spanish, with a
southern US accent, so they usually think that I am
European. If I try really hard to talk in Spanish like John
Wayne, they tell me that I am starting to sound like a
yanqui, which, of course, would not be appreciated by the
real Yankees.

Upon arrival in Argentina Atkins had deposited an
amount corresponding to 1,345.15 pesos in the American
Bank of Buenos Aires, *el Banco Americano*. (17) Those funds
was deposited under the name of Jim King, and they were
removed from the account by someone using the same name,
thus, as we showed earlier, John Atkins and Jim King were
the same person, and most likely both names were fictitious.
Another checkbook was also found in Atkins' possession,
which showed an account at the National City Bank of New
York that previously held 7,000 *pesos*. (18) Because the peso
and the dollar were of similar value in those days we assume
that this detail of evidence concerning the currency was
confused in the transcription; certainly a North American
who had not yet arrived in South America would have US
dollars deposited in a New York Bank and not *pesos*. (19)

**The Montevideo Broqua & Scholberg gun shop in a
photograph from the turn of the 19th and 20th
centuries.**

*Photograph from a special collection of the Museum of the
National Library, Montevideo - used with permission.*

Purchase of Weapons

In any case, it appears that Atkins was not lacking in funds for his adventures in South America. Leaving from Paysandú aboard a river steamer on the 5th of October, Atkins stopped in Buenos Aires to retire his pesos from the Bank and then proceeded on to Montevideo. Some of the accounts relate that in Montevideo itself he then purchased the arms used in the assault. (20) Others report that Pablo Martínez earlier purchased the arms in Buenos Aires, and that they were taken to Uruguay on the riverboat trip from Gualeguaychú with a stop in the Uruguayan port of Fray Bentos before arriving in Paysandú on September 21st. One newspaper refers to the testimony that Atkins purchased the arms in Montevideo as ridiculous, since the group knew Buenos Aires much better as a city, and most certainly there would be a greater variety of small arms to purchase in the larger city, not to mention better prices. (21)

But Montevideo did have very good private armories, and the *Broqua & Scholberg* gun shop and supply store was not surpassed by any other in the Southern Cone region. Broqua & Scholberg was a partnership between Uruguayan interests and the Belgian Scholberg & Gadet arms exporter. At the turn of the two centuries it was part of a chain of stores that included other large gun shops both in Argentina and Brazil. This large store, which sold everything from agricultural supplies to shovels to ammunition, which we today would more readily call a department store, was a major supplier of manufactured products and hardware to the city of Montevideo as well as to the interior of the country up through the first half of the 20th century. (22)

Shy Crook?

BROQUA & SCHOLBERG — Montevideo

Vista exterior de las Vidrieras frente á las calles Sarandí y Policía Vieja

Broqua & Scholberg's new store

A larger gun shop and department store was built in a major expansion in the early part of the 20th century.

Atkins, who by all evidence was the real leader of the gang, when once arrested preferred to step into the background. He was the one who bankrolled the adventure, did the planning and investigating and made all of the important contacts as well as adopted all of the significant decisions right up to the attempted robbery. But once the plan went awry Atkins was content to let Lewis appear as the leader, and evidently Lewis had the character and disposition to take that part. This was something they surely worked out in the few days of flight in case they did get arrested. The arrest photographs show Lewis looking straight forward, with either overconfident bravado, or he had much less to lose than Atkins. Lewis is always seen looking right at the camera, while in every photo Atkins lowers his head to avoid having his face registered well or recognized. It appears to us that Atkins wanted Lewis to get more attention, both in the testimonies and in the photos.

This intrigues us and indicates that Atkins had more to hide than did Lewis.

The Aliases

National Archives, Montevideo, Uruguay

My little 1989 French Peugot 205 parked in front of Uruguay's National Archives building.

As we have noted before the names used by our three *Apaches* were false names and so far no one has been able to ascertain even a hint of the real nombres that each of these men were given at birth. The one exception may be Pablo Garcia/Martínez.

pacho principal. Secciones: Armería - Cuchillería - Quincallería - Caja.

A partial view of the gun section in the Broqua & Scholberg department store - all types of short arms, rifles, air guns and shotguns were sold here. Some, like Winchesters, Colts and Webleys, were name-brand pieces, others were odd Belgian contraptions that one cannot find today, even in museums.

We attempted several searches for information on the three gang members in the National Archives of Uruguay, located in a rather ordinary neighborhood of Montevideo; graffiti and political slogans plastered on the walls. The help offered by the public employees was outstanding, but the differences in the recording systems used by the Salto regional authorities and those of the capital city of Montevideo were so disparate that finding the actual judicial record was impossible. The stacks upon stacks of criminal archives for the years 1917 through 1919 must be enormous in both size and number, because the large number of selected stacks brought for our perusal were just a representation of what remained in the basement of this building.

We could never find the actual number of the court case in Montevideo. There was a doubt as to whether it would have been recorded according to the date that the case was turned over to the national judicial system in Montevideo, whether it was recorded on the actual date that the jury trial began in Montevideo, or whether it was recorded at the end of the process.

Because the criminal records from Salto itself were fewer in number and more identifiable by date, my search in the archives was a bit more fruitful. In these records from Salto I was able to discover the annotation of the arraignment of the prisoners in the "Index" to the court cases. But the actual case files could not be found, even those of the earlier proceedings in Salto; those had most likely been sent on to Montevideo along with the prisoners.

The index for "Book Six of Arraignments", for the years 1914 through 1926, turned up the names of the three prisoners in *"Libro"* number 635, *"Folio"* number 72. This was the system that did not correlate at all with that of Montevideo, thus leaving us with a cold trail for encountering the actual court transcriptions.

But at least the three names are noted in the Index, listing two different last names for the Mexican: *"García, Martínez Pablo,"* and at the same time listing the given names of the two Americans. The annotation in the Index is seen in the following photo and then translated to English, and the actual cause of their arrest is mentioned briefly:

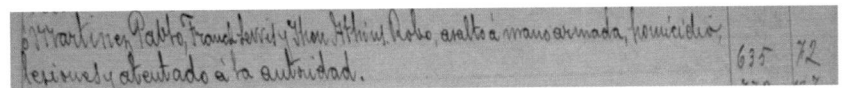

"Garcia [cut off in the above photo] - Martinez, Pablo, Frank Lewis, Jhon [sic] Atkins. Robbery, armed assault, homicide, injuries and resisting authority. 'Book' 635, 'Page' 72"

Frank Lewis

"Lewis seems the most capable of all. His words show great cunning; he has engaged in several deliberate contradictions, in order to put a stumbling block before the judge's actions..." (23)

As we have noted, Frank Lewis is the name that links previously to the Cassidy gang in Patagonia. His testimony before the judge in Salto comes across as a well-studied attempt to throw the Judge off any trail that might lead to his previous wanderings in Argentina. Atkins had already testified that he met Lewis in Valparaíso, Chile, which would give Lewis the benefit of having recently arrived in the Southern Cone. But later testimony by Martínez contradicts this and indicates that Lewis was added to the gang in Argentina some time before the trio arrived in Paysandu in September.

A group of journalists, who after the heist, interviewed Martínez in jail, also asked to interview Frank Lewis, this while Atkins was still "indisposed." Lewis also then told this group that he met Atkins in Chile. This interview, published the next day in the newspaper *El Paysandú*, had a few bits of information not seen in other reports. Here Lewis indicated that he was born to a George Lewis in St. Louis, Missouri. He said that his mother died when he was born and that his dad had eventually remarried, which was why he left home. A later account said that Frank Lewis was released from prison in Uruguay in 1945 and returned to his native state of Missouri. (24) Since "Frank Lewis" was a false name, it is most improbable that this personal history had anything to do with his actual previous life. And we also doubt the reports of his later return to Missouri.

All newspapers described Lewis' physical appearance as well-shaven, with protruding cheekbones, pale skin, thick, wavy blond hair, thin. (25) No height was given, not even approximate, and in the photos from the time of capture none of the gang looks to be tall, especially compared with the Uruguayans who surround the group, although Lewis appears a bit taller than the other two. Later photographs show that Lewis was significantly taller than his two cohorts. Our guess is that Lewis was at least five to six inches taller than either Atkins or Martinez.

Stop in Cuba?

Francisco Lewis, as he was named in some newspapers, said that he had left the US in February of 1917. He relates having gone to Cuba looking for work as a mechanic, but since Cuba was experiencing a revolution after a few days he decided to travel on to Panama and then to South America through Lima and eventually to Valparaiso and Buenos Aires. The papers comment on how his trip partially parallels that of Atkins and Martínez, of course this without Lewis saying that he met them along the way. (26) Since Lewis was a fairly sharp fellow, why would he talk about a trip that even *partially* parallels that of the two men whom he has said he only met recently in either Chile or Argentina? This appears to us to be false information with which he was trying to divert attention from his real travels in recent months and years.

Lewis had been with Atkins and Martínez enough in the recent weeks, perhaps months, in Argentina itself to have heard about their trips. That information, now stored in his own memory, would give him the most recent routes that his friends had used to get from the US to South America.

However, Lewis' reference to a revolution in Cuba does ring true, especially within the time frame to which he refers. In February of 1917 there was an uprising against the Government of *General Mario Menocal*, and forces led by *José Miguel Gómez* rebelled in several of Cuba's Provinces. And, most importantly, that month, the same month that

Lewis says he was in Cuba, the rebels captured Havana. If Lewis had truly been in Havana and then traveled south through the Panama Canal, he could well have arrived in the Chilean port of Valparaíso and there met Atkins. Nowhere does any testimony indicate that the three had been together in North America.

Lewis' information about the revolution in Cuba could also have come from reading the local newspapers. Newspapers throughout Latin America, especially those of the capital cities, have traditionally reported in quite some detail the wars, revolutions, government changes and cultural matters throughout the Latin American world. These countries, with a similarly shared culture, have always been much more aware of each other than has the United States been of them.

Mechanic and Driver

Martínez gives some revealing information about Lewis when he relates that they needed a driver of the new automobiles for part of their plan. According to Martínez they actually discovered Frank Lewis in the city of *Zárate*, (27) the jumping-off point along the Buenos Aires to Rosario routes. Zárate was where one could turn north to Entre Ríos Province and the port cities along the Uruguay River. It is here that Lewis joins the other two on their definitive trip out of Argentina to Uruguay. Zárate was a literal crossroads; a major hub where the main roads and the ever-important railroads, two main lines out of Buenos Aires, converged and moved north along the south side of the *Paraná* River system. Closer to Buenos Aires several large rivers, including the *Paraná*, came together to form the wide *Río de la Plata* - the River of Silver.

It is telling that while Lewis wanted to extend his association with Atkins by at least several months and another continent, Martinez put him joining the gang almost at the last minute. What is more realistic is that the Atkins/Brown/Martínez group made contact with Lewis earlier in La Plata where he was working at a meat packing plant. From all we have been able to learn about Lewis it appears that he was working at that plant, and later in Zárate, as an expert vehicle mechanic.

Ferry Trains at Zárate

A "ferrobarco" carrying freight and stock wagons

At Zárate traffic could cross this large river system by "train" beginning in 1907, this was when the *ferrobarcos*, made in Scotland, were first used to make this crossing. These were large barges that ferried trains from Zárate to *Puerto Ibicuy* in *Entre Ríos* Province. These "ferry trains", built to carry 12 passenger cars or 22 freight cars, were also used from about that time to transport freight trains directly to Buenos Aires. (28)

From *Zárate* to *Puerto Ibicuy* the three outlaws both "sailed the rivers" and "rode the train" north and eventually arrived in Gualeguaychú in Entre Ríos Province, from where they could catch a river steamer to continue their journey up to Paysandú. Gualeguaychú doesn't actually sit on the Uruguay River; there is an approximate 30-mile run from the city to the port. The group hired a car, which Lewis drove for this short hop on their odyssey. We will see that Lewis had had previous contact with the other two *pandilleros*, although the testimony is confusedly contradictory on this point. But it appears that when they *picked him up* in Zárate, he was actually doing honest work at a large meat packing plant there. (29)

All this makes Lewis an even more interesting character, because in all of the early Uruguayan accounts he is identified as the leader of the gang. But there is no real indication that he was the mastermind behind the assault, rather he was just a take-charge type fellow.

Most of the infrastructure still stands at this once busy river port now abandoned, but once the northern hub for the huge ferry trains.

In any case his mental acumen and ability to find quick answers as well as to throw off the judges and investigators from the real trail were noted on more than one occasion. His ability to speak Spanish very well, along with his playing dumb about that skill, actually gave him an advantage in the questioning; he would know exactly what the judge was asking before the translator could repeat the matter in English. This lead-time gave him valuable moments to already be working on his responses.

"Lewis is undoubtedly the most intelligent, quiet and observant, he was the director of the assault and was the

128

last who resisted the Paysandú police, not wanting to hand himself over." (30)

Swift Meat Packing Plants

Meat packing plant in Zárate

A detail shot of the Zarate Las Palmas Meat Packing Plant which shows the high level of mechanism, rails and the assembly line type production that characterized these British plants.

In later testimony Lewis gave a very interesting piece of false information; he said that he had been working most recently in Argentina in a Swift Meat Packing Plant when he was invited by Atkins to join in the Uruguay adventure. (31) In Zárate, Buenos Aires Province, there were no "Swift" plants. Was he saying this to throw off the investigation in case they might actually do some checking in Zárate to find out more about his recent past? That would have been a dead-end for the investigators. But the mention of a Swift Meat Packing Plant may be a link to Lewis' past in Argentina and even in Patagonia.

The Chicago based Swift Meat Packing Company invested in Argentina's growing beef industry in the early 20th century. In 1907 they took over a packing plant in *La*

Plata, Buenos Aires Province, and, of much more interest to us when Lewis mentions Swift, is that in 1910 and 1911 they opened two more plants in *Rio Gallegos* and *Puerto San Julián* in Patagonia. Puerto San Julián is in the region where the real Frank Lewis lived and worked in Argentina, and close to where the three Cassidy gang members actually met the Patagonian Lewis both before and after the famous robbery in Rio Gallegos.

In a later interview with Ríos Silva, our *uruguayo* Lewis did say that he had worked "three months" in the Swift plant in La Plata. And he also related that when he went to La Plata he had actually gone accompanied by Atkins. Further, somewhere along the way the trio had also stayed at the YMCA in Buenos Aires. A letter was found from Lewis to Atkins asking that he pick up some clothes he left at the YMCA, thus the investigations began to put together at least a two to three month link between Lewis and Atkins. (32) Does this mean that they had had some kind of contact before Atkins arrived in Argentina? Was it the shadowy McWiden or Brown that brought them together for the present venture?

Frank Lewis in Patagonia

The story of Frank Lewis needs more fleshing out concerning the Cassidy "associates" in Patagonia in the previous decade. We do know that the real Frank Lewis, the rancher on the *Río Chico* of Santa Cruz Province, and the "Frank Lewis" of Uruguay were definitely not one and the same person, although in Uruguay it has long been understood that the *uruguayo* Lewis was part of Butch Cassidy's gang.

Swift Meat Packing Plant, San Julián, Santa Cruz

The San Julián Swift Plant was opened in 1911 and closed in 1967.

In March of 1904 in Patagonia's Chubut Province two of Cassidy and Sundance's associates were involved in a robbery that resulted in their arrest, and it even led to the temporary arrest of Cassidy because one of the pair was found with a revolver belonging to Butch. The two are identified as Grice, no first name given, and Emil or Emiliano Hood. Grice is later identified as the teamster who was driving a horse-drawn wagon with supplies for the British *"Compañia de Tierras"*, the British "Land Company". A manager of the Company, on the same trip, was transporting in his case 5,000 pesos for payment of salaries once they arrived at their destination in Leleque, Chubut. After a night's stop, the manager, *Guillermo Imperiale*, could not find his bag, which, after a thorough search, showed up some 70 yards from the camp with the money missing. The only two suspects possible were Grice and Hood, who at the end of the trip were arrested and taken into custody by a Deputy Britto. In April Britto had to go to Ñorquinco, some distance from where the two were being held, this to deal with a murder committed by another North American, a gold miner named Charles H. Williams who had no connection with Butch Cassidy. Britto left the two thieves in another's custody, from which they quickly escaped and disappeared. (33)

Hood later shows up in the same Chubut area as the protagonist of multiple incidents, all outside the law. And now, under the new name of Robert Evans, he forms a team with a William Wilson, which perpetrates some of the most famous robberies, kidnappings and murders in Patagonia's history. The two were finally cornered in 1911, and after a shootout with the new Frontier Police they were both summarily executed. The Austrian head of the new *Policía Fronteriza*, Mateo Gebhard, was a Nazi before his time who grew weary of judges freeing his arrested bad guys on lack of evidence. Osvaldo Aguirre identifies the actions of this new police force as the beginnings of the *"herencia maldita"*, accursed heritage, which would plague the Argentine police and military forces, or more properly their victims, right up through the military take-overs of the second half of the 20th century. (34)

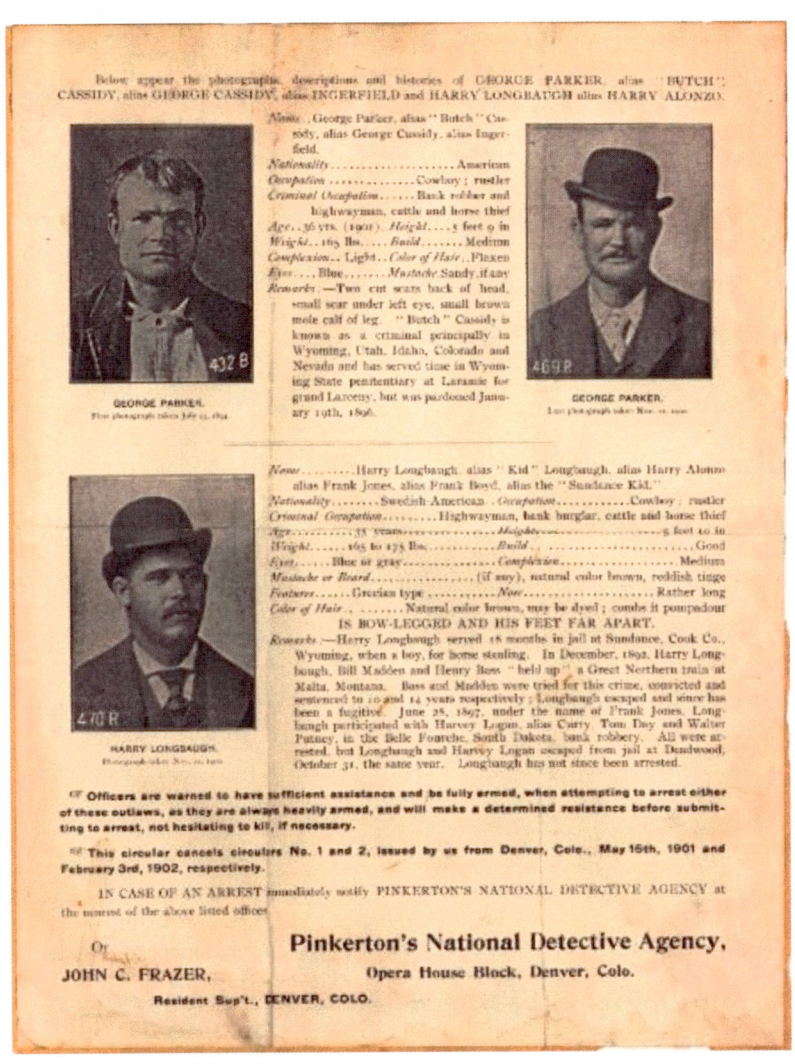

Pinkerton Wanted Poster for Cassidy & Sundance

The poster that helped to establish that Cassidy and the Sundance Kid were in South America.

Several have identified Evan's sidekick, Wilson, as Grice. But one witness, who had actually known Grice, later testified that Wilson was not Grice. And a local guide, Francisco Albornoz, who personally knew Wilson, when he saw an earlier photo of Grice from the time he had been in custody, said that the two could not be the same person. Anne Meadows has since identified Wilson as a Texan who had farmed near Billings, Montana, and who arrived in Patagonia too late to be considered part of the Cassidy gang. Unfortunately that photo of Grice has since disappeared from the Argentine police records. (35)

Cassidy & Associates in Patagonia

One of the few photographs showing some of the "Wild Bunch" in Patagonia

After the escape of Grice and Hood, Grice himself never showed up again in Chubut. But Hood/Evans did stick around, and was even seen with Butch Cassidy on his last trip into Argentina in 1906 when he returned briefly from Chile to try to sell off the last remaining assets that he and the Sundance Kid still held in Argentina. Recent personal correspondence with Dan Buck gave us the information that Grice was an Englishman who immigrated to the US in 1898 and then appeared in Argentina a few years later. We now know that Grice's first name was Herbert and that he worked on a ranch close to where Cassidy and Sundance lived and got involved there with the Cassidy associates, and then got into trouble with that major crime. According to Grice descendants he returned to North America about 1905 and had later run-ins with the law. (36) So Herbert Grice cannot be our Uruguayan Frank Lewis, even if he was part of the Rio Gallegos hold-up. So it is now the third unknown gang member on the Atlantic coast of Patagonia that we would like to know much more about.

In the same month that Hood and Grice broke free, April of 1904, Harry Place and Etta, the Sundance Kid and his companion, made a trip to the Atlantic Coast to take a steamer from Puerto Madryn to Valparaíso in Chile. The local papers at this Atlantic port commented with surprise that this beautiful woman had just ridden a horse all the way across Patagonia! Etta was already famous in Chubut for her riding skills as well as her handling of a Winchester. It is possible that some of the Cassidy associates made that trip along with Sundance and Etta. This trip was made at the same time that Grice disappeared from Chubut. Then *three* men appear nine months later further down the Atlantic coast to rob the Bank in Rio Gallegos, and, as we will note, both Grice and Hood have been identified as the possible authors of the Río Gallegos heist. The Río Gallegos crew was made up of either members of Cassidy's gang or Cassidy and Sundance themselves. Only two men were actually seen in Rio Gallegos itself, so a third rider kept his distance from town.

The Río Gallegos Heist

For the purposes of this study we would like to be able to identify the third man in the crew that carried off the robbery of the bank in Río Gallegos in February of 1905. There are two theories as to the identity of the two men who actually spent time in town, made a deposit in the bank, and later returned to carry out the heist. The first theory, which was repeated in Argentine newspapers and other accounts from the early 20th century, was that the two crooks were Butch Cassidy and the Sundance Kid themselves. More recent scholarship has placed Butch back in Cholila at the time of the theft, making his presence in Río Gallegos most improbable. The second theory says that the two gang members were Robert Evans and Herbert Grice (which is why we underlined the Grice/Hood incident in Chubut), although in these studies no one yet knew Grice's first name. It is not our purpose here to prove or disprove either of the theories, and they are *theories* because no absolute identification was ever made by the authorities in Santa Cruz Province. Rather, our interest has to do with the third man in this party who remains even more of a mystery. Since we know that Butch and Sundance left Argentina in search of new pastures, and we know that Evans was later executed by the Frontier Police, and with the new information on Herbert Grice's return to the USA, the only character in this chapter of outlaw history in Patagonia who totally remains in the shadows is the third rider.

Sheep Dip and Outlaws

Besides running a ranch Frank Lewis was also a sales representative for one of the main British companies that supplied a medication for sheep mange, known as *Little's Sheep Dip*. He sold this product to other sheep ranchers across Santa Cruz Province, and this explains how Frank met the group on the banks of the Gallegos River, far from his own ranch. This encounter happened right before the Cassidy gang set up their heist in Rio Gallegos city. The river meeting with the three Cassidy crew was about 140 miles south of the Lewis Ranch on the Chico River. After the bank robbery, and not yet having received the news of the holdup, Frank then hosts the three men on his own ranch. Since he had had no idea that they were outlaws he surely had earlier invited them to visit him on his ranch if they ever passed close by on their way back north.

So Frank Lewis, the rancher who had driven the sheep north to Rio Chico in 1894, met the *three* gang members both before and after the robbery of the Bank in the city of Rio Gallegos. Edward Chase, the American whose travels and exploits in Patagonia were published by Robert and Katharine Barrett, had several encounters with Frank Lewis that help us put into context the setting in which the Cassidy gang members met and got to know Lewis. Frank and William Lewis ranched an area that covered thousands of acres roughly located to the west of the Atlantic port cities of Puerto Santa Cruz and San Julián.

Relatives of James Lewis viewing El Río Chico, typical of the many small rivers in dry Patagonia.
Thanks to James Lewis for the photograph.

Scones and Hymn Sings

In the Barretts' book on Edward Chase's experiences in Patagonia from this very same time period, they quote Chase concerning another character, Bill Downer, an American sailor who, like Chase, puts his roots down in Patagonia. Chase's remarks about Downer have to do especially with his rough language and even rougher fists. During those days groups of English speaking immigrants and travelers showed up for Sunday get-togethers on the Lewis Ranch on the *Río Chico*; to sing hymns and eat hot scones and honey. According to Chase quite a few Anglophones made long treks on Sundays to the Lewis ranch for these special meets. Frank and William Lewis' mother was the one who would prepare the scones, and who one day rebuked a critic of Bill Downer who had made remarks about Bill's colorful language; Mrs. Lewis told him,

"I have known Willie Downer for years and I have never heard him use an indelicate expression." (37)

The point of mentioning Mrs. Lewis and the Rio Chico Ranch is that the *La Margarita* ranch was a known meeting place for British and American guests from all over the southern reaches of Patagonia. And it was right there that the three Cassidy associates show up after the Bank robbery in *Río Gallegos*. Our main question has to do with whether one of the gang members, the shadow rider who like Grice never returned to the Chubut Cassidy nest, might have stayed on in the Santa Cruz area, or maybe even have moved on further from there, but now with a new, borrowed, name. It would be even more fun to know if Cassidy and Sundance joined in a hymn sing at the ranch!

Had Frank Lewis related to the three that he was soon going to take over the family ranch further west towards the Andes? This move happened just a month or two later that same year, 1905, after which his brother, William Lewis, took over the *Río Chico* holdings. Perhaps a mention of the coming separation of the two brothers put our unnamed villain to thinking that borrowing a British name might keep him even more shielded from his Chubut outlaw past.

Nowhere in Patagonia where this person might wander would anyone ever mistake him for an Argentine or even a Chilean, but a North American just might pull off the ruse of being a British subject - he wouldn't be able to fool either an Englishman or an American on that account, but the fooling would normally be needed for Spanish speaking Argentines who would mostly not know how to distinguish between the two similar gringos.

Being known as a British rancher would also keep this re-named outlaw from suspicions that were falling on quite a few North Americans as the Wild West gangs were turning Patagonia into the Wild South.

Leaking Abroad

One good thing that we can say about the thousands of British and Welsh immigrants to South America is that they never became famous for forming outlaw bands, as did quite a number of North Americans.

In 1931 Rockwell Kent wrote in the introduction to the Barretts' book on Edward Chase, "A Yankee in Patagonia", that while Chase was a faithful representative in the southern lands of the North American spirit and integrity, sadly there were others of more dubious standards who also moved south; *"...while good men of crowded Europe go... to new lands, our worst, too often, leak abroad, wearing - it pays to advertise - the Stars and Stripes."* (38) This "leaking abroad" of some of our worst examples of American arrogance and thuggery was an export reminiscent of a later spectacle of cultural insensitivity known as the *ugly American*.

The Cold Atlantic Shores

There are references to a Frank Lewis residing in the port city of *San Julián* in this same period. We have not been able to find corroborating evidence to that effect, but up until the first months of 1905 the real Frank Lewis, along with his brother, ran the *Río Chico* ranch, *La Margarita*, located about 80 miles west, south-west of this port, then Frank himself moved even further west to run the family's second ranch.

Were the cold coastal Patagonian winds more favorable for a new Frank Lewis? Or was it a simple case of breathing freer far from the Andean exploits of the larger Cassidy bunch? One has to remember that Patagonia in the early 20th century was one of the most under populated regions of the world. The southern reaches of Argentina are something like Siberia; the coastal regions are inhospitable, wind swept and extremely cold in winter, although not as cold as Siberia itself unless one takes into account the wind-chill factor. The area closer to the Andes Mountains is actually much more tolerable, and it reminded Butch Cassidy of Wyoming and Montana, and it had, as he wrote his friends, even milder winter weather than his old stomping grounds.

Until today Patagonia remains the least populated region of South America. Back then, in any particular region of Patagonia, just about everyone knew everyone else, so one could not melt into a large population like that of Buenos Aires or Santiago. Therefore a move of a 1000 or more miles, from Chubut to Santa Cruz, would have been a most practicable solution for avoiding identification and arrest for someone like our mystery gang member. So a name change for our new "Frank Lewis" would not just be handy, it would be necessary if he wanted to escape his association with the Wild Bunch.

The Lewis who showed up in Uruguay 14 years later was now an experienced mechanic and driver of the new automobiles. In 1905 there were very few automobiles in Argentina, not to mention far-off Patagonia. But the establishment a few years later of the Swift meat packing plants in San Julián and Río Gallegos would require the hiring or training of a group of qualified mechanics. The Uruguayan Frank Lewis' mention of working for the Swift company could have included a stint at one of the Patagonian meat packing plants, most likely the San Julián plant which is close to our area of interest, and is also where a mention is made of a Frank Lewis actually residing.

Even before the arrival of the new automobiles with internal combustion engines, all of these large meat packing

140

plants, including those that Swift built in Argentina, were highly mechanized. If Lewis had a mechanical ability he could well have started working on the machinery in the San Julián plant even before getting started on the newfangled cars.

James Lewis and the Patagonian Lewis Clan

One of the later exchanges of both emails and telephone calls I was privileged to have was with the real Frank Lewis's grandson, who lives in Santa Cruz Province of Argentina, and who still operates the *Lewis* Ranch, *La Margarita*, on the Chico River. I found James Douglas Lewis' name and other information online when looking for Lewis connections in Patagonia. Besides managing the family ranch, James is director of tourism for the historic port city of Santa Cruz.

James Lewis of Santa Cruz, Patagonia, Argentina

Lewis is Director of Tourism for the historic southern Atlantic port of Santa Cruz. James is grandson of Frank Lewis - the real Frank Lewis.

Our phone calls and correspondence were yet another link in the chain of gratifying experiences as well as discoveries of living connections to the history I had been

141

studying for some years. Even though Argentina and Great Britain went to war over the Falkland Islands in the 1980's, the links to the people and culture of Great Britain in the southern lands of Argentina are wide-ranging and well documented. Many of the British settlers and *British* natives of the Falklands, among who were many sheep farmers, ended up in similar occupations in Patagonia.

The real Frank Lewis was the first European to be born in Tierra del Fuego, and this to parents who had until recently resided in the Falklands. Even today James Lewis works to maintain the ties that the *Anglo-Argentinos* have with the *Kelpers* of the Falkland Islands. All Anglo-Argentines see the Argentine-British War of the 80's as an unfortunate interruption in a positive link of cultures and peoples that now goes back at least 150 years.

It was James Lewis who informed me that his grandfather, the real Frank Lewis, sold Little's Sheep Dip medication all over the south of Patagonia. And, as we mentioned, this was most likely how Frank Lewis was found many miles south of his own ranch when the Cassidy gang appeared on the Gallegos River.

Osvaldo Aguirre in his otherwise well documented book on the Cassidy bunch in Patagonia, throws doubt on the three gang members actually having had a second meeting with Frank Lewis, "on the Chico River, close to Conche Peak." This encounter doesn't exactly fit Aguirre's sequence of happenings after the Rio Gallegos robbery, so he gives little importance to Frank Lewis' report, and further says that the meeting was a matter of hearsay:

"...but this version was never confirmed, and in the light of later facts, it appears as a product of confusion and fear." (39)

Evidently Aguirre did not have access to the Edward Chase material, and, further, no contact with the actual Lewis family still living in Patagonia. Several witnesses corroborated the visit of the three Cassidy gang members at the Lewis ranch. And the English speaking Britain's and Anglo-Argentines, as well as Americans like Chase, would not easily mistake the identity or the wanderings of an

American gang in their midst. Nothing we know about the real Frank Lewis of Patagonia points to him being a confused or fearful fellow - just the opposite, he was a renowned pioneer of sheep farming in that region, he was a skilled carpenter who built many of the first houses and buildings across Santa Cruz Province, and he boldly traveled through the land of Indians and *pumas* selling his special brand of sheep dip.

As we have pointed out, it was *after* the actual robbery that the three Cassidy bad guys showed up on Lewis' ranch, La Margarita. Frank Lewis recognized them from their earlier meeting further south, and only later did he hear the news about the robbery. It didn't take him long to put two and two together, so he then traveled down to one of the Atlantic port cities to inform the authorities that the gang had passed through his ranch.

Lioness Hotel

Lewis' grandson, James, also clued me into the visit of the same Cassidy gang in 1905 at *Hotel La Leona*, this further to the West near the outlet of *Lago Viedma*, a glacier-fed lake located about 40 miles north of the famous *Lago Argentino*. The police of Santa Cruz interviewed the Hotel personnel after the robbery in Rio Gallegos, and seeing the photos of Butch Cassidy, Sundance Kid and Ethel Place, they identified them as the three *Gringos* who had stayed a few days at the hotel.

Along with the identifications made by Edward Chase and Frank Lewis, together with those of the personnel of Hotel La Leona, it looks almost certain that the real persons who carried out the Rio Gallegos heist were Cassidy and Sundance themselves. While no one in Rio Gallegos saw a woman accompanying the two outlaws, witnesses did see her at the hotel much further to the west. And witnesses further south clearly saw the *third man* accompanying the two who held up the bank.

Conche Peak, near where the outlaws showed up on a visit to the real Frank Lewis

The Lewis Ranch along the Chico River, in the distance: Conche Peak.

Thanks to James Lewis for the photograph.

For the purpose of this investigation, which did not set out to prove or disprove the movements of Butch Cassidy and the Sundance Kid in southern Patagonia, it is the figure of the third unknown gang member that is more important for our thesis concerning the later Uruguayan gang. Our information is circumstantial, and until the "Uruguayan" Frank Lewis is more positively identified, we can only surmise that the mystery Cassidy gang member of Patagonia is the same person who later turns up as the tall American driver, expert shooter and mechanic of the later gang of *Apaches*.

Frank Lewis and the Spanish Language

The last bit of telling information concerning our *uruguayo* Lewis we found in a smaller Paysandú newspaper, *El Diario*, from its October 20, 1917 edition. All of the north

Uruguay newspapers and even the court records note that both Lewis and Atkins were not able to speak Spanish. In fact the newspapers of Montevideo later relate that the jury trial itself lasted much longer than the actual facts warranted, precisely because all proceedings and testimonies had to be translated into English for the two Americans. Earlier the *Diario Nuevo* of Paysandú gives the novel information that it was MacFarlane's good friend, George Armstrong, who served as translator for the Salto court officials right after the arrest of the three. (40)

Then the report goes on to say that,

"The two Americans are not able to clearly express themselves in Spanish..." (41)

The Salto Tribuna newspaper employs even stronger terminology when it says;

"The first two absolutely don't speak any Spanish and they depend on Martinez as their translator." (42)

Several newspapers reported that immediately after the arrest, on the walk of the prisoners to the Hervidero Ranch, the two North Americans kept their mouths shut. Thus there was no early sense of whether they spoke only English, a bit of Spanish... or more. But one of the Paysandú policemen later told the *El Diario* reporter that when the gang was first arrested, seated on the ground at the Hervidero Ranch and surrounded by guarding officers, that at a certain moment, when a few of the guards had distanced themselves from the three, Lewis took advantage to speak to Martínez:

"...he told the Mexican, in an imperative tone, in clear Spanish: 'Don't admit anything!'" (43)

Frank Lewis, the Spanish speaking "Apache"

For foreigners, Spanish does not come out of the mouth *clearly* - not without years of experience in both hearing and speaking the language. Nothing we know about Lewis, from his testimony or that of his two partners, places him earlier in Mexico or any other Spanish speaking country to the north for an extended length of time, so his good Spanish appears to have been picked up in the Southern Cone. Another group of journalists, who talked with Frank Lewis for the articles that came out on October 24th in both Paysandú and Salto, began the section on Lewis in the *El Paysandú* newspaper saying that in order to interview him they had to ask for a translator. Lewis was deliberately covering up his familiarity with the Spanish language. (44)

So this cocky American who testified that he first met Atkins a few months earlier in Valparaiso, Chile, and who said that he also arrived in the Southern Cone from the US recently, was definitely hiding what had to be years of
146

immersion in the Spanish language and culture. He even got the grammar right when he spoke to the Mexican, something that comes exceptionally hard for Americans who first step into the Spanish-speaking world.

Lewis to the left, keeping his mouth shut

The other revealing item is his use of the word *admit*, which in Spanish is *declarar*. A North American bad guy when telling his partner to keep his mouth shut would never use the word *declare*, rather he would say something like, "don't say anything," "don't admit anything," "don't breathe a word," or one of several more colorful forms of expression from the outlaw language of his time; e.g., "don't rat on me", although this *ratty* expression has its origins in Yiddish and likely comes from the later North American Mafia scene.

"Declare" is something you do with the contents of your luggage in customs; it is an almost quasi-legal term in English. Nations declare... Judges declare... individual persons also declare... but usually expenses on a form, or an

147

official takes their declaration. What they do not do is outright declare something when the police catch them. Upon being caught they might *sing*, but not *declare*. (45)

On the other hand it is quite common and proper to use the word "*declarar*" in Spanish for these kinds of encounters or admissions. For Lewis to use this word shows a familiarity with the *way* things are said in Spanish. If he were new to the Spanish language he would have said, "*No diga nada*"; don't say anything, or "*no admite nada*"; don't admit anything, but instead he easily uses a form of speech that only years of listening and practice could have put on his tongue for those circumstances.

Another reporter, working for the Paysandú newspaper *El Telég*rafo, was the one who had first reported on this exchange between Lewis and Martínez. This reporter writes that Lewis tried to cut off Martínez after the Mexican had started giving out all kinds of information; e.g., where the horses had been left, who were their accomplices, and such. The *Telégrafo* journalist says that at this point Lewis lost his cool,

"...*on the Hervidero Ranch he lost his patience, and giving the Mexican an elbow, in a low voice he told him to shut up.*" (46)

This reporter, while paraphrasing Lewis' statement heard by the policeman, did not say whether Lewis said what he said in Spanish or English. But up to this time neither of the Americans had said anything to anybody; they were maintaining a strict silence, especially in Spanish. Therefore the issue of which language was spoken didn't stand out as important for the reporter. The point is that the policeman who had overheard the exchange *understood* what was said. If Lewis had been speaking in a low voice to Martinez in English, a different language from that of the policeman, the policeman would not have comprehended the exchange. It would be most improbable that a Uruguayan country policeman would have studied English; this was a language used mainly in the cities and commercial centers of Uruguay and mainly among the Anglo-Uruguayans who were arriving and investing in Uruguay's economy. If the policeman had even had a chance to study another language during his school days, it almost certainly would have been French, the main foreign language studied in Uruguay up to the second half of the 20th century.

The more precise newspaper account, with the direct quote, comes a day later and is the result of the second journalist inquiring further with the policeman who had heard the exchange, and this reporter then wrote in his article the exact words that had been spoken in Spanish.

Two Patterns

Concerning both Atkins and Lewis, among the false information given, among the facts garnered by investigators and the press, and among the various contradictions between testimonies, two patterns stand out:

First: Atkins did not want his past criminal career in the US to be highlighted; he put forward Lewis as the leader of the gang, he tried to avoid being photographed at any clear angle, and he, like all in the gang, used several false names. He was covering up a past up north.

Atkins was the one who bankrolled the project, or at least he was the one holding the cash to make it possible. Was he connected with other criminal elements in the US? Was he the one who put up the funds for the heist, or did others provide that investment? And who was his slippery partner Sam Brown/McWiden who accompanied him in Buenos Aires and Montevideo, only to disappear later?

It is about Atkins and his elusive partner that we have the greatest paucity of information. We have not even a hint as to their connections up north, nor about any previous criminal past. There has to be a past and there has to exist somewhere information that will give us an idea of why Atkins and associates traveled all the way to the Southern Cone specifically to carry out a bank robbery. Were they running, like Cassidy and Sundance earlier, from a criminal past, from the law, from the Pinkertons and whoever else wanted to bring them to justice?

Second: Lewis worked hard to cover up what could be a Southern Cone past. He was glad to be pointed out as the leader of the *American* gang of Apaches; he almost sought opportunities to be identified as someone from further north. He very clearly gave contradictory testimony about his time in Argentina, and most telling, he did not want anyone to know that he spoke good Spanish.

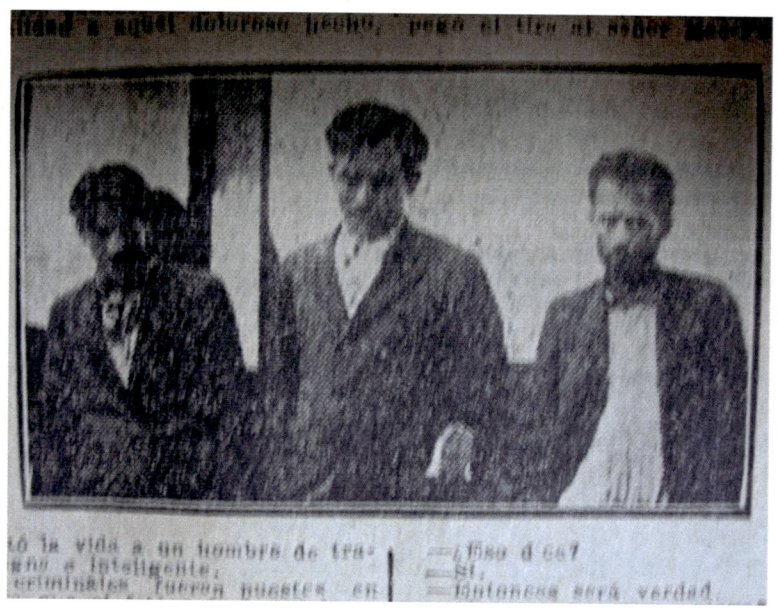

The Apaches when transferred from Salto to Montevideo

Atkins, to the left, continues to avoid the camera, Lewis, in the middle, is now in better condition and showing his greater height, Martínez to the right with a doubtful look.

Lewis' Age?

The one fact given about Lewis that would bring into question a past in Argentina was his declared age. *La Prensa* of Salto writes that Lewis himself declared his age as 19, although another source, perhaps from the court proceedings, lists his age as 28. (47) If he had been 19 at the time of the Salto heist there could be no way that he had a previous 12-13 year history in Argentina. And even at 28 that would be impossible; that would have made him a juvenile 15 or 16-year-old when arriving in Argentina, similar to Martinez' testimony that would have put him on a firing squad for Pancho Villa at the same age. If Lewis, possibly our shadow rider in Santa Cruz Province, was in his late teens or into his twenties when he had arrived in Argentina 13 years previously, (48) he would now be into his thirties and most likely close to 40. Could the court officers, for example, mistake a 35 or 40-year-old for a 19-year-old? It would be more likely that they would not question his age if the court in 1917 established it at proximately 28.

It is common that people of one racial and cultural type have a hard time guessing the age of other types with whom they have had little contact. But Uruguay in the early 20th century was already the most European country in the Americas; (49) most of its population was made up of immigrants from Europe or children of immigrants. And besides, there were British and American citizens living in Salto itself, some of these having a personal hand in the interviews with Lewis himself. So if his given age had been off by a huge margin, it surely would have been noticed and questioned quite quickly.

The other doubt thrown on Lewis' stated age of 19, or even the 28 years mentioned elsewhere, is a cultural one; at that time, and especially in the South American setting, a young whippersnapper in his 20's would never be accepted as the leader of anything. The Latin culture has traditionally placed a premium on age, even when not justified, and it is most difficult for a truly *young* person to be acknowledged as a leader in any association. All who had contact with the group naturally accepted Frank Lewis as the *jefe*, even though we now know that Atkins was the true power behind the throne. For Uruguayans at that time in history the idea that a young person would be the leader or spokesperson for a business group would be literally unthinkable. So the easy acceptance of Lewis as the head of this band clearly tells us that they saw in Frank Lewis a minimum of 30-40 years of life and experience.

The main issue in this line of the investigation does not have to do with Lewis' testimony about his own age; he could have been trying to throw off the investigators concerning that data also. Until we have more information and better photos of Frank Lewis we cannot state with certainty that he was the bogus Frank Lewis of Argentina, our elusive rider of Patagonia in the 1904-1906 period. However he is anything but a young kid.

Along this line the other pattern we see in our *uruguayo* Frank Lewis, whom we are getting to know from almost 100 years downstream, is a person with much experience. He does not come across as a youngster just getting started in a life of crime. He knows what he is doing with guns, with cars, and in tough situations. He keeps his cool under fire, and he actually takes charge when it is necessary. This is not a young punk learning the ropes.

And, as we have shown with some detail, Lewis was fluent in Spanish, something that would not be compatible with the age he gave unless he had grown up somewhere close to Mexico instead of in Missouri which he claimed as his home. And, if he had grown up in Texas or along the border of Mexico, almost certainly the Uruguayans would be saying that Lewis' accent was more *American*, like that of Atkins.

Tantalizing Hints

The main story that we have been laying out in these pages is about the gang that arrived in Salto, Uruguay in 1917 and committed a wretched crime. The history of that episode in the life of this peaceful city in northern Uruguay, as well as the lives touched by the double tragedy, not to speak of several Wild South shootouts, is the story that we are filling out in these pages with a certain completeness.

Yet, many questions remain, especially about this criminal gang called *Apaches* in the Southern Cone newspapers. In the future we may be surprised by a totally different explanation for the tantalizing hints we have found, especially from the testimony and reports concerning Frank Lewis. So far those hints only appear to fit into a mosaic that includes a previous past for Lewis in Argentina - and those hints point to a connection with a North American criminal association, either one that had South American links through the "cowboys" who showed up for the Buenos Aires *Rural* each year or with Cassidy's Wild Bunch, as has long been believed in Uruguay. When other, new, historical data does come to light, those few pieces of the puzzle may well fit into another completely different picture. Until then we will keep looking south rather than north.

References: Chapter 5

1. I ran a further Google search for any surname Mecuel, anywhere in the world; I got nine hits, which means that Mecuel is a very rare word. All of the answers were from businesses that would be glad to charge me for looking up the last name Mecuel. On two of the sites they did list the names Adrien Mecuel and Alain Mecuel, which sounded to me like a come-on, for which I was not going to pay good money to further my investigative instincts. And glory be, with a broader search I actually found a real person, just one out of the hundreds of millions who had other names, and he had a *first* name Mecuel; a Mecuel Hutber who arrived in New York as a German immigrant between 1851 and 1891. And knowing how the US immigration officials were good at changing the spelling of hard-to-pronounce names, our poor Mecuel from Germany may well have arrived in the United States with a name similar to but not exactly like Mecuel.

2. Rios Silva, "El Asalto al Banco de Londres, Empiezan las Contradicciones," *Tribuna Salteña*, November 6, 1917, op. cit., p. 4, col. 4

3. Rios Silva, "El asalto al Banco de Londres, Aparece Mecuel e insinúa el asalto," *Tribuna Salteña*, November 3, p. 8, col. 1

"El asalto al Banco, Juan Akins (sic) o Jaime King," *Tribuna Salteña*, Salto, November 6, 1917 p. 4, cols. 3-4

4. Daniel Buck and Anne Meadows, "Wild Bunch in South America, Neighbors on the Hot Seat: Revelations," WOLA Journal, vol. V, no. 2, Spring/Summer 1996, p. 13

5. "Mayor" - *Jefe Político*, literally *Political Chief* - the Districts that make up Uruguay were governed by Officers appointed by the central Government, at that time they were not elected. Even today in the interior of Uruguay some mayors, who now are elected in democratic elections, administrate an interior city and a whole corresponding District or section of the country, rather than just their particular urban center.

6. *"cara lapina"* is the description of Martinez's face. *Lapina* is not a word in Spanish and most likely comes from the French word *lapiner/lapina* which has to do with agriculture, country, etc.; thus a country or peasant face.

7. The complete text of the Buenos Aires Bank's letter in Spanish:

> Buenos Aires, Octubre 30, 1917
>
> Señor don Bernardo Gómez
>
> Jefe Político del Salto
>
> Uruguay
>
> Muy señor nuestro,
>
> Recibimos hoy su telegrama en el cual nos pide usted le informemos a nombre de quien corresponda la libreta de cheques numerada del 881 al 890, a cuyo mensaje hemos contestado con fecha de hoy, como sigue:

"Libreta pertenece Jim King, guacho*, pelo alazán. Llegó de Norte America Abril último, Partió para Paraguay

mediados Setiembre, dícese acompañado de indio mejicano llamado Gonzalez o Garcia, 21 años, muy hablatino.

Detalles carta

Jim King llegó a este país en el mes de Abril de este año, y el día 17 del mismo mes vino al Banco para tratar con nosotros acerca de cierta remesa de dinero de un tal Sam Brown, ambos gauchos* norteamericanos.

Dicho Sam Brown ahora nos informa que estuvo con Jim King en los Estados de Texas y California, de los E.U., así como en la ciudad de la Paz, Baja California, Méjico. El Segundo es un hombre de unos 25 años de edad, de pelo casi rojo, poca cultura. Es un hombre bastante callado, pero según los informes que hemos obtenido aquí, parece embriagarse con demasiada frecuencia.

El señor Brown no conoce a ningún miembro de la familia King, si es que la tiene, ni nos pudo informar el lugar de su nacimiento. Se nos dice que durante el tiempo que permaneció en la Argentina, antes de partir para el Paraguay no se dedicó a trabajar en ninguna forma, y que cuando se fue iba acompañado de un indio mejicano, como de unos 21 años de edad, cara lapina y muy charlatán, llamado Gonzalez.

Habiendo referido a nuestro libros, nos hemos cerciorado que Jim King paso por el Banco el dia 29 de Setiembre, pidió el saldo de su crédito en cuenta y lo retiró mediante su propio cheque; de manera que la fecha de su partida fue más bien a fines de ese mes y no a mediados, segun informamos en nuestro telegrama. Al tiempo de retirar su cuenta nos informó que era su intención irse a Montevideo.

Nos permitimos incluirle en la presente un espécimen de la firma de Jim King, así como una copia del estado de su cuenta con nosotros, según el cual podrá usted cerciorarse que dicha cuenta está cerrada.

Sin otro motivo por el momento, saludan a usted muy atentamente." *

*sin firma, ni nombre - Note: there is neither name nor signature included with the published letter.

Rios Silva, "El asalto al Banco de Londres, Finalizando," Tribuna Salteña, November 7, op. cit., p. 5, col. 4

Gaucho: The term gaucho employed in the letter to describe the two Americans is a word no longer used in that context concerning foreigners, it has traditionally referred to the South American cowboys, often of Indian and European mix, who roamed the Pampas and the open reaches of Argentina, Uruguay and southern Brazil. But in the context of this letter it almost certainly means *cowboy*. The more proper Spanish word for cowboy is *vaquero*, but in Argentina in those days the cowboys happened to be *gauchos* - and evidently the North American cowboys were included in the title. We have not seen any modern reference to cowboys from up north as anything but *vaqueros*, so this use was peculiar to that time.

The reference in the letter to the second man more logically refers to Sam Brown, not to King/Atkins, because that was the order of the letter - the grammar is a bit confusing on this point. The reference to the second man as having "almost red hair" might refer to either King or Brown. The penchant for drunkenness was not one of King/Atkins' weaknesses, and to say that King/Atkins had little culture does not coincide at all with the later reports of Atkins' responses when being questioned by the Salto Judge.

8. Rios Silva, "El asalto al Banco de Londres, Siguen los viajes," *Tribuna Salteña*, November 4, op. cit., p. 5, col. 3

9. *"Es un tipo locuaz y cínico; no tiene de apache nada más que la apariencia, pues oyéndolo conversar degenera en un charlatán."*

"El Asalto al Banco, Nuevas Declaraciones...," *La Prensa*, Salto, October 21, op. cit., p. 1, col. 2

10. Rios Silva, "Ecos del Asalto al Banco, Entra el Suceso en un Nueva Faz," *Tribuna Salteña*, November 1, p. 5, col. 2

11. "Más Ecos de lo de Salto, Habla Pablo Martínez," *El Diario*, Paysandú, October 24, 1917

12. Rios Silva, "El asalto al Banco.Empiezan las Contradicciones," *Tribuna Salteña*, November 6, op. cit., p. 4, col. 4

13. *"Si Vd. trae un perro, y lo ve mal, ¿no lo va a defender?"*

"Los Asaltantes al Banco de Londres, Con Pablo García," *El Paysandú*, October 24, op. cit., p. 1, col. 4

14. *"Atkins da la impresión de que es un tipo sincero. Su relación no inspira dudas al respeto. Por otra parte parece que su estado de salud es bastante grave, habiéndose pensado en trasladarle al Hospital."*

"El Asalto... Nuevas...," *La Prensa*, October 21, op. cit., p. 1, col. 2

15. Rios Silva, "El asalto...Juan Atkins o Jaime King," *Tribuna Salteña*, November 6, op. cit., p. 4, col. 3

16. "Los celebres apaches...El siniestro terceto," *La Prensa*, October October 19, op. cit., p. 1, col. 4

Note: A strong American accent, *más accento yanqui*, usually refers to someone speaking with a pronounced southern accent

17. Rios Silva,"El asalto. Donde combinaron el plan," *Tribuna Salteña*, November 6, p. op. cit., p. 4, col. 4, Note: The US Dollar and the Argentine Peso were almost at a par, the smaller dollar amounts and 15 cents change included in

this total could have come from a small difference in exchange rates or even from a bank charge when the funds were deposited.

18. "Los Salteadores...Bien forrados," *El Telégrafo*, Paysandú, October 20, p. 2, col. 4

19. It is not stated if the checkbook that was found in Atkins' possession had his name printed on the checks, which would have been Jim King. If that were the case, then his real name would be apparent, or at least the false name could be traced back to New York. But while Scotland introduced checks with the owners name printed on each check in the early 1800's, and Great Britain followed with some checks thus printed, in the United States only a few Banks printed the owner's name on their checks even in the early 20th century. The banking system in the US seemed to be more concerned with methods to protect bank checks from a later alteration of the amount on check than with displaying the owner's name. Thus we doubt if any name would be found on the checks or checkbook that "Jim King" still had in his possession.

20. Rios Silva, "El Asalto...Siguen los viajes," *Tribuna Salteña*, November 4, p. op. cit., 5, col. 3

Rios Silva, "El asalto... Donde combinaron el plan," *Tribuna Salteña*, November 6, op. cit., p. 4, col. 4.

"El Asalto...Viaje de los bandidos," *La Prensa*, Salto, October 24, op. cit., p. 1, col. 3.

21. If Atkins did purchase the arms in Montevideo, especially the two Remington Carbines and perhaps the Semi-Auto Colt .45 Pistol, along with ammunition and two clips for the Colt, then he would have transported them by steamer on his way back to Paysandú. Moving a significant amount of arms from one country to another, even back then, would bring up the issue of customs possibly making an examination of the luggage and then questioning the need of one person possessing so much fire power. By purchasing

the arms in a Uruguayan city and transporting them *within* the country there was no danger of having to pass throughcustoms at the end of the voyage. "Within" legally, in any case, because one couldargue that the steamer had touched international or even Argentine waters on its the way to Paysandú.

22. Rios Silva, "El Asalto...," *Tribuna Salteña*, November 4, op. cit., p. 4, col. 3

"El Asalto... Nuevas...,"* *La Prensa*, October 21, op. cit., p. 1, col. 2

*Here is mentioned the opinion that it was Martínez who brought the arms from Buenos Aires to Paysandú

23. *"Lewis parece el más hábil de todos. Sus palabras demuestran gran astucia; ha incurrido en varias y deliberadas contradicciones, para poder oponer tropiezo a la acción del juez..."*

ibid., "El Asalto al Banco, Nuevas Declaraciones...," *La Prensa*, October 21, p. 1, col. 2

24. Alberto Moroy, "Cuando Uruguay importaba asesinos de EEUU," online magazine: El País Viajes, Montevideo, May 18, 2012

http://viajes.elpais.com.uy/2012/05/18/cuando-uruguay-importaba-asesinos-de-eeuu/

25. Note: In the Southern Cone culture blond hair does not signify light blond, rather it can be anything from lighter brown to platinum blond.

26. Rios Silva, "El Asalto...Francisco Lewis," *Tribuna Salteña*, November 6, op. cit., p. 4, col. 5

27. "El Asalto...," La Prensa, October 21, op. cit., p. 1, col. 2

Rios Silva, "Aparece Lewis," *Tribuna Salteña*, November 4, op. cit., p. 5, col.2

28. These *ferrobarcos* actually had to navigate two river systems to make the total crossing, *Paraná de las Palmas* and *Paraná Guazú,* and the trip could take from four to ten hours depending on river conditions. Not until 1977 did a series of long bridges connect Buenos Aires Province with Entre Rios Province, beginning from this same jumping off point, *Zárate.* Soon after this crossing, as one moved back south and east, and as the huge river systems approached the wide outlet to the sea, the various river channels flowed into a swampy delta region where even today bridge crossings are not commercially nor structurally viable.

29. Rios Silva, "El Asalto al Banco de Londres, Entra el Suceso...," *Tribuna Salteña*, November 4, op. cit., p. 5, cols. 2-3

There were three large "British" meat packing plants functioning in the early 20th century in Zárate, Buenos Aires Province: Smithfield, Las Palmas - the oldest, begun by James Nelson in 1885, and the third, located right on the Paraná River named El Anglo - begun only in 1916 in an outlaying neighborhood named Villa Angus – this doesn't sound like the plant at which Lewis worked since it was not in Zárate itself. It would be more than difficult to find out with which Meat Packing Plant Lewis worked, because all closed down earlier in the 20thcentury, and Lewis worked there only temporarily.

"Los Asaltantes del Banco de Londres," *El Paysandú*, Paysandú, October 24, 1917

30. *"Lewis es sin duda, el más inteligente, reservado y observador; el fué el director del asalto y fue el último que se resistió a la policía sanducera a la que no quería entregársele."*

"El asunto de los apaches, El sumario y los réos," Diario Nuevo, October 22, p. 2, col. 5

31. "Confesión de Lewis," La Prensa, Salto, October 21, 1917,

We add here two quotes that give local color to Lewis' possible sojourn in San Julián on the Atlantic coast of Patagonia. The first is included in the stories about William Norris, 1868-1951. We only found this in Spanish, which we translated back to English. Norris worked in the cattle business in Patagonia and left some very interesting notes, including a run-in in 1907 with two thieves who evidently were Evans and Wilson.

http://patlibros.org/wn/anecdote.php

The following quote has to do with the Swift plant in San Julián, but comes from a visit to the ruins of the plant, which would have been after 1963, so it is an added comment that could not have come from William Norris himself.

"The Swift Meat Packing Plant in San Julian was originally built around 1910 to process cattle, as well as sheep. Cranes in the area where the cattle were killed were three feet higher than normal. There were also remains of high fences around the pens. When asked why, we were told that the animals that were brought to the plant at that time were so wild that they could jump like deer. This livestock came from the ranches of the Pre-Andes Ranges as well as from Indian land. "
Next is a historical note about the buildings and living arrangements of the Swift Plant; San Julián was basically a company town that depended on the Swift business.

"The Swift company had three buildings for staff accommodation; one was for regular employees where they could cook meat in a hallway that divided the two wings of the building. Another was for qualified personnel; cooks, porters, foremen, watchmen, and identified with the No. 50. It was an excellent masonry building of two floors, which though it was rather plain, was quite comfortable. The third building was called Siberia, where the common laborers lived; inside sheets of metal divided it into sections, it was

very cold, and that's why it was named as it was. At the entrance there were houses, one was for the chief engineer and the other was destined for the accountant."

The Swift Plant of San Julián was rocked by the major labor troubles that affected most of Patagonia in the early 1920's, and known as la *Patagonia Rebelde,* the harsh working conditions in the cold south and the poor pay were never questioned by anyone who knew the real situation.

http://www.oni.escuelas.edu.ar/2003/santacruz/283/historia.htm

"El Asalto...Confesión de Lewis," *La Prensa,* October 24, 1917, op. cit., p. 1, col. 6

32. Rios Silva, "El asalto al Banco de Londres, Detalles desconocidos," *Tribuna Salteña,* November 7, op. cit., p. 5, col. 3

33. Aguirre, op. cit., pp. 128-132

34. ibid., Aguirre, pp. 357, 359, 371-372, 379

35. Buck and Meadows, WOLA Journal, op.cit. p. 1

"El asalto al Banco," La Prensa, October 26, p. 1, col. 6

36. Daniel Buck, email to the author, April 15, 2014

37. Robert and Katharine Barrett, 'A Yankee in Patagonia," op.cit, p. 207

38. ibid., Robert and Katharine Barrett, p. viii

39. *"pero la versión no fue confirmada, y a la luz de hechos posteriores parece fruto de la confusión y el temor."*

Aguirre, op. cit., p. 170

40. Later analysis of legal and police errors in the events after the assault included calls for the defense lawyers of the three criminals to request the annulment of the testimony that had been translated by Mr. Armstrong because he was a close friend of the deceased.

"¿Qué hace la justicia?" *La Prensa*, October, October 25, p. 1, col. 1

41. *"los dos americanos no alcanzan de expresar claramente el español..."*

"La Prisión de los Apaches, Las declaraciones," *Diario Nuevo*, Salto, October 19, p. 1, col. 4

42. *"Los primeros dos no hablan absolutamente nada en Español y se valían de Martínez de intérprete."*

"El Asalto al Banco...Los delinquentes en Paysandú," *La Prensa*, October 20, op. cit., p. 1, col. 2

"La indiada en el Salto, Los delinquentes han estado en Paysandú," *El Diario*, Paysandú, October 17, p. 1, col. 4

43. *"...le dijo al mejicano, en tono imperativo en claro español; '¡No declare nada!'"*

"Ecos de la Indiada de Salto," *El Diario*, Paysandú, October 20, 1917, p. 1, cols. 5-6

As quoted below this same newspaper, the day before, related, as did all newspapers, that the two Americans did not speak any Spanish, but it added a note of doubt as to whether the Americans were that slow when it came to Spanish. Evidently the reporter who wrote these lines smelled something fishy, and by the next day's report he had sought out the testimony of the policeman who had heard Lewis speaking in proper Spanish.

"An interpreter was designated for their declaration, as these individuals, whether by deceit or by truth, do not clearly express themselves in Spanish."

"Para la declaración de estos se designó un intérprete, pues los individuos, sea por maña o por verdad, no saben expresarse claramente en español."

"La indiada en el Salto, Los criminales ante la justicia," *El Diario*, Paysandú, October 19, 1917, AM Edition, p. 1, col. 3

44. "Los asaltantes al Banco de Londres...con Frank Lowis (sic)," *El Paysandú*, October 24, op. cit., p. 1, col. 4

45. Even "make a declaration" when it is translated from Spanish to English almost always comes out as "make a statement." In English declare is only used in combination with another word when an official "*takes* a declaration," which can also be expressed as "*receives* a declaration." The corollary to this is when an individual *gives* a declaration. These uses are always found in a legal setting. By contrast, upon arrest or confrontation the villain might admit, confess, sing, blurt out, etc., but it is only later in the police station or in a court setting that he might go so far as to "make a statement" or even "give a declaration". But simply "declare," no.

46. *"...tuvo en el Hervidero un ímpetu de impaciencia y codeando al mejicano, le dijo en voz baja que se callara."*

"Cómo se efectuó la captura...Revelaciones del mejicano," *El Telégrafo*, October 19, op. cit., p. 2, col.3

47. "El asalto al Banco. Ultimas informaciones," *La Prensa*, October 20, op. cit., p. 1, col. 2

48. William Wilson, Robert Evan's unfortunate sidekick, arrived in Argentina from the US when he was only 19 years old and was killed for his troubles at the ripe old age of 26, so it is safe to assume that other "associates" of Cassidy and

Co. could have arrived in South America at a quite young age.
Buck and Meadows, WOLA Journal, op.cit. p. 1

49. They have a joke in Uruguay that works both in Spanish and English - you are supposed to answer each line with the word that best fits the phrase:

"The Mexicans descended from the....answer: Aztecs.

The Peruvians descended from the....answer: Incas.

The Uruguayans descended from the...answer: Boats."

All of them came from Europe and got off a boat.

CHAPTER SIX: "ONCE IN THE DANCE..."

Una vez en el baile...

"Lightning. Once it has forked, hot-white, from sky to earth, there is no going back"

Ally Condie, Matched

This phrase used throughout Latin America; *"una vez en el baile...,"* is rhetorical; the phrase doesn't have a second half, which, of course, is understood. "Once in the dance..." you have to keep dancing until the dance is over. If you get something started, it's up to you to finish it. The plans and actions of this gang have inexorably set in motion a series of actions and circumstances and choices that will now take them accelerating towards a destination that none in the group has fully taken into account. Of course any criminal gang like this has to be sufficiently determined and bold to take the risks of such a venture, or they would never have set out on the outlaw paths in the first place.

© Richard Dean Young

Dayman River Camp
Cattle crossing at the *Paso de la Cadena*

El Paso de la Cadena de los Laureles, today this continues to be an important livestock crossing.

On the 10th of October the band left Paysandú for Salto; they were mounted on the three "excellent" horses. On Saturday, the 13th of October, they arrived at the main Dayman River crossing point, *el Paso de las Piedras*. They didn't settle at their final camping spot from which they would ride out for the assault until the next day, Sunday. That final camp was made at a crossing of the Dayman further east known variously as *Los Laureles* or *El Paso de la Cadena*, and at times by its complete name, *El Paso de la Cadena de Laureles*.

Paso de la Cadena was an alternative crossing of the Dayman River about 13 miles to the east and upstream from the main crossing. Its name means "The Crossing of the Chain" - evidently there was a chain that crossed the stream at that time, perhaps to grab onto in high water and flood season. Back at the main Dayman crossing the Paysandú-Salto road ran in a north-south direction. After the gang rode north from Paysandú to this main Dayman crossing, instead of crossing the river they turned east passing through the countryside along the southern bank of the Dayman River to eventually arrive at the Paso de la Cadena crossing. They made this ride in order to get a lay of the land for their escape route after the assault on the Bank. (1)

The gang carefully chose this more easterly location to make camp before their incursion into Salto. This ford of the Dayman River was mostly off the beaten track, although it was used in those days, just like today, as a main livestock crossing. The regular vehicle, cart and horse traffic, which plied the main highway, today Route 3, would not come this far east. It gave the outlaws a somewhat secluded place from which to strike, and also a place to leave their horses and other supplies that could be retrieved later.

The Salto newspaper, *La Prensa*, reported later, on October 24th, that when the three arrived at the main Dayman River crossing on Saturday, October 13th, the day before setting up their final camp, that, while Atkins and Lewis stayed on the south side of the river, Martínez then took the horses on to Salto to get them shod. The gang would later abandon the car used in the holdup at this same crossing. From this later information we understand that the outlaws did not immediately ride east to their camp spot, but that Lewis and Atkins waited south of the main crossing for Martínez to return with their newly shod horses.

Drinking Buddies

The guard manning the check point just north of the river, Alfredo Cuadrado, seeing Martínez riding north with several horses ordered him to stop and asked if he had papers for the three horses, for which he immediately produced the bill of sale.

Afterwards they both went across the road to a *pulpería*, country store and watering hole, belonging to a Mr. *Catáneo*, and shared a drink. We will see that when the gang comes speeding by a few days later, after the holdup in Salto, this same *pulpería* and this same officer will play a role in the attempts to stop and apprehend the Tin Can Gang.

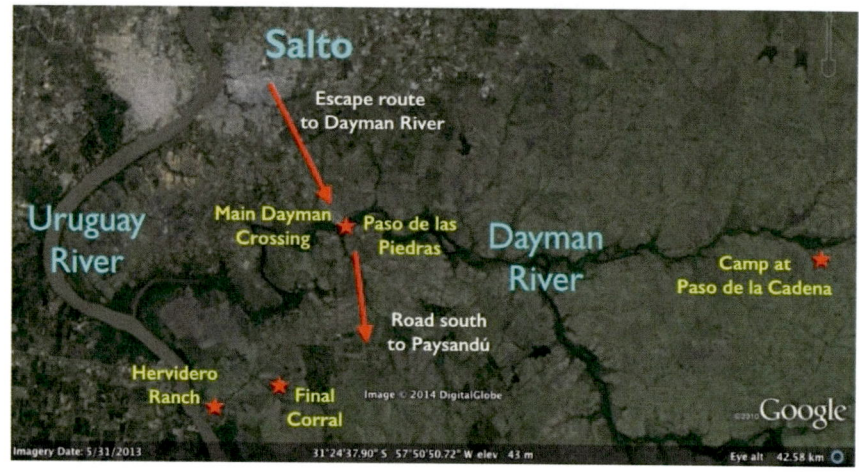

Map of the Salto/Dayman Area

Area from Salto to the Hervidero Ranch and Corral where the outlaws were finally captured.

Underlying image from Google Earth, 2013

El Peón and the Camp

According to later testimony of the Apaches, they had hired a laborer, a Black Uruguayan, *"un peón negro"*, (2) to watch their animals and supplies until they returned to the *Paso de la Cadena*. It would seem logical that they found this worker in the vicinity of their camping spot and hired him for that purpose, and this only for the two to three days immediately before and up to their return after the assault.

The field where they camped is still an open grassy area that runs from south to north as it slopes down and narrows before reaching the Dayman River. This "river" is really just a stream except at flood time.

@Richard Dean Young

Paso de la Cadena camp for the Tin Can Gang

Area where the gang camped and left their horses at Paso de la Cadena - view from the south towards the north and the Dayman River

Another reason for having their camp in this rather secluded corner was that after the heist they were planning to head north to Brazil, and even talked about going further to Paraguay. North would be a direction that few would expect them to flee. Crossing back over directly into Argentina would be the more logical choice, but that would also be the escape route to first be patrolled. While at the camp they made several excursions on horseback to get to know the territory and especially to scout out at least the first part of their northward escape route.

Buried Booty

According to later testimony, Atkins had buried some of their remaining capital near the camp spot with the purpose of picking it up after the robbery. Since he had withdrawn over $1,300 dollars, in pesos, from the Bank in Buenos Aires, and since the costs of the excursion into Uruguay, along with the horses, arms and other supplies would not have added up to anywhere near half of that amount, the money buried near *Paso de la Cadena* had to be an important sum for those times. There might also have been extra funds from the robberies in both Paysandú and Salto to secure until their return from the big bust.

@Richard Dean Young

Gonzalo and Tito Panissa, 2007

Ranchers who own a good sized Estancia near Paso de la Cadena.

Tito and Gonzalo Panissa, owners of the San Antonio Ranch, south of *Paso de la Cadena*, recounted to me how treasure hunters have dug up the open areas around the crossing for the past 90+ years. (3) The money had been buried using several trees for reference according to Atkins' testimony. Just how far away from the camp he dug his hole, and just which trees were used have never been discovered, so hopeful treasure hunters still show up from time to time to tear up the surrounding real estate. Most likely Atkins rode some distance from the camp to stash his funds, certainly he would not want the hired man seeing where he was digging a hole, and probably didn't want the other two Apaches knowing either.

Declarations to the Judge

After the capture of the bandoleros, the District Judge of Salto, Doctor *Mariano Pereira Núñez* Jr., took the declarations of all three criminals. These statements were recorded at the police headquarters by Núñez' clerk, the notary *Jorge Castro*. (4) The gang entered in multiple contradictions, especially as to which ones were responsible for the planning and financing of the assault. But some basic facts did come out that added to the larger picture of how the assault was put together and carried out.

Model T Getaway Car

One detail that became clearer is how the Ford Model T was *procured* for the use of the gang. (5) Atkins, Lewis and Martínez set up their camp on Saturday, October 13th, and then on Monday, October 15th, the day before the actual hit,

Martínez returned to Salto. Later information indicated that all three went to Salto that day, thus the other two could return to the camp leading Martínez's horse.

¡Traición!

A Molinos Campos Painting from Argentina depicting the treasonous act of pulling a gun during what should have been a duel of knives.

Martínez stayed the night in a house of ill-repute run by a woman named Servanda Rodríguez. This residence was located on the street *19 de Abril*, between the streets *Julio Delgado* and *Hervidero*, about 6-8 blocks from the bank itself, and a few blocks closer to the Uruguay River in an area of bars and other such "businesses." (6) Martínez invited those present to share a beer with him, and danced the tango with several women.

When the morning came Martinez called for a rental car from the same residence. The owner, Antonio Casaretto, and his driver-mechanic, Juan Figueredo, soon appeared with a red Ford Model T, with the license number 249. (7) In the phone call Martínez had explained that he had two American businessmen waiting at Paso de la Cadenas, and that they wished to see some country property as they were looking to buy a ranch. When the vehicle approached the crossing, about 200 yards from the camp, Lewis and Atkins stepped out of the bushes and greeted the surprised men with raised rifles and ordered them out of the car. Figueredo then drew a knife and said indignantly;

"That's not how 'men' kill each other; come on, let's fight!" (8)

To which Martínez laughed and ordered him to throw down his knife. Figueredo, who was now thinking the better of his outburst and bravado, and also contemplating three weapons aimed at him, obeyed the order.

Airborne Poncho

The three then boarded the Ford, and with Lewis driving headed back to Salto. Figueredo yelled after them to not be such heathen to take his poncho, which they threw out of the car without slowing their march.

Lewis, in later testimony, said that he then inspected the car, which was not done near the camp, because they had taken off immediately after "requisitioning" the Model T. After the inspection he then told the others it would not do the job; it wasn't fast enough because the motor was worn, and the carburetor was placed much too low for a river crossing. (9) He was right on the mark with his mechanical observations.

There are several indications that by this time in the plot Lewis had grown quite weary of Martínez, and the three had a heated argument about whether the car would do the job.

© Richard Dean Young

Paso de la Cadena Bridge

A later bridge and cobblestone approach at this crossing of the Dayman River.

By the time the car had been requisitioned and the three drove off, it was already past midday. The two unfortunate men on foot had no other choice than to set off back up the road to Salto. After covering about four miles they came to a country store that had a phone, but their call arrived too late because the assault at the bank had already gone down.

20-Mile Crawl to Destiny

In the first confusing days after the attempted *steal on wheels* several of the newspaper accounts related that the two rental car men were tied to a post and later freed themselves. That did not happen and contradicts the flying poncho incident; the two were simply left on foot near the river. Since the actual carjacking happened a prudent distance from the river, before the vehicle even approached the river crossing, the two taxi men never saw the camp or the horses on the other side of the stream. I myself stood at approximately that same spot and nothing could be seen of the other side of the river, let alone the area of the camp.

The gang arrived at the bank at approximately 1:55 p.m. Therefore their drive into Salto, about 20 miles over country roads, took them over one and a half hours. That would be an exceptionally slow crawl, even for a Model T. This time lag coincides with Lewis saying that somewhere along the path he had made the inspection of their newly acquired transportation.

References: Chapter 6

1. "El Asalto al Banco...Aprensión de los Criminales," *Diario Nuevo*, Salto, October 18, p.1, col. 3

2. *peón negro*: the use of the word *negro* in River Plate Spanish does not always indicate a person of Afro-American descent, although it did mean just that in the newspaper accounts of this incident. Uruguay does have a minority of Afro-American citizens. The word can often mean a person of darker coloring, and even in families a member with a bit darker skin may often get the nickname *Negro*. Generally, the term does not carry racist overtones.

3. Panissa, Tito and Gonzalo, Interview at the Panissa ranch, north Paysandú District, May, 2009

4. "La prisión de los apaches, Las declaraciones," *Diario Nuevo*, Paysandu, October 19, 1917, p. 2, col. 3

5. "El Asalto al Banco de Londres...En vísperas del asalto," *La Prensa*, October 24, op. cit., p. 1, col. 3

6. Taborda, 1947, op. cit., p.86

7. "El asalto al Banco de Londres, En vísperas del asalto," *La Prensa*, October 24, op. cit., p. 1, col. 4

8. *"¡así no se mata a los hombres; si quieren vamos a pelear!"*

Taborda, op. cit., p. 87

In the Gaucho tradition of Argentina and Uruguay it was considered unmanly to fight with firearms, those were the weapons of the weak; real men fought with the traditional *facón*. In fact most Gauchos only carried a knife, refusing to arm themselves with the new-fangled firearms.

9. Rios Silva, "El Asalto al Banco, Los amigos se juntan," *Tribuna Salteña*, November 7, 1917, op. cit., p. 5, col. 4

una vez en el baile...

An Argentine Molinos Campos painting; "Dancers with Guitars." Molinos Campos' paintings appeared on a series of calendars in Argentina during the middle of the 20th century, they are quite hilarious, poke fun at the gaucho tradition, and are favorite finds in old bookstores and antique shops.

CHAPTER SEVEN: STEAL ON WHEELS

The original Bank of London building was located to the left, where later stood the building of the newer "Caja Obrera" Bank. The former MacFarlane residence still stands to the right.

The Salto Bank of London (1) opened its doors each week day at 1:30 in the afternoon. One of the two bank guards, Mr. *Hermelindo Meloni*, an Italian immigrant who had arrived from Genoa in 1895, showed up for work on Tuesday, October 16th, accompanied by his wife, María Rossi, and their five-year-old daughter Dora. Mrs. Meloni and her daughter were taking advantage of the trip into town from the *Cerro* neighborhood to do some shopping after accompanying Mr. Meloni to his job. (2) The other employees would have arrived at about this same time, and the bank manager, George MacFarlane, arrived using an inner door at the rear that linked the bank to the manager's family residence next door. This door entered from back patio area of the house.

Open for Business

At approximately 1:55 p.m. a red Model T Ford drove up and parked across the street from the Bank of London, located at Nº 43 Sarandi Street, between Rivera Street to the south and Artigas Street to the north. The Ford was parked pointing north because then, as now, this was a one-way street. Three men crossed the street and entered the bank but left the motor running, the hand crank starting system on these old Fords was known for being *cranky*. Mr. Meloni actually opened the door for the three men and then returned to his seat beside the door. Two of the men headed towards the counter, and almost immediately Meloni heard people running inside the rear office area, so he stood up only to have a gun rudely pushed into his temple by Frank Lewis who had a finger to his lips motioning for silence. (3)

The MacFarlane residence until October of 1917

The official residence of the bank manager, next to the bank

"Not One Step!"

At this point the Mexican had jumped up on the counter
that separated the right entrance area from the left office
area and ordered in Spanish *"¡Ni un paso!"* "Not one step!"
Atkins, at the same time, was pointing his gun at the teller
and an accounting employee in an office to his left. Then
Martínez ordered one of them to take Atkins to the bank's
safe. MacFarlane was in a side office to the right, towards the
rear of the main office area and only steps from his own
office. He was seated at a small table using a typewriter
when he heard the ruckus, but he couldn't see what was
happening because a tall desk blocked his view. He then
leaned forward to look into the main office area behind the
counter; immediately Martínez pointed his revolver directly
at the manager and ordered him not to move.

MacFarlane ignored the order and crouching low he
went running directly to his office where he grabbed a pearl-
handled revolver out of his own desk drawer.

Odd Shots and a Wrestling Match

As soon as MacFarlane disappeared into his office, Atkins abandoned his two charges in the left office and bank safe area, ran through the office where MacFarlane had been sitting and followed him into his office. Two shots were then fired inside this office; these shots were not fired together, rather there was a short time-lapse between the first and second. These were fired while the two men were caught up in a wrestling match. MacFarlane's shot went straight down into the floor; which indicates that Atkins had grabbed him from behind in a bear hug right after he picked up his revolver. A shot from Atkins' gun hit the baseboard just inches from the door where he had entered - this shot, which was heard some seconds later, was fired from a position parallel to the floor, because by this time MacFarlane, who was physically much stronger, literally got the upper hand and had thrown Atkins to the floor where he had him pinned down on his back. The *El Paysandú* newspaper gives the information that there was a mark on the floor where someone's shoe had slipped "violently" - this was surely from Atkins' sole as he went down under the exceedingly greater force of MacFarlane. (4)

A drawing of the Bank of London after it became the Uruguayan 'Banco Caja Obrera'. *The car at the front and the people on the sidewalk are quite out of perspective.*

In a telegram expressing his condolences for MacFarlane's passing, his previous boss and personal friend, Theodore Bourse in Buenos Aires, mentions that he and MacFarlane had often talked about the security situation of the bank and how to guarantee its safety. That MacFarlane now owned a gun had to be part of his personal response to these conversations, and Bourse says quite clearly that he always knew that *Mac*, his colleague and good friend, would be ready to confront any attack on the bank. (5)

Atkins later said that MacFarlane, with his own gun, had repeatedly hit his right wrist, trying to get him to release his weapon. Atkins showed bruises on that wrist where the bank manager had hammered it with his own revolver. It was while he was in this position, flat on his back on the floor, with MacFarlane attempting to rid Atkins of his weapon, which Atkins' gun actually fired and sent the bullet skimming along the floor to pierce the baseboard beside the door into the office.

"It appears that one of the shots fired by this subject [Atkins] was fired along the floor, the precise strange direction of the projectile could not be discerned well because its trajectory introduced it into the baseboard." (6)

The trajectory of this shot is not that "strange," knowing from later testimony just what happened in the office, and it is important because it shows that MacFarlane had the outlaw pinned to the floor where, in a sense, Atkins was "facing" the door through which he had recently entered. Atkins' right hand, parallel to the floor, was roughly aimed back at the point from which he had entered the room. We do not know if he pulled the trigger by design, or if MacFarlane's blows to his hand caused the detonation. MacFarlane himself, leaning over and subjecting Atkins, was facing away from the door therefore he could not see when another entered from behind.

Fatal Body Blow

From both testimony and evidence it is apparent that MacFarlane could have shot Atkins instead of trying to disarm him. All this happened within seconds, and in the midst of MacFarlane's dominating Atkins, Martínez came running in and observed that MacFarlane had Atkins pinned to the floor under him. Martínez would say later that he could not even see Atkins' head because MacFarlane's body blocked his view. Martínez then shot MacFarlane through the right side of his torso. (7) A group of journalists from several papers later interviewed Martínez in the Salto jail. When they asked him *why* he had shot MacFarlane, he did not directly answer their question, rather he merely said that at first he was going to shoot MacFarlane through the head, but when he realized that the bullet might pass on through and hit Atkins, he had to shoot him through the body.

Mr. Jorge Macfarlane

Meses antes de su muerte, en pose para «Tribuna Salteña».

This photo of MacFarlane was taken several months earlier, and was printed in La Tribuna newspaper the day after his death.

While MacFarlane was overpowering Atkins and holding him to the floor, Martínez, after what was only a slight hesitation, deliberately shot him with the intention of doing the most damage possible. The bullet passed through MacFarlane's body, at an angle that would not permit it to hit Atkins who was directly below MacFarlane. As we wrote earlier, this projectile first penetrated the right lung, then passed through the heart, and was later removed from the upper part of the left lung.

MacFarlane was kneeling over Atkins in the process of subduing him when he was shot; one article gives the information that a knee of his pants was marked with dust from the floor; this was his left knee because he was leaning over towards that side to deal with the gun in Atkins' right hand. Right before the fatal shot MacFarlane had had both hands busy dealing with the gun in Atkins' hand, this with Atkins flat on his back, so MacFarlane's upper body would have been angled up above that of Atkins, his lower torso about 13-14 inches above the floor, and his upper torso about 24-26 inches above the floor and leaning slightly to his left where both hands were busy with Atkins' right hand. Thus for Martinez to shoot at the angle he did, he had to have pointed the pistol directly at MacFarlane's right side, and then fired at an upward angle aiming through the body. The bullet would have entered about 7-9 inches below his right armpit. This was a deliberate shot, calculated in the moment, but designed to kill and remove the threat to his partner.

According to the autopsy done the next morning by the Doctors Sosa and Olarreaga, the bullet was from a Colt pistol; a full-jacketed .45 military-type round. (8)

1911 Colt Semi-Auto .45 ACP

The 1911 Colt pistol, made from a design by the Belgian gunmaker Browning, had been ordered by the US Military as a man-stopping small arm whose cartridge would have the same effect on human beings as a shot from the famous .45 Long Colt. The "old" .45 Colt had been one of the magnums of the 19th century. No one gets shot with a .45 Long Colt or a .45 ACP Colt cartridge and remains standing, the shock is just too great. This is why the 1911 Colt was the favorite sidearm of US forces in both World Wars, other than the fact that it never quit working, clean, dirty, wet or otherwise.

Later testimony by both Atkins and Martínez indicates that it was Atkins himself who entered the bank carrying the .45 Colt semi-automatic pistol. A clip from this pistol was found on the floor of MacFarlane's office after the would-be thieves fled from the bank. Atkins had actually run after MacFarlane with this pistol in hand, and then Martínez used that same pistol to shoot the bank manager. Therefore MacFarlane did actually get Atkins to release the pistol, and Martinez would have had to pick it up to make the fatal shot. It appears that MacFarlane's blows to Atkins' gun hand not only caused one shot to be fired, but also activated the magazine catch button, either directly or by a hit to Atkins' right thumb, and then the force of this punishment finally knocked the pistol from Atkins's grip and sent it sliding along the floor for Martinez to pick up.

Salto Antiguo

A downtown view from a few years after the bank assault

Securing the loose gun was Martinez's first reaction since the Colt was lying free on the floor - he instinctively grabbed it before MacFarlane himself could take it up. All witnesses said that Martinez was waving a *revólver* when seconds before he had ordered everyone to stand still in the main part of the bank. We know that Martinez practiced with and carried at different times at least two different revolvers. He himself, as we noted earlier, testified that he entered the bank carrying an imitation of the Smith & Wesson revolver, probably chambered for a .38 cartridge.

Martinez may or may not have realized that the magazine had been ejected from the Colt 45, but it would still have one bullet in the chamber - enough for the job at hand. We can't enter Martinez' head from our vantage point and suppose that he instinctively knew that the Colt .45 was the hardest hitting short gun that any of them carried. All we know is that he used it, and that he fired one shot.

Down, But Not Quite Out

When MacFarlane received the paralyzing shot he collapsed on top of Atkins, mortally wounded. But the amazing physical strength and top condition of this British sportsman amazed all the medical practitioners who had a direct part in treating Mr. MacFarlane that day; he was shot through the lung *and* the heart at about 2:00 in the afternoon, and he lived until 7:50 that night. After the autopsy none could believe that this was actually possible, and none had ever witnessed such stamina and amazing human strength after a similar mortal wound. At that time in history there was no possibility of a medical solution for George MacFarlane once he had been so severely wounded, and he had just been moved to the operating table at the local hospital when an attending doctor indicated to the surgeon that MacFarlane had finally expired.

Bullet through the Heart?

We have consulted with cardiologists, referenced medical literature concerning wounds to the heart, as well as interviewed law officers who have seen many gunshot deaths and witnessed autopsies. We asked about the possibility that someone could actually survive a gunshot wound *through* the heart for the almost six hours that George MacFarlane remained alive.

All concede that a gunshot wound from a large-caliber pistol that penetrated even one of the ventricles or chambers of the heart, or the aorta or atriums at the top, would not be survivable for more than five to ten minutes, let alone several hours. And a gunshot wound, or other puncture wound, that compromises two of the heart's chambers is usually fatal in an even shorter time. There is ample medical literature of persons surviving knife wounds to the heart, or pellets from pellet guns, or individual pellets from shotguns...

"In contrast, large-caliber gunshot wounds result in fatal gaping cardiac defects" (9)

In recent decades the rate of patients arriving at trauma centers in the US with penetrating gunshot wounds to the heart has now surpassed that of knife wounds. Until WWII there were very few successful surgeries on the heart for any kind of penetrating wound, then during WWII Dr. Dwight Harkin was able to successfully remove "intercardiac projectiles" from 13 soldiers, and all lived. (10) But even now with advances in emergency techniques as well as in surgical procedures, only 11% of victims with bullet wounds to the heart survive *until* they arrive at trauma centers. We could find no statistics on how many of these were also saved. (11)

The medical doctors who performed the autopsy on MacFarlane concluded that the .45 caliber bullet had passed through the right lung, then *through* the heart, and lodged in the upper part of the left lung. Martínez fired an upward angling shot through the center of the torso. We know this both because of where he was standing, above and to the right of MacFarlane, and also because of his deliberately choosing an angle for the shot that would not endanger his companion who was held to the floor on his back by MacFarlane.

A fairly simple exercise will confirm this trajectory. You stand behind a person who is resting on his left knee with his torso angled above the floor. His arms should be extended down as if subjecting another person's right hand and wrist. You will see that the natural position of the shooter's right hand when the palm is held against the side of the kneeling subject, with or without a pistol, aims at a 45° downward angle in relation to the floor and also points at a slightly upward angle in relation to the body. Since Martinez did not want his colleague to be hit, he closed his wrist so that the projectile would pass on a plane parallel with the body, and that action increased even more the upward angle of his aim in relation to the torso. He wanted the bullet to pass through the body where it would do the most damage, so both this parallel line and the upward trajectory are natural and not forced.

If the angle of the bullet took it through the lower part of the heart it could possibly have penetrated only the lower right ventricle, because that chamber reaches further down towards the base of the heart itself. But with that large a hole punched through the walls of the heart *and* a major chamber there is no medically known way that the heart itself could close the wound or form a clot;

"If the defect in the pericardium is large, rapid exsanguination and death will occur." (12)

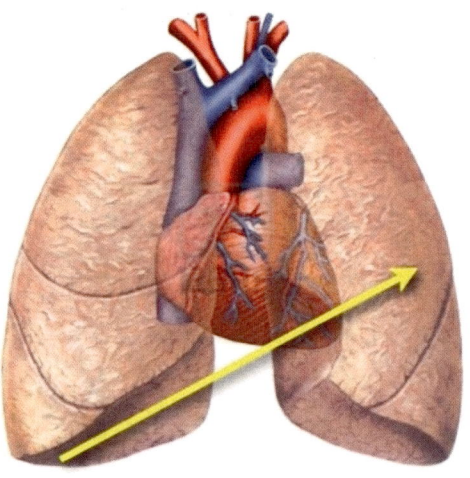

A heart and lung diagram with an arrow added showing the possible trajectory of a bullet passing through the lower muscle of the heart.

There are two possibilities that we can imagine, and which have some medical substantiation at least as theories. The first is that the trajectory of the bullet sent it at an exact upward angle through the right lung so that it penetrated the muscle at the very base of the heart without entering the right ventricle itself. At that angle it would also be impossible for the bullet to compromise the smaller left ventricle, and it would have lodged finally in the central part the left lung. With this angle of the projectile Martinez would have had to shoot MacFarlane from a point even further

190

down his body, some 10-12 inches below the armpit and below the rib cage itself.

The only problem with this theory is that the autopsy reported that the projectile lodged in the *upper* part of the left lung. However, it is known that athletes, especially those who have been active since adolescence, often have larger lungs and larger heart muscles. Sometimes this enlargement actually results in a pathological hypertrophy of the heart, but we would need to have a much more complete report as well as the measurements of MacFarlane's internal organs to be able to establish this as a firm hypothesis.

The second possibility is that the bullet passed through the top of the heart and did not compromise the left atrium, the aorta, or any of the larger arteries or veins. The walls of these vessels are quite tough and a slowed-down projectile *could* have squeezed on through without actually fatally penetrating these major tubular structures. (13) If even one of these large chambers or tubes had been perforated, death would have been quick if not almost instantaneous.

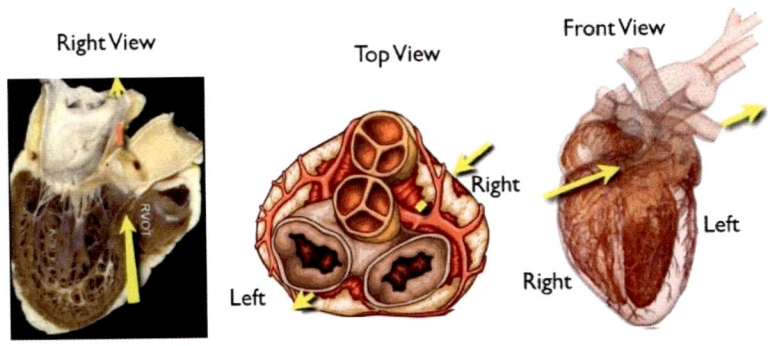

Upper heart trajectory

In these three diagrams the bullet passes through the top of the heart without affecting the larger vessels.

The advantage of this second theory is that it accords with the bullet lodging in the upper part of the left lung, and the heart would have shown the entrance and exit wounds as reported in the autopsy. The information we have from the autopsy does not confirm, or deny, this trajectory.

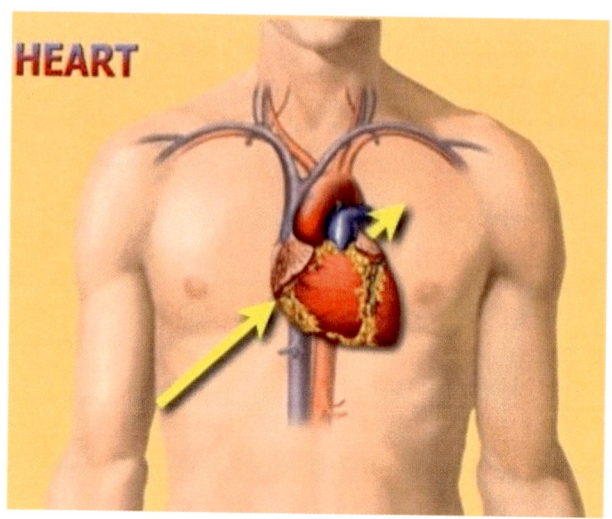

The tilting heart

The human heart does not sit straight up and down in the chest, rather the base points markedly to the left while the top leans over to the right. The angle that Martinez's chose for his shot was not forced, rather it was on the same plane as the body, and his purposefully closing his wrist to aim along this plane and to keep from shooting down towards Atkins, caused the bullet to take a sharp upward path through the torso causing the penetration of the heart to be literally from side to side and through its upper part.

My brother, Dave Young, a state policeman, armorer, and court-appointed expert witness on ballistics as well as gunshot wounds who lives in the Pacific Northwest, gave me some background on the Colt .45 slug that passed through a good part of MacFarlane's torso. The Colt pistols in those days used the standard US issue 230 grain round nose brass jacketed bullet, as was informed by the autopsy.

"It was never designed to do massive damage to tissue, just to make a big hole and if it hit a bone, it would break it. I have seen round-nosed slugs that went completely through chest cavities and out the other side that caused little

bleeding, and some of the folk, so struck, didn't even know they were shot till later when they found blood on their shirt. Round nosed bullets at their low velocity, 700 FPS or so, do not cause severe tissue damage when passing through the body, they just push the tissue aside and slide on through." (14)

Thus the .45 slug, when it finally passed through the heart, would not have done major damage to the tissue. Rather it would have made a hole that could at least partially close if it were through muscle tissue and not through one of the chambers of the heart or one of the large vessels at the top. If either had been the case, the simple function of the heart's *pumping* would have immediately forced massive amounts of blood out of the heart into the chest cavity.

Dave goes on to say that the projectile would have already done its major damage at the entry point in the first tissue it encountered including the right lung. When it reached the left lung it had slowed down considerably and then stopped.

"By the time it reached the heart it was about like getting shot with a slingshot, it had just enough velocity to do a little damage. The major damage was to the right lung and surrounding tissue on the way in. Heart muscle is very very tough, it never stops exercising. MacFarlane's heart and other muscles in the area were most likely in fine shape, and besides, he was engaged in some tense activity when he was shot. If the Doctors say the heart was hit, it surely was. The damage it received could have been minor, but not survivable." (15)

The simple facts we have on which to base our theory are those that MacFarlane survived for almost six hours after being shot, and that two medical doctors attested that the bullet had passed through these vital organs. The records of the *Sanatorio Salto*, whose building still functions as a hospital in Salto but under completely different management, no longer exist.

The doctors who performed the autopsy asserted that the bullet passed through the heart, but no mention was made of it compromising either of the ventricles or any of the larger arteries or veins. We assume they did not dissect the heart itself to further show the cause of death. These doctors were not forensic pathologists, and the observation of an entry and exit wound to the heart itself was sufficient for their purpose in determining the cause of death.

MacFarlane's internal injuries, even without a traumatic penetration of any of those critical components of the heart, were sufficient to cause his death. That he survived such a brutal gunshot injury for that extended time is still a marvel and a testimony to his physical strength and stamina. To have survived a *"fatal gaping cardiac defect"* (16) for that same amount of time could only have been miraculous.

Window of Opportunity

The three shots inside the bank had already drawn the attention of passersby, and the Bank teller, who actually had a firearm at hand but was too spellbound to reach for it, waited until the three bandits had passed out through front door before he went to the window to raise the alarm. One newspaper gives the account that this employee, named *Avellanal*, picked up a pistol with the intention of stopping the three intruders. (17) But this comes from a report the day after the attempted robbery when many of the details were still not clear. It is possible that the teller reported at first that he had taken the bold step of grabbing his pistol, but later testimony by other bank employees gives the lie to this, and even shows that the teller was too frightened to approach the door of the bank to holler for help, and decided that the window was the safer place from which to sound the alarm.

The Second Guard

An employee named *Echeverría* had actually escaped ahead of MacFarlane towards the rear of the bank when the ruckus started in the main office; he passed through a bathroom that had two doors and ran quickly to the far rear of the Bank and entered the storage room where the bank kept supplies and paper. The second guard, a Mr. *Della Britta*, was in this same room - having been sent there to fetch office supplies. Echeverría briefly told him what was happening up front. Neither guard, Mr. Meloni beside the Bank's main door nor Mr. Della Britta in the back storage room was armed that afternoon, and it isn't clear if they had *ever* carried sidearms while "guarding" the bank. Bank robberies were unknown in Uruguay up to that point, so it may have seemed almost pretentious to walk around with a firearm.

Several of the other employees took advantage of the commotion in the manager's office to escape the bank through the front door. And one worker, *Popelka*, instead of running out, ran in; more precisely he ran to one side... to the Bank's large safe, climbed a ladder that was up against the side, and hid himself on top. Popelka's closeness to the happenings did provide a corroborating witness to the actual gunshots that were fired; he said he first heard two loud shots and then a third that was "softer" - this would be the third shot that Martinez detonated right up against the side of MacFarlane. Whether the Mexican had the barrel pressed against MacFarlane's side, or whether he shot from an inch or two is academic, the closeness of the shot reduced the sound of the explosion. MacFarlane's side would have received important powder burns, and if the pistol were held tight against his side there would have also been evidence of gases from the cartridge entering the body at that point - although it is doubtful that information like this was gathered as evidence at that time in Uruguay's history.

Sunset on Salto City Center

Salto's Cathedral today

Courage too Late

Della Britta, the second guard, in the meantime was looking for whatever kind of weapon he could find and settled upon a metal bar with which he went running along a side corridor between the bank and house hoping to keep anyone from exiting out of the front of the bank. When he got to the street, the car with the three criminals aboard was already pulling away. This shows how quickly matters accelerated inside the bank once MacFarlane ran for his gun. It is possible that all of these steps were through in a period of three minutes from when the Apaches entered the front door of the bank to when they rushed back out that same front door to their waiting vehicle.

George's Painful Walk

After the outlaws ran out of the bank George MacFarlane was able to actually pick himself up off the floor and walk to the back of the Bank and through the back passageway into the patio area where at least two of his children were playing. Some of the accounts say that before he did this, his wife, upon hearing the commotion and shots, had entered the bank from the rear and helped her husband to their bedroom. Other accounts say that MacFarlane arrived in the house on his own, saying something to the children playing in the patio before arriving at the bedroom, where he then found his wife with their smallest child. We will see later that these accounts about how MacFarlane and his wife found each other were based on either hearsay or conjecture.

All accounts agree on the fact that after MacFarlane arrived in the bedroom his wife Daisy then tried to stop the bleeding, and that either she or employees of the bank sent for medical personnel to come immediately. MacFarlane was quoted as first saying to his wife in Spanish, "A North American wounded me." Then, later, when asked how he was doing, he answered in Spanish, *"Lindo no más"*. This is a figure of speech which roughly translated means "I'm OK". And then he exclaimed over and over again during the afternoon, "We won! We won!" MacFarlane was exhilarated and exceedingly proud that his actions had kept the gang from stealing anything from the bank. While he knew that he was severely wounded, he did not realize how gravely. All accounts say that he was lucid, excited, running on adrenaline, and able to converse with visitors all afternoon.

Daisy's Anxious Walk

In my interview with Elena Miguens in Salto in May of 2009 a different version was discovered concerning the intervention of Daisy MacFarlane. (18) Elena's mother, Dora, five years old at the time, remembered with clear detail what happened in front of the bank that afternoon. No doubt talking over these matters with her mother, María Rossi, and with her father, Hermelindo Meloni, the guard inside the front door of the bank, helped to settle the experience in her young mind. But young children who witness critical events often have those memories indelibly implanted into their consciousness the rest of their lives.

Dora with sister and parents

Dora, upper left, perhaps 10 years after witnessing, along with her mother, the walk of Daisy from her house to the Bank

Dora and her mother had only left Mr. Meloni at the bank half an hour before the assault, and when they heard the commotion and people calling out that there was an attempt on the bank. They, along with many other curious folk, went running back towards the bank. Meloni's wife would not be one of the "curious" ones; she was most likely horrified that something might have happened to her husband. When Mrs. Meloni and little Dora arrived in front of the bank right after the Apaches had made their exit, a huge crowd had already formed on the street in front of the bank.

"At 2:05 a group of several hundred had gathered in front of the Bank building, and minute by minute the crowd kept

growing. Numerous persons, friends of Mr. MacFarlane who have their residences close to his, came to get information... showing on their faces indications of deep pessimism and concern." (19)

The huge crowd in front of the bank kept Dora and her mother from crossing the street to the sidewalk directly in front of the Bank, but Dora clearly remembered seeing the bank manager's wife leave the front of the MacFarlane residence and cross over to the bank. Dora later told her own daughter, Elena, with whom I spoke, that she remembered with clarity the look of worry on the face of the small, blond woman who hurried to the front door of the bank. (20)

These kinds of memories are quite valuable, and usually are much more exact than the speculations of those who later attempt to put together the chain of events. And the physical description of Daisy MacFarlane, passed down to Elena Miguens by her mother Dora, is the only verbal description we know of concerning one of the people most severely affected by the events of that day.

Daisy had been relatively near the front of the house when the events were unfolding next door in the bank; most of the living quarters in these traditional houses were much closer to the front of the property than to the rear, but it was at the rear of the property that the passageway connected the two buildings. The first employees that escaped through the front door could have gone to the door of the house to inform Daisy of the happenings. But we seriously doubt that this was done by those first out the door, because these employees were thinking of saving their own hide and would not want to be anywhere near the front of the bank when the robbers came out armed and perhaps shooting. In any case, if they had stopped to notify the banker's wife, she might well have crossed over to the bank before the felons came running out to the car, and that did not happen.

Daisy could have arrived in time to help her husband on his painful walk through the back of the bank and finally to their bedroom, but it is apparent that she arrived too late for that, this because of the reference to George MacFarlane speaking only to his children as he passed through the back patio. And since Daisy did not appear again at the front door of the bank, she must have followed her husband's steps through the back of the bank and into their house, most likely just seconds after MacFarlane had taken that path himself.

El edificio asaltado

"The Assaulted Building"

A photograph from the time of the attempted robbery. The main door was just to the right of the opening in center of the building. Daisy would have gone directly to this door, just a few yards away from her own front door.

What is logical is that the second guard, Mr. Della Britta, after he arrived at the street, then went to the door of the residence to let Daisy know about the attempted robbery, this after seeing the hooligans get away in their vehicle. Or it could have been one of the other employees who had stayed and realized that MacFarlane had been gravely wounded who then went to tell his wife about the attack. The bank would have had a rule that bank employees were never to enter the living spaces of the residence through the rear passageway. Thus any bank employee would immediately, and logically, think of doing the *proper* thing and go to the front door of the house - which was the formal, correct thing to do.

Some of the children indeed were playing in the rear patio area of this long extended property. Several accounts say that Daisy was in the main bedroom with her youngest daughter, aged three at the time, therefore if she had answered a call at the front door, the shortest distance to the bank and to her husband's office was by leaving through her front door and entering through the front door of the bank. And that is exactly what little Dora and her mother witnessed. (21) Dora and her mother watched Daisy leave the front door of her residence and walk over quickly and anxiously to the front door of the bank.

So Daisy entered the bank through its front door and then hurried into her husband's office only seconds after he had picked himself up off the floor and painfully made his way toward the rear of the establishment to enter the family residence through the rear passageway. Daisy then followed George's path to the rear of the bank and on into their own living spaces.

Wheezing Getaway

When the bandits made their hurried exit from the bank, without the loot they had planned on taking, they scrambled into the still-running Ford and excruciatingly commenced their getaway. A Civil Guard, a type of public watchman with almost the status of a policeman, who in this case was not armed, had heard the commotion and gunshots from down the street. He came running up right when the three Apaches rumbled off in the Ford, so he took off running after the car, blowing his whistle as he ran.

The car painfully accelerated north two and a half blocks, turned right, to the east, on *Brasil Street* and continued at the highest speed possible eleven blocks to then turn right again, south, on the street *San José*, which in two blocks became *Dr. Washington Beltrán* Street. Beltrán was the street that further to the south opened into the route that led to the crossing of the River Dayman at the *Paso de las Piedras*. This route south was the main road to Paysandú and other cities along the Uruguay River.

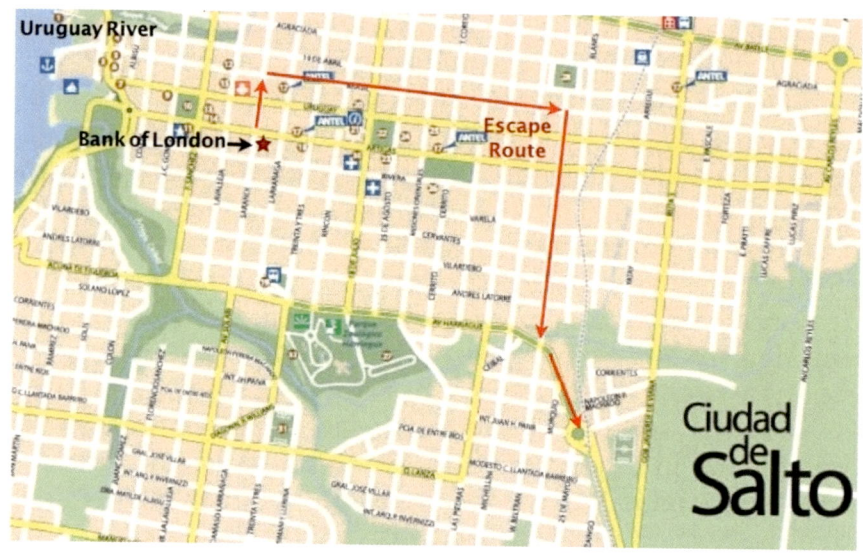

Salto and the escape route of the red Ford

The Ford's owner later said that the motor was not in the best of conditions, and that the taxi had previously received a lot of hard use. The gang had counted on a properly running vehicle; instead they got one that needed an overhaul. Thus their speed through the city and then onto the open road to Dayman would not have been anything like that of a race car - one reporter commented that a horse could have caught up with the Ford at any point along the route.

A curious remark appeared in the *Diario Nuevo* newspaper the next day among its criticisms of the slowness of the Salto Police in reacting to the crime. This was that the police chief himself had been standing on the corner of Uruguay and Larrañaga Streets; one block east of where the Ford traveled north and one block south of the Ford's route after it turned east on Brasil. The article claimed that the Police Chief had to have seen the car and its three occupants crossing both Uruguay and Larrañaga streets. Next to him was a parked car; therefore the newspaper asks why didn't he immediately go in pursuit of the bad guys. (22) The same newspaper repeated its criticism two days later and it appears that the "new Ford" that was parked on the corner was not a police car, rather a private automobile, which, of course *could* be commandeered but mostly would not be, because that was similar to riding off on someone else's horse. (23)

Downtown Salto 1923

A downtown view of Salto from the year 1923, looking down Uruguay Street towards the river to the west. The Police Chief had been standing on a corner close to this location when the Apaches drove north crossing Uruguay Street before turning east one block later. Looking west down Uruguay he "may" have seen the car cross Uruguay Street, and then if he turned and looked north he "may" have seen the Ford again one block away as it crossed Larrañaga Street.

And at about a minute from the escape of the three Apaches, and at over two blocks distance from the bank, it is doubtful that the police chief even knew yet that an assault had gone down at the bank. So seeing from the distance of a full city block that a car with three occupants was passing by, and not at a speed that would seem out of the ordinary, it would not have raised enough suspicions in the police chief's mind to take a private car and go in pursuit of three individuals who happened to be driving by. He may well have heard the guard blowing his whistle from a block away, but the guard would have crossed Uruguay Street at least some seconds after the Model T, and the chief of police, at best, may have only wondered if the whistle blowing had anything to do with the car carrying three men.

For the people along this route, seeing the red Model T coughing along as best it could with its three passengers, it would not have appeared like any kind of spectacle. Cars generally did not speed within city limits in those days. The dangers of running over pedestrians or colliding with slower moving horse-drawn carts or even mounted riders were very real. So Frank Lewis, doing all he could to coax the car along and put the maximum distance possible between the Apaches and any pursuing forces, appeared to be driving like a responsible citizen.

Wild Cities

Over the next several days the newspapers, those of Salto and Paysandú, not to mention major newspapers in the bigger cities of Montevideo and Buenos Aires, expressed their collective stupor that such a heinous crime and major holdup could ever happen in their relatively peaceful neck of the woods. Even though the smaller cities of Uruguay and Argentina had their issues with the *big* cities of Montevideo and Buenos Aires, they did not instinctively think to look towards these urban centers, which had their own problems of gangs and delinquency, for the comparisons with which to measure the earth-shaking crime just committed in their quiet corner of the woods.

Rather the examples they looked for to express the immensity of their horror and outrage were the even larger cosmopolitan centers that tended to monopolize the news; both business and cultural and, not least, criminal. So just as today when the worlds' attention continues to be unevenly concentrated on the major western centers of business, culture and misconduct, so back then; the worst they could think for calling up as examples of crime run amok came not from Montevideo or Buenos Aires, rather from London, Paris and New York.

The same Salto newspaper that commented on the faults of the police chief as well as of the whole Police Department complained about the institutional anarchy;

*"...which the people of Salto have already been suffering, and now they are amazed contemplating the presence of Apaches, **worthy of the great Paris or of cloudy London**." (24)*

While we now understand the origins of the "Apache" terminology as coming from the gangs of Paris, we can understand even more the horrific feeling in this society after a gang had perpetrated, right in their midst, the type of crime and scandal that they had only read about in their daily newspapers, and which for them could only happen continents away.

Today's Comparison - The Wild West

In Uruguay today, where crime seems to be getting out of hand, they no longer use the metaphor of the "wild cities"; today the cultural comparison is the "wild west." While Uruguay's situation is nothing like some other Latin American countries, just the impression that things are getting out of hand produces much local hand-wringing and anxious finger popping. Moreover, both government spokespersons as well as journalists themselves have the tendency to compare the latest shoot-out, bank heist or other symptom of lawlessness not with the gangs of New York, Paris or even Chicago (as they would have 50 years back with this last *mafioso* stronghold), but rather with the *Wild West* of the United States. This is a much greater testimony to the influence of Hollywood's Westerns, and Italy's..., than to any kind of studied criminology. Since I hail from that same "Wild" West I try to put things in perspective, but the influence of all the cowboy flicks and shoot-em-ups far outweigh my humble attempts to bring out the actual facts of the case.

El drama de ayer en el Banco de Londres

El gerente Sr. Macfarlane, gravemente herido, fallece horas después

Los apaches no consiguen robar nada

Un suceso a la manera neoyorkina

Todos los detalles del extraordinario acontecimiento

"A New Yorker Type of Event"

The headlines of the Salto Tribuna newspaper the day after the attempted death and adds the curious comparison of the assault to criminal happenings in New York: "An incident in the 'a la' manner of New York".

I tell those who will listen that between the Civil War and the turn of the 19th and 20th centuries, west of the Mississippi River there were only 600 homicides caused by firearms in the whole Peaceful West. Of course this didn't include Indian Wars and other such "official" mayhem. But in Uruguay today, and I would guess around the world, there is an indelible picture implanted that out West they were having shoot-outs and street duels every day. Of course in that fantasy Wild West nobody would have survived. Yet statistically, while that same Wild West was supposedly experiencing lead winging by in all directions, just *one* of the years in that same period saw over 600 firearms related homicides solely in the city of New York.

Out West. Where just about everyone had a gun, but very few were used on another human being.

So back in 1917 the press, at least, understood where the more notable sources of crime lay, and with the exception of the use of the "western" Apache title, their pointing to New York, London and Paris rang more true than the Wild West comparisons of today. Such a horrendous crime in their midst could only be explained "a la" manner of New York. And even though the *Apache* title was technically linked to the Old West of the USA, it's lineage in Uruguay and Argentina was rather one of the most notorious crime capitals of the world; Paris itself, as we indicated in the first chapter.

References: Chapter 7

1. In the Gaucho tradition the Spanish name of the bank: *El Banco de Londres y Río de la Plata.*

2. Elena Miguens Meloni - my interview with the granddaughter of the bank guard, Salto, May 2009.

3. "Una banda de apaches operando en el Salto...Las primeras noticias," *La Prensa*, October 17, op. cit., p. 1, col. 2

4. "Sobre el asalto al Banco de Londres," En el Banco," *El Paysandú*, Paysandú, October 19, 1917, p. 1, col. 4

5. "El Asalto al Banco...Telegramas de pésame," *Tribuna Salteña*, October 19, op. cit., p. 4, col. 1

6. *"Parece que uno de los disparos hechos por este sujeto (Atkins) fue desde el suelo, precisamente uno cuyo proyectil no podía precisarse bien por la extraña trayectoria que tenía, habiéndose introducido la baja en el zócalo."*

"Los celebres apaches.el siniestro terceto," La Prensa, October 19, op. cit., p. 1, col. 4.

7. "El Asalto...Por qué fue muerto Macfarlane," *Tribuna Salteña*, Salto, November 1, 1917, p. 5, col. 2

"El asalto al Banco...Nuevas declaraciones," *La Prensa*, October 21, op. cit., p. 1, col. 2

8. "Un Atentado Audaz en el Salto, La Autopsia," *El Telégrafo*, Salto, October 17, 1917, p. 3, col. 1

9. Samir R. Kapadia and Eric J. Topol, "Textbook of Cardiovascular Medicine", 3rd Edition, Lippincott, Williams & Wilkins, Philidelphia, 2007, Chapter 38: *Cardiac Trauma*, pp. 698-699

10. Reyes L.H., Mattox KL, Gaasch W.H., Espada R., Beall A.C., "Traumatic coronary artery-right heart fistula," *Journal of Thoracic and Cardiovascular Surgery*, 1975, vol. 70, pp. 52-56

11. Meredith JW, Trunkey DD. Thoracic gunshot wounds, In: Ordog G. J., ed. "Management of gunshot wounds," New York, Elsevier, 1988, pp. 283-293

12. Kapadia and Topol, op. cit.

13. Most diagrams of the heart show the flow of blood through the organ, few show clear details of the actual separations in the heart, usually called *septums*, with are muscle type tissues. The outer heart muscle, which encloses the right ventricle, also continues up over this ventricle and continues inwards and upwards towards the upper middle of the heart under the right atrium. And though a valve is present at that point, this separating tissue surrounds the valve at that level. When one sees a dissected heart, this continuing muscle or septum, which is quite thick, presents itself as a possible entrance point for the bullet along the upper extreme of the right ventricle. The projectile would have continued at an upward angle that would take it through part of the higher *oblique septum* that separates the left and right atrium. A slow moving bullet could have done just that as well as continued to slide on past the aorta and important arteries to finally have exited the heart and then lodged in the upper part of the left lung.

14. David Young, email to the author, October 19, 2013

15. *ibid.*, David Young

16. Samir R. Kapadia and Eric J. Topol, op. cit. p. 698

17. "Una banda de apaches...El asalto al Banco," *La Prensa*, October 17, op. cit., p. 1, col. 2.

"El drama de ayer...Manifestaciones de los empleados del Banco," *Tribuna Salteña*, October 17, p. 2, col. 3.

18. Elena Miguens, interview, 2009, op. cit.

19. *"A las 2 y 5 minutos se había formado frente al edificio del Banco, un grupo de varios centenares de personas, y minuto por minuto iba creciendo. Numerosas personas amigas del señor Macfarlane, que tienen su domicilio contiguo, acudían a informar. .se retiraban de allí*

mostrando en su rostro indicios de un hondo pesimismo y preocupación."

"Una Banda de apaches....Las primeras noticias," *La Prensa,* October 17, op. cit., p. 1, col. 1

20. The term blond, *rubia*, in the Southern Cone Spanish culture is not necessarily a reference to the hair color, rather mostly to the skin-tone of the person. When we first arrived in North Argentina in 1978 I remember several referring to me as a *rubio* when I still had dark black hair, the older ladies also worried that I had to be constantly sick because I was so pale.

21. The buildings and houses, in those days, were constructed on lots that often continued all the way to the center of the block. The traditional block in Uruguayan cities measures about 278 feet on each side, which means that the properties in the middle of the block could extend almost 140 feet towards the center. The houses built on these lots were much, much longer than they were wide. Towards the back of a lot one can find open patios or garden spaces, and even more common, usually towards the front, is the presence of alternating living and kitchen and washing areas, at times interspersed with patios, these often open to the sky.

Most of these traditional, European-type houses, would have a small greeting parlor at the front, followed by a living room for formal occasions. Beyond this, sometimes alternating to one side or the other, would be a dining area, bedrooms, the kitchen, bathrooms, etc. The MacFarlane residence had its main door in the middle, with tall shuttered windows on each side - we assume that this first passageway continued towards the rear through the middle of the house. Depending on whether, after the formal spaces, the bedrooms came first or the kitchen, the main bedroom, where Daisy was said to be at this time, would not have been more than 40 to 60 feet from the front of the house, and that makes Daisy's location much closer to the front than to the rear of the lot where the two properties had their inner connection.

22. "Los Apaches en el Salto...La Acción Policial," *Diario Nuevo*, Salto, October 17, p. 1, col. 4

23. In those days keyed ignitions were unknown, only first introduced by Chrysler in 1949, and while some cars were outfitted with alarms for a warning when an unauthorized person tried to get the magneto turning, the vast majority of automobiles did not have any kind of a secured ignition system. After all, horses didn't have a secured ignition system either....

24. "...la viene sufriendo el pueblo del Salto que ha tenido que contemplar, sorprendido, hasta la presencia de apaches, dignos del gran Paris y de la nebulosa Londres."

"Los Apaches...La Acción Policial," *Diario Nuevo*, October 17, op. cit., p. 1, col. 5

CHAPTER EIGHT: MARK OF HONOR

The Hermelindo-Rossi family with Dora, the youngest, standing behind her mother María. Also seated is Hermelindo Meloni, the Bank Guard.

Anxiously, he touched the lump on his head again, then felt his injured leg, groaning. "The whole affair is a mystery to me," he said. "Who would want to steal anything from me?"
"Perhaps a thief...?" ventured Julius.
Henry Winterfeld, Detectives in Togas

Elena Miguens related a marvelously colorful anecdote about her grandfather during the holdup that adds a unique personal touch to this story. After I had visited both Paysandú and Salto in 2005 on my first investigative trip, the *Telégrafo* Newspaper in Paysandú ran a story about my visit in a later Sunday supplement on the 28th of August, this about two weeks after my stay in Paysandú. The newspaper office sent me a copy of this Sunday Magazine,

"*Quinto Día,*" with the two-page story that included photos of myself taken by a newspaper photographer in their archive room while I was taking my own photos of the newspapers from 1917. The story in the supplement was titled, "The Near West" (1) and it included information from their own 1917 editions about the attempt on the Bank of London in Salto as well as an interview with me about my interest in the history of the *Near West*.

The Old West brought near

Richard Young studying the old newspaper archives for information and clues about the Tin Can Gang.

Two years later the office of the *Telégrafo* sent me contact information for a woman in Salto who had recently run across the supplement. She had read the article and then wrote to the Newspaper asking to be put in contact with me. As we mentioned earlier, this person was Elena Miguens, the granddaughter of the guard who first greeted the criminals at the front door of the bank.

I later called Mrs. Miguens and we talked briefly about what she knew concerning her grandfather and the holdup. Not until May of 2009 was I was able to make another trip to the Paysandú-Salto region, and on that trip I set up an interview with Elena and her family in her home right outside of the city of Salto.

Elena Miguens, granddaughter of the bank guard

Elena Miguens of Salto, daughter of Dora, and granddaughter of the guard, Hermelindo Meloni and his wife María Rossi.

The memories that Elena shared, having heard them from her mother, who was five years old at the time of the assault, were still clear and form part of the living heritage of a working-class family whose lives had been personally stamped by the most famous bank heist in Uruguay's history.

Elena told me of the experience of her mother and grandmother who had hurried back to the bank when the alarm was sounded, and of them having seen Mrs. MacFarlane crossing over to the bank from the residence next door, as related in the previous chapter. But the next story she told adds some *Old West* flavor to the happenings - more properly we could call this some *Wild South* flavor.

Hermelindo Meloni

A photo of Hermelindo Meloni from his national identity card, taken some years after the assault.

Little Dora and her mother had heard on the street that there had been a shooting in the bank, but they did not find out right away if Dora's dad was unharmed. And the piece of color we have to add to the story comes from her Dad's experience when Frank Lewis put the revolver to his head.

Not only did he put the barrel of the revolver up to Hermelindo Meloni's temple and motion with a finger to his lips that Meloni keep silent, he kept the business end of the barrel there firmly against his temple. Elena said it was his right temple, because he had been sitting to the left of the door, and Lewis drove home the urgency of his command by maintaining the revolver firmly in place for at least a minute.

Mr. & Mrs. Meloni

María Rossi and Hermelindo Meloni in their later years.

During this time Mr. Meloni said that one of the gang members, who we now know was John Atkins, was leading a bank employee to the safe to open it. Pablo Martínez, from his perch on top of the counter, gave the order to this employee,

"Don't resist!" (2)

That was when Atkins suddenly ran after MacFarlane and all hell broke loose in the manager's office. Both Martínez and Lewis also immediately went running to the office, just seconds behind Atkins. Thus the revolver was abruptly removed from Mr. Meloni's temple.

The mark of honor that Hermelindo Meloni received... a round, red mark impressed with force by the revolver's muzzle into his right temple... *didn't go away for three days!*

Now when I start to complain about *pressing* matters, I stop and contemplate Mr. Meloni's experience that afternoon in Salto.

References: Chapter 8

1. "El Cercano Oeste," Quinto Día - *El Telégrafo*, Paysandú, August 28, 2005, pp. 6-7.

2. "¡Qué no resistas!" Elena Miguens, 2009, op. cit.

CHAPTER NINE: SHOOTOUT AT DAYMAN

El Paso de las Piedras, Historic Crossing of the Dayman River at Dayman Hot Springs

"Still, he figured, sometimes you've got to do what you've got to do, and then sometimes you've just got to run like hell after it's done."
Derek Landy, Death Bringer

When the three Apaches exited the bank to board the still running Ford Motel T, they were even more determined to take their previously planned escape route. Instead of heading for the road that opened to the east, which would have taken them in the apparently logical direction, straight to their waiting horses at the *Paso de las Cadenas* camp, they headed south, south-east on the main road to Paysandú. Their intention was to throw off the authorities by going directly to the main river crossing at the Dayman Hot Springs. After that they planned to turn east to get their animals. This was the first route they had scouted on horseback. If you drive south out of Salto today, you take the very same road the Tin Can Gang bumped along in their desperate reach for freedom almost 100 years back.

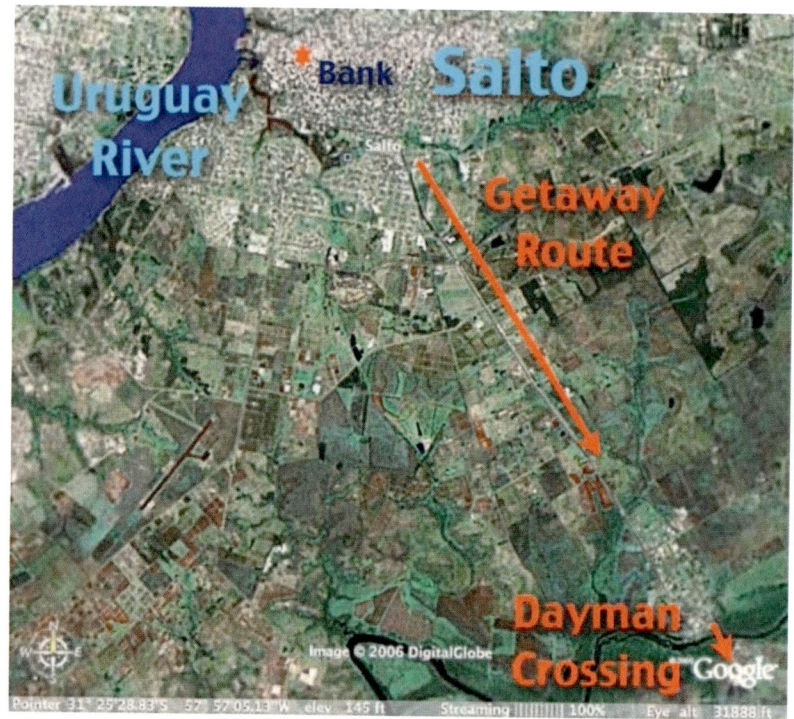

Escape Route

The chosen route south was along the main road from Salto to Paysandú
Underlying image from Google Earth, 2006

Of course, they had counted on no immediate persecution by Police officers in several other vehicles. Their original plans called for surprise in the robbery itself and some lead-time to depart the city without calling attention to themselves. They would be just another group of foreigners taking a ride in one of those new automobiles... Instead, their slow dash south in the stolen Ford took on a spirit of urgency.

The hand-drawn map, shown on the next page, was published in the Montevideo newspaper *La República* on October 23, 1917. (1) It is somewhat out of perspective with relation to distances, and the Dayman River ends up being at least a kilometer wide; which would be at least 10-15 times its actual width, while the Uruguay River is close to twice its real width. The Apaches would have needed a ferry to cross the little Dayman River as represented on this map.

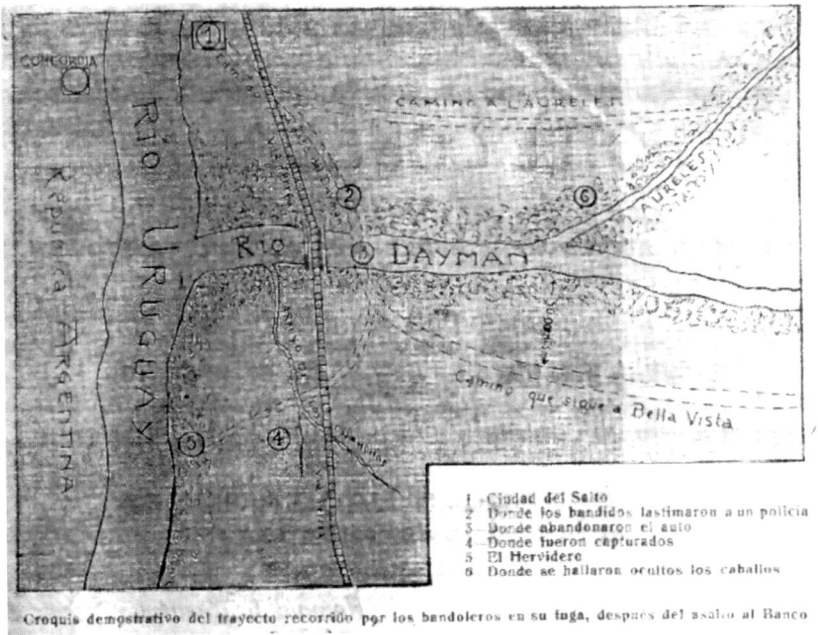

1917 hand-drawn map of the Dayman area

The upper road "Camino a Laureles" actually led out of Salto itself.

But several details do help us; first there is a road heading off east at the top middle of the map, this leads more directly towards Los Laureles and the gang's horses. This road, in point of fact, left the city of Salto even more to the north and later branched off south from the easterly route, which today is National Route 31. Their turn south in the city itself shows that they had already decided to take the different more direct run towards the Dayman River.

Today the same more easterly route still takes one to the *Paso de la Cadena* crossing and the old camp spot. They had come into the city on this road, and in the same car, earlier that same day. We believe that they never planned on returning straight to their camp spot using this more direct route. They assumed that the taxi's owner and his mechanic would have already informed the Police about where they had been held up and the car had been taken. And more importantly, the run to the Paso de la Cadena crossing, where they had made camp, was three times longer than the short haul directly to the main crossing of the Dayman River south of the city. A pursuing force would have had a fairly good idea about where to find the Apaches if they had taken this longer, more easterly road. And now with the Model T barely plugging along, (2) the pursuing vehicles, with multiple armed officers, had a good chance of catching up with them even before they reached the closer river crossing, let alone their waiting horses.

Model T "Pickup"

A Ford Model T approaching another river, this time under more peaceful circumstances.

This nearer Dayman crossing offered a wiser spot for their retreat; a place which they could easily defend once they were on the other side of the river, much like a military retreat that looks for those physical obstacles that can slow down the advance of the pursuing forces. Then from this easily defendable crossing they could work their way back to Los Laureles and their waiting horses.

The spot marked #2, which on the hand-drawn map indicates where the policeman was wounded, is also wrongly identified, because the officer was in reality shot to the south of the river, after arriving there on horseback in an attempt to cut off the Apaches. This point on the map, #2, may well correspond to the police checkpoint about two thirds of a mile north of the Dayman River.

The Salto police had quickly called the telephone installed at the watering hole, *la pulpería*, across from this checkpoint near the Dayman River Crossing. They also made a later call to the Paysandú Police headquarters, in both cases asking that the car carrying the three fugitives be intercepted. The first call, to the tavern at the Dayman crossing, went out at approximately 2:15 PM, just 15 minutes after the episode at the bank. The second call to the Paysandú Police Headquarters didn't go out until 3:00 PM, which, we will see, was strongly criticized. They also called the customs office of the Salto Port, asking that they launch their two patrol boats on the Uruguay River. These boats were normally used to stop contraband passing from Argentina into Uruguay. And several cars, loaded with armed officers, left Salto, about 10 to 15 minutes after the red Model T had started its run to Dayman.

Slow Speed Chase

© Richard Dean Young

The Dayman River and the crossing point

The small Dayman River spreads out and becomes shallower where a geological formation interrupts the flow of the stream.

Frank Lewis, knowing that organized pursuit would only be minutes behind, prodded the frail Ford almost beyond its limit, and the outlaws lumbered past the Dayman guard post at precisely at 2:15 in the afternoon. (3) About two minutes later they arrived at the main river crossing of the Dayman, *El Paso de las Piedras*, the Crossing of the Rocks - or Rocky Crossing. If, as it is reported, the gang had entered the Bank of London close to 1:55, and if the incidents in the bank took about 3 minutes in all, then the drive to the Dayman River crossing would have taken about 15 to 17 minutes. There were exactly 6.46 miles from the Bank of London to the Dayman River crossing. (4) If the trio did this run in 15 minutes, they would have averaged an overall speed of 26 miles per hour. Even with this moderate speed we know that Lewis pushed the motor so hard that it was damaged even worse than before the escape.

With the outside times being approximate - the arrival at the bank at 1:55 and the arrival at the river at 2:17 - it is logical to say that the overall episode, from the entrance by the outlaws through the bank's front door to arrival at the river, transpired in approximately 22 minutes.

For all of the actors in this tragedy, those 22 minutes appeared to be breaking Einstein's law of relativity, not that any of the individuals involved were yet aware of Einstein's work, which was first published in 1905; Einstein's theories were published in their day, but not in their world.

Time for each one had slowed down to an eternal crawl. With the speed at which brains were running and hearts were beating, not to mention the Ford's failing motor screaming at its maximum revolutions, the whole wild mess was pumping adrenaline through their systems, along with anguish, doubts and multiple calculations throbbing through frontal lobes... It was the same for MacFarlane, Daisy, the police and the Apaches. In this dream-like state, where all hell was spinning down into a chronological black hole, but where the conscious thought of each person seemed lodged in a never ending time-warp, each one was sincerely wishing that the trance would just get finished and that time and circumstances would please return to their normal, boring regularity. But, as they say, too many things had just gotten smashed to have any hope of getting them fixed again. Boring regularity for some would be a sad, broken life, for others a jail cell, and for two... a grave.

Worn Ford, Deep Ford

Later reports say that the motor of the Model T had been severely damaged by the "high speed" escape from Salto - the car also had one flat tire and a side panel from the hood was abandoned somewhere along the way, this to allow the engine to run a bit cooler. (5) When the gang arrived at the river, the several cars carrying Police officers, who had the advantage of greater speed in vehicles that were in much better condition, were now just a few minutes behind.

Even though Lewis could not know exactly how far back the pursuing caravan would be, he had a pretty good idea that they were easily beating his time, so with this urgency he drove the car straight into the water in the very center of the crossing. The magneto got soaked and the Model T stopped running after barely entering the water. Not having seen the actual car in the river, some reported that the Ford stopped "mid-stream". But the depth of the water and other testimony points to the car stopping only about 5-10 feet into the river.

Later Dayman Bridge

The "New" Dayman Bridge built in 1923, after which most traffic stopped using the ford at Paso de las Piedras.

The magneto was the apparatus on the Ford Model T that supplied the electrical spark for the engine to keep running; it was a large flat disk that was basically attached to the flywheel at the front of the motor. When the lower part of the motor entered the water, that same water penetrated the engine housing, the magneto got soaked and shorted out - thus the motor stopped functioning. The only way to get it going again was to get the car onto dry land, wait for the magneto to dry out, and then try crank-starting the motor again. With the car partially submerged in even fairly shallow water that option was out of question. The problem was not the water, it was time.

The Salto newspaper, *La Prensa*, commented that since they entered straight into the river from the road, instead of along to one side of the main crossing, that the water had therefore been too deep for the car. (6) This was local knowledge that the gang did not have; a previous walk through the river at the crossing might have alerted them to the fact that the midsection of the crossing would be too deep for the Ford.

Martínez had crossed over there more than once with the horses, but not being conversant with the operation of these new carriages called automobiles, he had not noticed anything unusual about the depth of the water.

Local Horse Sense

I approached a similar stream crossing in the mountains of North Argentina back in the 1980's. Some Gauchos had just crossed the stream on horseback and came in my direction. Because I didn't like the look of the water's depth, I got out and asked the two riders if my Ford Falcon could get through the stream without difficulty. They told me, sure, that trucks crossed through there all the time. The reference to trucks made me even more doubtful, but the stream was not that wide so I gunned the car into the water. Fortunately the momentum and speed got me to the other side - but in the middle the car went right down into a hole and back up out, the water had come halfway up the driver's side window! ...which fortunately I had rolled up. Those two gauchos may have had local knowledge, but years later it occurred to me that their view was similar to that of Martínez, if a horse could get through, then why not a car?

Greetings and *Gritos*

When the car came laboring past the check point and the *pulpería*, these located about a kilometer or two thirds of a mile north of the Dayman crossing, (7) Martínez waved at his buddy, Sergeant Alfredo Cuadrado, with whom he had shared a drink a few days before. Martínez called out

"Greetings, Sergeant!" to which Cuadrado responded, *"Greetings, friend!"* (8) Just 30 seconds later someone came running out of Cataneo's tavern yelling to the guard that a call had just come in with orders to stop the car.

Some later criticized the Salto Police for the lateness of the phone call to the guard station. But by the time the Police had arrived on the crime scene at the Bank and had received sufficient information about the Apaches and the car they were driving, and by the time the same officer(s) could get back to the Police Headquarters on foot three blocks away, the 15 minutes could easily have passed. There is no indication that any of the bank employees had called the police after the attempted robbery, and even if they had done so, their major concern would have been to report that the manager had been shot, and since none of the bank employees who stayed inside the bank had actually gone out to the street, they would not have immediately known any details about the getaway car.

Right after the attempted robbery and the shooting of MacFarlane, all accounts speak of someone calling urgently for medical personnel to come to the Bank Manager's aid. If someone did call the Police Headquarters from the Bank it could well have been five to ten minutes after the shooting and the escape - and since several police officers did arrive soon after the assault, making a call from the Bank to the Police Headquarters might have seemed superfluous. The phone system in the city was manned by operators who personally took all calls and *plugged in* the caller to the recipient; this *after* checking that the recipient's phone line was free. After taking all these steps they would ring the recipient's phone and announce the incoming call. Anyone who has memories of the good-ole-days of the operator-run systems and *phone plugs* for the exchange of calls, will be aware of the long waits that often accompanied a simple phone call.

We have found no information as to how the police were officially informed of the tragedy that took place just three blocks from their offices, but we do have quite precise information about when the call was made from the police station to the *pulpería* across from the guard post at Dayman, and that time-lapse does seem reasonable. Even today with cell phones and GPS, one constantly hears of tardiness in responses to attacks and holdups, and some of those responses have gone even more horribly awry than did this police response in Salto back in 1917. And even our famous "dedicated" phone network, 911, that many rely on to speed up the official pursuit, at times can serve more to slow things down.

Hot Pursuit...

From the Dayman checkpoint Sergeant Cuadrado took off running behind the Ford, revolver in hand and behind him came *Policarpo Cabrera*, carrying a Mauser rifle. Cabrera was responsible for a boat or raft used for river crossings. This craft was tied some 300-400 yards up-stream, to the east of the crossing. The shallow water and rocks at the actual Dayman crossing were not that helpful for floating across in a boat.

A local policeman at the turn of the 20th century

Photograph from a special collection of the Museum of the National Library, Montevideo - used with permission

As we mentioned, as soon as the Ford entered the water at the crossing, the motor stopped and the three men got out. There are reports of them trying to push the car on across the river, but almost immediately a firefight started and the car was forgotten.

Also at the guard post was Civil Guard Florentino Mongelos, some report his last name as Mujelo, who immediately grabbed his Mauser rifle and mounted a horse. The different reports are a bit confusing on the next steps, but we have worked them out as follows: The guard, Mongelos, immediately rides down to the river close to where the boat was kept, and from there, using his Mauser, shoots at the fugitives five times.

A more detailed report, put together later, states that his shots came from about 350-400 yards to the east of the crossing. (9) The Mauser rifle, a Uruguay Mauser Model 1908, chambered for the 7x57 cartridge, was a superior firearm to the Remington Carbines that the gang was carrying, but it was evidently in the hands of an inferior marksman. And, if Mongelos did not get off his horse to do the shooting from that distance, then those shots were basically *tiros al aire*; shots in the air. The five cartridges in the clip were all he had available, because he never reloaded his rifle. The fact that Mongelos fired from a spot further up the river - in reality too far from the crossing for any kind of marksmanship with the rifle's open sights - is connected with his next move. Mongelos then crosses the river, still on horseback, and circles around towards the south, this in an attempt to cut off the retreat of the three *Desesperados*.

Dayman Rocks

*The rocks where Lewis hunkered down to fire his carbine,
getting himself wet in the process.*

Return Fire

When Mongelos fires the shots from upriver, Frank
Lewis immediately crouches behind some low rocks at the
river's edge and commences to fire back with his carbine.
This first exchange of fire produces no victims, and while
this shooting is going on the other two policemen, Sergeant
Alfredo Cuadrado and Policarpo Cabrera, are approaching
the river from the north, running right down the main road...
at least we think they are still running.

Although the exact placement of the guard post and the
tavern are unknown, we believe that the guard post was
located where today the road to Paysandú continues its
southeasterly direction to the bridge over the Dayman. But
back in 1917 at this point, about 1 kilometer north of the
river, the main road made a turn more directly south. The
checkpoint seems to have been located at this place, and

from this spot on today's road, one either turns in the more southerly direction towards the old river crossing and the built-up village with its thermal baths, or one stays on the main road from Salto that soon arrives at today's bridge.

The road south to Paysandú and the Dayman River crossings.

The old road to the river ford continued the straight line of the road from Salto, the path to the boat crossing as well as the modern road to the bridge took a more southeasterly turn.

Underlying image from Google Earth, 2006

We believe that this more southeasterly stretch of the modern Route 3 was previously the old trail that led from the guard post to the boat crossing. Back in 1917 this path would have opened out to the boat launch and the place where the mounted officer stopped and fired. The checkpoint was not in any sense "close" to the river because the other two running officers did not arrive to join in the firefight until the mounted officer had already crossed the river and approached the crossing from the south, this after stopping to fire his carbine.

After firing his rifle at the river's edge Mongelos crosses over to the south side of the Dayman almost at the same spot where the bridge was built a few years later. Because this officer is mounted, he arrives quite quickly at the river 400 yards upstream from the crossing, using the path from the guard post to the river. The other two officers, who have taken off running, guns in hand, are still moving south on the old road towards crossing. They have to cover the approximate one-kilometer distance on foot. In all of the accounts Sergeant Caudrado, Martínez's drinking buddy, does not even take part in the gunplay at the river; did he get too winded to arrive before the fireworks were over?

The other policeman, Policarpo Cabrera, does finally arrive at the river from the north and threatens the Apaches with the second Mauser rifle. (10) This should give him the advantage over the outlaws if he knows how to use the rifle properly or is sure of himself with an excellent high-powered rifle. Evidently he does not and is not, because when both Atkins and Lewis aim their carbines at him, he drops his gun and pleas for his life saying that he has children to raise. The outlaws let him go and then continue on across the river. (11)

Right before this, in his attempt to cut off the retreat of the three fugitives, Mongelos has managed to move through the brush and trees to the south of the river. Different accounts give conflicting information about the next shots fired, but we have put together the only timeline that fits the known facts. In this scenario, when Mongelos arrives from the south, about 50 yards from the river and still in thick brush, Lewis fires his carbine and kills Mongelos' horse with one shot.

A Remington Model 14 Pump Carbine, in production between 1912 and 1936.

The Remington rifle that Lewis was using (see notes on chapter two) was chambered the new .35 Remington round - since that time a favorite deer and bear cartridge in the US, but a quite rare cartridge to find in Uruguay, even today. It is a bullet that at medium ranges, 50 to 150 yards, packs an extraordinary punch and most certainly can knock down and kill a horse, especially at the approximate 70-yard distance from which Lewis was firing. And not only were the bullets hard hitting, when the remaining Remington ammo was captured, it turned out that the slugs were *"balas dun dun"*, meaning that they were hollow point rounds - something that is prohibited in any wartime cartridge, and which turns the bullets into an almost explosive round.

Next, Mongelos' dog, that has been following the horse, makes a run at one of the men in the river, either at Atkins or Martínez who are now ahead of Lewis and nearing the south shore. Lewis easily dispatches the dog with another shot. The dog, even if a large one, and most dogs following the Gauchos and their horses in Uruguay and Argentina are small to medium size, has no idea what hits him when the Remington missile arrives. Pooch is exploded into dog heaven in milliseconds, and doing burial detail for the poor beast would now required two shovels; a sharp one for digging and a wide one for scooping up the scattered pieces.

Looking south, straight across the Dayman crossing.

Officer Down

Mongelos, now without his Mauser, his horse, and his dog... moves closer in towards the south bank of the river and the firefight continues. But concurrently the three outlaws are themselves approaching the same south bank of the river in their urgency to distance themselves from the other vehicles and officers they knew are bringing up the rear. Mongelos has only his sidearm to confront three men armed with carbines, revolvers and a Colt pistol, and he soon takes a bullet to his right leg - this fired by Atkins. (12)

Later reports identify the slug as coming from a revolver, this coincides with the Colt Frontier .44-40 that was never turned in. While the reports are confused, it seems that Mongelos is the one who first orders the group to surrender - this make sense since he is mounted, and even though he has taken the time to cross the river and arrive by a roundabout trail, his mode of transportation puts him in harms way either before or about the same time that Cabrera shows up on the north bank of the Dayman.

© Richard Dean Young

Colt Single Action Frontier Revolver, cal. .44-40

We believe this particular revolver was used by Atkins to shoot the guard at the river.

Mongelos was fortunate to have been hit in the leg by this lighter revolver round, and not with a slug from the carbine that Lewis was shooting with devastating accuracy, because a hit from this high-powered cartridge could well have severed his leg or caused massive bleeding and death. Even so, the .44-40 Winchester slug, with which he was hammered, was a cartridge that packed a serious punch; like the .45 Long Colt it was one of the two 19th century *magnum* rounds, and it was used in both revolvers and rifles.

Mongelos, upon taking this shot to the leg, which is not in the least a superficial wound because he later has to be carried across the river to be taken back to the hospital, drops like a rock. The absolute shock of this large bullet can put down just about any large man.

As we mentioned, some accounts relate that the Model T Ford has stopped mid-river, but the fact that Lewis is soon out of the car and crouched behind rocks to do his shooting points to the vehicle having barely entered the water, most likely just a few yards. In the middle of the stream there are no protruding rocks for Lewis to crouch behind. It is possible that Atkins and Martínez have even started to push the car on through the crossing, but the quickly accelerating shootout and the armed officers approaching down the road convince them that pushing a car under a hail of bullets is not the wisest option.

The Dayman *Paso de las Piedras* had been used for centuries as a crossing, but that was usually done with animals and carts, as well as people fording the river on foot. In the early 20th century the crossing was just starting to be used by motorized vehicles, but it was much more suitable for trucks and higher mounted rigs. Some of the ranchers, as we will see, also had cars and regularly crossed the Dayman River at this point, but they had worked out that their smaller cars could only make it across in the shallower parts to either side of the central crossing area, and they certainly would not have entered the river racing like the Devil was behind, as Frank Lewis did that day.

In the early 1920's a modern bridge was constructed about 500 yards to the east of the crossing, and today on the north side of the old Dayman Crossing, along the old road down to the river, there is a built-up area of hotels and spas taking advantage of the plentiful hot springs that from time immemorial have flowed down from the higher ground into the river, right at the crossing.

The "new" Dayman Bridge, built in 1923

Florentino Mongelos, shot in the leg, is now out of the fight, lying on the ground and certainly in great pain. The other two guards can only now watch as the three men carefully climb up the south bank of Dayman River and enter the vegetation. There are no details concerning what Sergeant Alfredo Cuadrado does, he had taken off down the road armed with a revolver, but his contribution to the firefight, if any at all, is ineffective. There are also no accounts of the wounded officer, Mongelos, taking any more shots at the gang, (13) but his presence immediately to the south of the river, down but still armed, has to be part of the reason the group moves more in a southwesterly direction, rather than southeasterly, as they leave the river.

Holed Up

The three fugitives then hole up on a large island in the middle of the Dayman River, this island is located about a half mile to the west. The island is completely covered by brush and trees and makes a more than adequate hiding place.

Thick brush on the south side of the Dayman River crossing

The shots from the east by Mongelos with the Mauser rifle, as well as his closing in on the gang also from the east along the south side of the river, were definite factors that kept the group itself from turning east after crossing the river, and thus continuing on toward their waiting horses. The three guards at the river had no way of knowing that the Apaches' camp was further to the east along the same river, but the fact that the mounted officer had shot at the outlaws from the east and then attempted the pincer movement, also from the east, had the effect of pushing the gang to the west instead of back towards their waiting horses.

To get their camp and their horses they would have still had a 13-mile trek through the countryside from this Dayman crossing. The river island, just to the west, looked like a much safer bet for the time being. The gang knew that a whole caravan of cars, loaded with police officers, was bringing up the rear and would arrive at any minute. Any attempt to move eastward, where the countryside didn't offer the same consistent cover of vegetation, would have put them in contact with a much larger group of armed lawmen. And a pursuit in an easterly direction would be through this more open countryside, and by officers who in all likelihood *could* get their vehicles across the river. So east did not look promising.

© Richard Dean Young

The larger Uruguay River about a mile south of the Hervidero Ranch buildings

The rock formations along the Uruguay River shore are similar to those on the Dayman River. Most of the rock formations in Uruguay are Pre-Cambrian.

Within a few minutes of the gang disappearing into the brush, the first pursuing car arrived from Salto with several policemen. In that car was Salto First Deputy Juan J. Bajac, who immediately crossed the river on foot, armed only with his revolver. Bajac then tried to get some sense of the trail left by the three fleeing criminals. (14) This officer was blissfully unaware of the danger he was facing from the three bandits, especially from Lewis who had now shown himself to be a cool-headed sharpshooter. He eventually gave up his solitary pursuit and returned to the north side of the river. Two other cars arrived soon after, and after getting the wounded officer back across, one of the vehicles took Mongelos to a hospital in Salto. A total of 30 policemen was the first larger contingent that arrived in several cars to begin the pursuit of the Apaches. These were under the orders of a Deputy Borges. (15)

Goin' After Bear

Years ago in Eastern Washington State my younger brother and I were hunting elk in the foothills of the Cascade Mountain Range. We had been walking up a narrow valley with a light snow cover when we saw huge bear tracks heading in our same direction. The tracks were large enough for a Grizzly, one of which we had sighted a few years earlier near Mount Rainier. We soon came upon a section of deep brush and trees in the middle of this valley, similar to the tangle of brush on the island in the Dayman River. My brother Dave went around one way, I went around the other. When we met at the far end there had been no bear tracks coming *out* at any point. We looked at each other, and without a word kept going up the valley *hunt'n elk*. A bear in deep brush is about the most dangerous wild critter that one could ever stupidly mess around with... and three armed, desperate criminals holed up in deep brush would be just about as dangerous for any fool in a rush for martyrdom.

The newspapers said that the policemen, civil guards and soldiers, who later arrived, actually "beat the brush" looking for the three *bandoleros*. But, in actual fact, they merely surrounded the island, and all the next day, Wednesday, nobody was foolish enough to go on in for bear.

Slipping Away

The three spent the night on the island surrounded by at least 60 officials, and early on the second day, while avoiding one officer who came to within 40-50 feet of their hideout, they took advantage of his going down to the main river branch to drink by slipping away and leaving the island across the southern branch of the Dayman.

They then made their way along the south side of the Dayman River all the way to where it flows into the Uruguay River. A Police report at the end of the second day, Wednesday, said that they had found footprints right at the confluence of the two rivers, but up to this time no confirmed sighting of the fugitives had been made. After this the Apaches turned south and eventually ended up at the "not so OK Corral." By the end of their sojourn along the Dayman River and then south through the Hervidero Ranch they had covered well over 20 miles on foot.

Hornets' Nest

Eventually more than 350 men gathered to pursue and capture the gang of three. Most of these were policemen and Army troops from the Salto and Paysandú districts. When once the gang crossed the Dayman River, the southern part of the pursuit fell under the authority of the Paysandú police force. At the same time the 3rd Battalion of the Uruguay Infantry, headquartered in Salto, loaned 120 men for the search, 110 by other calculations.

Troops of the 3rd Battalion on parade in Salto

Photograph from a special collection of the Museum of the National Library, Montevideo - used with permission

The first group of army troops numbered 30 and was transported to the Dayman River in a truck that had been loaned for this purpose by the utility company *ULEN*. Then another 80 troops arrived in army trucks early in the morning on Wednesday, October 17th, and the combined Police-Army search started at 4:00 AM. Col. Jaime Bravo led the army personnel, and the police forces were under the command of Salto First Deputy Bajac. (16) There was also a large contingent of Civil Guards who arrived to help in the search. There is no information as to who was their commanding officer, most likely they were put under the command of the Salto Police at the scene of the escape across the Dayman River.

The Salto police officer, Bajac, believing that he had the three fugitives surrounded on the island, kept the major part of his troops there all day Wednesday. At the same time the soldiers and civil guards along with the Paysandú Police concentrated on beating the brush that day from beyond the Dayman River Island all the way to the Uruguay River. We now know that the gang had slipped away from the island and had headed west towards the Uruguay River. The concentration of troops beating the bushes along the whole remaining length of the Dayman River had to be the major reason that the three eventually turned south. Several patrol boats were guarding the Uruguay River itself so that the three could make no attempt to cross or swim back to Argentina.

El batallón 5.o de infantería en el Salto

El 5.o de Infantería entrando al cuartel por la calle Rivera—El coronel Victor Cantón y el mayor Constante Baldizzone, primer y segundo jefe—La corporación de oficiales—(Fotografías tomadas instantes después de arribar el 5.o a esta ciudad.)

Fifth Battalion of the Uruguayan Army

*The Fifth Battalion which was later posted in Salto,
replacing the earlier 3rd Battalion*

When the Apaches made their plans to hit an easy target in Uruguay, with the light security at its banks and the absolute absence of any previous bank holdups in the country, they literally had no idea of the *hornets' nest* into which they were stepping. The immediate concentration of troops and policemen in a concerted, organized search - some questioned whether it had been that well *organized*, but the huge number of officers involved in the search is not disputed - would have been impossible and impracticable in neighboring Argentina. Even after the Wild Bunch bank robbery in Rio Gallegos, Patagonia in January, 1905, the police could only put together a posse of five men, three officers and two volunteers - this to go after a gang that had lifted a record take from a Southern Argentine bank. (17) And in December of that same year when Butch Cassidy and the Sundance Kid hit the bank in Villa Mercedes of San Luis Province, even though the whole city was turned upside down by the robbery and ensuing firefight, only nine men were found to set out in pursuit of the gang that had just raised the funds to bankroll their move to Bolivia. (18)

Novel Official

After our *uruguayo* Wild Bunch was captured and the judge in Salto pulled the first information out of them, the police were ordered to check out their camping spot further up the Dayman River. There are only bits and pieces of information about what happened there; some newspapers refer to a "beating of the bushes" at *Los Laureles* where the Apaches had made their camp and where their horses were waiting. But the same concentrated attention was not given to the original campsite of the gang as to those areas where they were actually thought to be hiding.

First a *sub-oficial*, a low-ranking officer, from the San Antonio police station about 10 miles north of the camp spot was sent to the Paso de la Cadena area to look for the horses and the reported *Negro* who was watching them. When this officer arrived at the crossing at Los Laureles he saw a man next to the horses, at whom he immediately took a couple of hurried shots, but then had no idea if he had hit his target. Newspapers picked up on this edgy policeman and, tongue-in-cheek, called him the *"the novel official... beater of the bushes at the Laurels."* (19) This same official later returned with two other policemen and this time they did beat the brush as well as find the horses still there. Of course the watchman was now long gone leaving no trail of blood. They encountered two rolled-up raincoats covered with horse manure and also found packed on the horses themselves supplies; more canned food, and some maps which showed their intent to head north towards Brazil and then Paraguay. (20)

There was no mention in these newspaper accounts of the buried treasure at the Laureles camp. The speculation about this loot started later - and, as we mentioned in chapter six, it continues until today. Did the watcher know something about that horde? We sense that its location was chosen by Atkins so far from the camp, out of sight of watchman and cronies, and evidently so well selected that nobody will ever be able to find it.

References: Chapter 9

1. "El asalto al Banco de Londres de Salto," *La República*, Montevideo, October 23, 1917, p. 5

2. "Los apaches en el Salto, La Policía," *Diario Nuevo*, Salto, October 17, 1917, op. cit., p. 1, col. 4

3. We know that they passed the guard station at 2:15 because that was the time that the call had been made to the pulpería - the call arrived just seconds after the car passed. After the phone call it would have taken the car, at its average speed from Salto to river, just over another two minutes to actually arrive at the river itself. Thus we can say they arrived at the Dayman crossing almost precisely at 2:17 in the afternoon.

4. *"Desde la sucursal del Banco de Londres hasta el sitio en que se verificó el último encuentro, hay 4 leguas: 10 kilómetros y 400 metros..."* "From the Branch of the Bank of London until the site in which the last encounter was verified, there are 4 leagues: 10 kilometers and 400 meters..." This equals 6.46 miles. In the city the car would have been going 10-20 miles per hour at the most, and this included two hard right hand turns. The longest part of the run was the straight shot from Salto to the Dayman River, where they could have maintained a 30+ mile per hour speed, but it is doubtful they ever got the 40 mph speed that the Ford Model T was purportedly able to obtain.

"El asalto al Banco...¡cómo se escribe la historia!" *La Prensa*, October 17, op. cit., p. 1, col. 3

5. "Una banda de apaches...El automóvil de la hazaña," *La Prensa*, October 17, op. cit., p. 1, col. 4

6. *ibid.*, *La Prensa*, October 17, p. 1, col. 3

7. Note: this article refers to the guard post located to the north of the Dayman River that figures in several encounters with the Apaches; the exact data given is that the guard post was located 8 kilometers from the city of Salto. Usually these distances are calculated from downtown to the point mentioned. That would then place the guard post only 5 miles from Salto, or 1.46 miles north of the river crossing, the crossing itself being 6.46 miles from downtown. But the actual curve in the road, where we think the guard post was located is only about one kilometer, 2/3 a mile, north of the river. This distance would make sense if the 5 miles (8 kilometers) were calculated from the edge of the city, not from downtown.

"El Asalto al Banco de Londres...El viaje de los bandidos," *La Prensa*, October 24, op. cit., p. 1, col. 3

8. "El Asalto...A balazos con la policía," *La Prensa*, October 24, op. cit., p. 1, col. 4

9. "Ecos del suceso.¿Dónde están los bandoleros?" *La Prensa*, October 18, op. cit., p. 1, col. 3

10. "El asalto al Banco... Nuevas declaraciones," *La Prensa*, October 21, op. cit., p. 1, col. 3

11. "El Asalto...A balazos con la Policía," *La Prensa*, October 24, op. cit., p. 1, col. 4

12. "Una banda de apaches...En el paso del Dayman," *La Prensa*, October 17, op. cit., p. 1, col. 3

13. "Un Atentado Audaz...La Persecución," *El Telégrafo*, October 17, op. cit., p. 2, col. 5

14. "Una banda de apaches...Concentración en Dayman," *La Prensa*, October 17, op. cit., p. 1, col. 3

15. "El Asalto al Banco...Las tropas avanzan," *La Prensa*, October 24, op. cit., p. 1, col. 4

16. "Una banda de apaches...Concentración en Dayman," *La Prensa*, October 17, op. cit., p. 1

"El asalto al Banco...¡Cómo se escribe la historia!" *La Prensa*, October 20, op. cit., p. 1, col. 3

17. Osvaldo Aguirre, op. cit., p. 165

18. ibid., Osvaldo Aguirre, p. 217

19. "oficial novelero. batidor de los montes de Laurels"

"El Asunto de los Apaches," *Diaro Nuevo*, Salto, October 22, p. 1, col. 4

20. "El asalto al Banco. Los Caballos de los Apaches," *Tribuna Salteña*, October 19, op. cit., p. 4, col. 3

CHAPTER TEN: THE BOILER AND THE CANS

"Vice may triumph for a time, crime may flaunt its victories in the face of honest toilers, but in the end the law will follow the wrong-doer to a bitter fate, and dishonor and punishment will be the portion of those who sin."

Allan Pinkerton

The inner patio of the main building on the Hervidero Ranch

My first trip to Paysandú and Salto in 2005 soon had me knocking at the door of the *Hervidero* Ranch; more literally, opening a series of gates. After letting myself and my little Peugeot 205 through about four stock gates between the main Paysandú-Salto route, and driving some eight miles almost to the coast, I came across the main ranch building as well as several outbuildings, a small dairy, sheds for equipment, and cattle all over the place. In my high school years we had lived on the edge of a small city in the Yakima Valley of Eastern Washington State. Each year I would purchase a baby calf or two that were orphaned when their mothers died in birth, and the bottle feeding, raising and caring for a couple of animals introduced me to the "cattle" business. I actually worked on a ranch where we had to deal with cattle, horses, etc., but most of my work as a young kid was during the summers in the fruit harvest in the large orchards of the Yakima Valley - driving tractor, picking up the boxes of fruit, sitting in an outhouse when my friend tried to knock it over with a tractor... Driving onto this ranch brought back vivid memories, and aromas, from my teenage years.

El Hervidero main ranch house

Menacing Archeology

I was received at the Ranch by Luisa Amaro, who at first was wary of my reasons for showing up - when she found out that I was not an archaeologist, just a simple historian, she was visibly relieved. She told me of the ongoing debate they were having with a group of archaeologists who had done some digging near the farm house, and were sure they had found the original camp of General José Artigas, Uruguay's Liberator, who fought the Spanish and helped win independence, although he was never accepted as one of the first leaders of the new country.

Luisa and her brother had very little interest in having the ranch house and surrounding area set aside as a national park. The family had already ceded to the Government a section of their ranch further south along the Uruguay River where previous scholarship had identified the old Artigas camp spot. (1)

Luisa Amaro and ruins on the Hervidero Ranch

But when I started asking Luisa about the events of 1917 we easily moved our way forward in history from Artigas to her grandfather, great-uncle and others in her family who had played a role in the dramatic happenings during the two days when the police and army troops were scouring the ranch trying to find the Tin Can Gang.

© Richard Dean Young

General José Artigas, Uruguay's Liberator

A set of tiles on the wall of the inner courtyard of the Hervidero main ranch building - depicting General Artigas looking out from this same ranch across the Uruguay River.

The "Loco" Amaro Brothers

Lisa told me about her great uncle José María Nicanor Amaro who had been born in 1866. Now in 1917 he and Luisa's grandfather, Carlos María Amaro, were known as *"Los Locos"*. They were some of the few ranchers in the area who owned a car. And the "crazy" tag came directly from how they drove their new *automóvil*. José María, especially, would play the part of the daring Baron; he would lower the car top, put on his goggles and beret, and with a long scarf flowing out behind, speed like the Devil through the countryside.

José María Nicanor Amaro, owner of the Hervidero Ranch

A story not published in the newspapers relates that the day after the tragedy, Wednesday, October 17th, when the Apaches were moving south from the Dayman river towards the Hervidero Ranch house; José María was returning to the ranch from Salto, and at a sharp curve on the dirt road leading to the main house, the two Americans stepped out of the bushes, rifles in hand, and made threatening signs for Amaro to stop. Alongside José María in the car was his nephew, also José, Luisa's Uncle. Instead of stopping, *El Loco* gunned the car on through the curve and fortunately the criminals did not fire. If they had fired, almost certainly they would have had a wrecked car on their hands and perhaps another death or two to account for. (2)

This encounter points to another fact about the path that the Apaches took through the Hervidero Ranch territory. They were later apprehended about two and a half to three miles to the east of the Ranch house, but there are no sharp curves in the road in the last four to five miles before it arrives at the main ranch buildings. Most have surmised that the three moved basically south, near the shore of the Uruguay River and only at the end of their trek did they move inland along the road that crossed the stream and landed them finally in the corral along this main ranch road. Instead they appear at least four miles inland during the day, and try to stop the Amaro vehicle on the last sharp curve before the road makes its fairly straight run to the ranch. They had scouted the road even further east, deliberately looking for a place at which a vehicle would have to slow down. None of their wanderings through the Hervidero Ranch took a straight line at any point in their attempt to escape.

View of Ranch and the Uruguay River

Paysandú Deputy Araújo and the Southern Search

On the day of the assault, Tuesday, October 16, after the gang had made its getaway across the Dayman River, Deputy Elías Araújo, chief officer of the 7th Rural Section of the Paysandú District, was ordered to take charge of the operations based at the Hervidero Ranch for the capture of the gang. (3) Araújo was accompanied by his assistant Deputy Geroncio López. They set up their headquarters at the main ranch house of *La Estancia el Hervidero*.
254

The Boiler

Hervidero means boiler or boiling, because the Uruguay River, at a spot close to the ranch house, has a low, wide course that at times almost appears to be "boiling", this from the rapids effect caused by the shallows in that section of the river. In fact, this is one place where it is possible to ford the river, especially when the level is low. Although approaching from the Argentine side one encounters a fairly strong current right before reaching the Uruguay shore, then some tall bluffs make a landing difficult. It was precisely this characteristic of the Hervidero shore that led the archeologists to begin searching for Artigas' original camp close to the ranch house.

The Uruguay River as seen from the Hervidero ranch house

In 1898 Luis Alberto Herrera wrote about the Uruguayan Civil War of 1897 and he mentions the Revolutionary troops using the Hervidero Ranch as a base. He gives a detailed description of the river at this point as well as the setting of the main ranch buildings:

"The Hervidero is one of the most protected openings in Uruguay, the river at this point measures 15 to 20 blocks across. The name of this site on the river has to do with some shoals disturbing the waters and producing a kind of boil. This results in the main current moving away markedly from the coast of Argentina, with the channel running mainly along the eastern shore. Added to this strategic advantage is the fact that at the Hervidero, the bank raises up quite high over this side of our nation's river, which serves as an excellent platform [for the troops]. On the heights of this rise is the large main building of Mr. Amaro's ranch." (4)

The Noose Tightens

On this critical day after the attempted Bank heist, one group of policemen and soldiers camped at the Dayman crossing; they were surrounding and guarding the island where they believed the three were still holed up. Meanwhile Deputy Araújo made his way to the Hervidero Ranch to oversee the more southerly part of the operation. A larger group of soldiers, policemen and civil guards had set out to beat the brush, beginning from the island on the Dayman River, and continuing all the way to where the Dayman empties into the much larger Uruguay River.

The Nicanor Amaro brothers, los locos, seated at left and standing with shotgun

The day before, the Mayor of Paysandú had driven by car, along with several police officers, to the Dayman crossing from where he began to oversee the Paysandú police involvement in the search. (5) He later went over to the Hervidero Ranch itself. Thus the Hervidero Ranch became the main hub for most of the operations to apprehend the Apaches. The Ranch was strategically important because it was one of the few that had a telephone installed at this early date. The telephone line was linked only to the city of Paysandú, but from there messages could be relayed on to Salto.

One can see why the family itself, now two generations separated from the actual happenings, still has guarded many details and helpful anecdotes concerning the capture of the Apaches. Family and ranch life continued on normally right at the center of operations, and the Amaro family hosted and fed the many officials and other police personnel who happened to be present at the ranch headquarters. Thus, just about everything that happened related to the southern part of the search and the actual capture of the gang, not to mention telephone calls to and from the ranch phone, conversations among the policemen themselves, etc., were all witnessed by young and old in the extended Amaro family.

On Wednesday morning, October 17th, a Police boat set out from Paysandú to the bar of the Dayman River where it flows into the Uruguay River. On board was the Paysandú Inspector of Police, Major González. Later that same day, at two in the afternoon, the boat *"Chapicuy"* sailed from the dock of the *Nuevo Paysandú* Meat Plant, and this launch carried 20 agents of the Rural Police. Both boats were sent to the area to help patrol against the gang attempting any crossing to Argentina. But it does seem that the 20 Rural Policemen were there to help the search on land. (6)

The Hervidero Ranch had been connected by telephone line to the city of Paysandú just a few years earlier. Of course, there did not yet exist a major system of phone lines linking far flung ranches with every city in reach, nor with neighboring ranches, as would be true today in the outback of Uruguay. As we mentioned, back then the phone line only linked the Hervidero ranch house to the city of Paysandú. Because of that direct link, and the fact that a reporter for the *Telégrafo* Newspaper was immediately dispatched to the ranch, the news about the pursuit and capture of the gang was much more complete in the Paysandú *Telégrafo* newspaper than in the several newspapers in Salto.

Hervidero Ranch Scene

Regional Rivalry and Politics

The *Telégrafo* newspaper of Paysandú had had to catch up with *La Prensa* of Salto about the immediate happenings concerning the attempted robbery itself, as well as the news of the first hours of the pursuit. But after that one sees the Salto newspaper printing statements like "We have just heard from Paysandú..." Salto itself was only 12 miles away from the operation headquarters on the Hervidero Ranch, 12 miles as the crow flies, or by river - and somewhat further by land, while Paysandú was at least 60 more miles to the south.

© Richard Dean Young

Outbuildings and Barns on the Hervidero Ranch

A certain rivalry between these two Districts of Uruguay has been traditional, and the fact that the police of Salto could not capture the criminals in their own territory, and had to cede leadership of the search operation to the Paysandú authorities, was a hard pill to swallow. At least the criminals, when captured, were then returned to Salto, but the glory of the chase and the capture went to the backward country fellows further south, not even to the Paysandú metropolitan police force.

There already existed some feelings of serious discontent against the police force in the Salto district, because the criticisms of this body of officers for not apprehending the criminals in Salto territory were quick and cruel. Even with the more flowery use of language that is common to Spanish publications of the time, the anger expressed against the Salto police, just a day after the capture of the gang, was palpable, and while there was an element of wounded pride in the communications, very likely the harsh words flowed from previous discontent over security issues.

Inside the patio of the Hervidero Ranch main building

"The glory belongs to the Paysandú Police for having captured the three authors of the assault, this after an investigative action which was serious, persistent and well directed, without the exaggerations and exhibitionism, which characterize our Police, and have left them in the most ridiculous and shameful failure." (7)

What was even more embarrassing was the report in the *La Prensa* newspaper, also on October 19th, that when Col. Jaime Bravo, of the 3rd Infantry Battalion stationed in Salto, immediately offered troops to concentrate forces at the Dayman River, the police Colonel Córdoba:

"...vainly answered him that the Salto police had more than enough troops to capture the 'bandoleros'." (8)

Added to this was the fact that most of the Salto police force had gone to the Dayman River, and instead of following the trail of the Apaches, and the tin cans... had instead stayed surrounding the island on the river where they assumed that the three were holed up.

260

The first army troops had not arrived until later that first night, as we mentioned earlier, when they were able to help in part of the search through the rest of the night. The newspapers commented that an immediate acceptance of the offer of the Army troops might have made a difference. It is doubtful whether the extra troops would have speeded up the capture of the gang - what these editorial comments and factual statements do show is that the Salto society on the one hand was not that pleased with previous police lack of efficiency, and on the other, even more importantly, the whole society of Salto had taken a belly blow to its collective consciousness with the holdup, and especially with the killing of MacFarlane.

Memories of a Civil War

The other background to this malestar, anger and discontent, is that Uruguay had just come through its final Civil War just 13 years earlier in 1904. The Districts along the Uruguay River were the center of the rebellion against the Central Government, and this discontent in a sense played out in the Uruguayan politics of the 20th century, during which the two main parties, with two distinct visions of what Uruguay should be, the *Partido Nacional* or *Blancos* (the Whites) - who had literally been behind several of the Civil Wars that plagued Uruguay-, and the *Colorados* (the Reds) - the more liberal, progressive party - alternated time and again in government. Although the *Colorados* continued to dominate in the city of Montevideo with its concentration of half of the country's votes, therefore the Reds won the major number of the elections.

Comandante, J. Trías.—Mayor, M. Trías (hijo).—Coronel, M. Trías.—Comandante, A. Burgueño.—
Mayor, S. Burgueño.—Mayor, S. Devainlat.—Capitán, A. Trías.—Teniente, F. Barrios.

"Blanco" Officials, Uruguay 1904 Civil War

Notice the Gaucho-type dress that characterized the interior of the country, but not always the more cosmopolitan cities like Salto. Photograph from 1905.

The Mayor of the Department of Salto had been appointed by the *Colorados* in the Central Government, and, of course, the *Blancos* didn't take kindly to that. In several of the newspaper accounts that severely criticized the Mayor as well as the performance of the Salto Police, there was a clear political bias, along with some true grievances, so the matter was much more complicated than just a simple case of police incompetence.

"Everything, then, is a consequence of the same [incompetence]: bad personnel and worse organization. Mr. Mayor, whose appointment left the population speechless, because until then he was the illustrious Mr. Nobody, and then one good day out of Arapey, he precipitously appears to take nothing less than the post of Executive Officer; Mr. Mayor, we repeat, is not a fit or suitable person for that position, and anyone saying that the local police have improved their performance during his tenure would be far from the truth." (9)

According to a Paysandú newspaper, it was only at 3:00 PM on the day of the assault that the Salto Police finally called the Paysandú Police to the south asking for their assistance in capturing the three criminals. This was at least 30 minutes after the shootout at the river, and certainly *after* the gang had entered into Paysandú territory. And it is curious to read in the first edition of one Paysandú newspaper concerning the assault, this on the 17th of October, that the day before, the 16th, when the gang hit the bank, their newspaper had received a call about the holdup at 2:30 PM. They did not specify who made this call 30 minutes after the bank assault, and 15 minutes after the gang arrived at the border of the two Districts - yet the Police of Salto did not get around to calling their colleagues to the south for another 30 minutes *after* the Paysandú newspaper had been informed by private parties. (10)

One area in which the two police departments were able to cooperate to good effect, after these first blips in the system, was with the use of the telephone lines that connected the Hervidero Ranch to Paysandú, and the separate line that connected the two cities. The phone company in Paysandú was a private business owned by a Mr. Carlevaro, and the company in Salto, *La Nacional*, was owned by a Mr. Julio Rivero. During the search for the bandits the calls back and forth with the information shared were considered so important that Mr. Carlevaro had agents patrolling the full physical extension of the phone lines night and day. (11) And in Mr. Rivero's company the female phone operators put in extra long hours; according to one newspaper, they did this voluntarily. (12)

Tin Cans

When the gang crossed the Dayman River and then headed west on foot, the Uruguay River lay only about eight miles west - but the reality of the land and the sinuous course of the Dayman River made that trek at least twice as far. And if they had kept closer to the small Dayman River, where there was more natural cover, the trek would have been even longer and the landscape much more difficult to traverse, especially the closer they stayed along the river having to move through the deeper brush. And it was precisely along the Dayman River and its verdant banks that the police-soldier contingent was literally beating the bushes.

On a few hunting trips in Uruguay I have delved into some "river" brush, and later swore that I would never, ever do that again. The choking tangle of plants, low trees, vines and especially the thorn-bearing species in this tangle, all come close to my most gruesome dreams of Purgatory. And Purgatory was just what these three bandits were experiencing in the 40 hours they managed to keep clear of the authorities.

And the hasty meals on the run, discarding without a thought those tin cans, as mentioned in the preface, was the witless giveaway of their trail in one of the more careless moves that a group of crooks could have made. It reminds us of the brainless thief who broke into a store and among the stolen items took some nuts - the trail of nutshells all the way to his house was the perfect giveaway of a perfect fool. Several of the newspapers mentioned the police finding the tossed tin cans, and one dismisses this as not being factual. Luisa Amaro told me the same story, just as it had been handed down through her family from first hand accounts gathered from the police who had actually closed in on the Apaches.

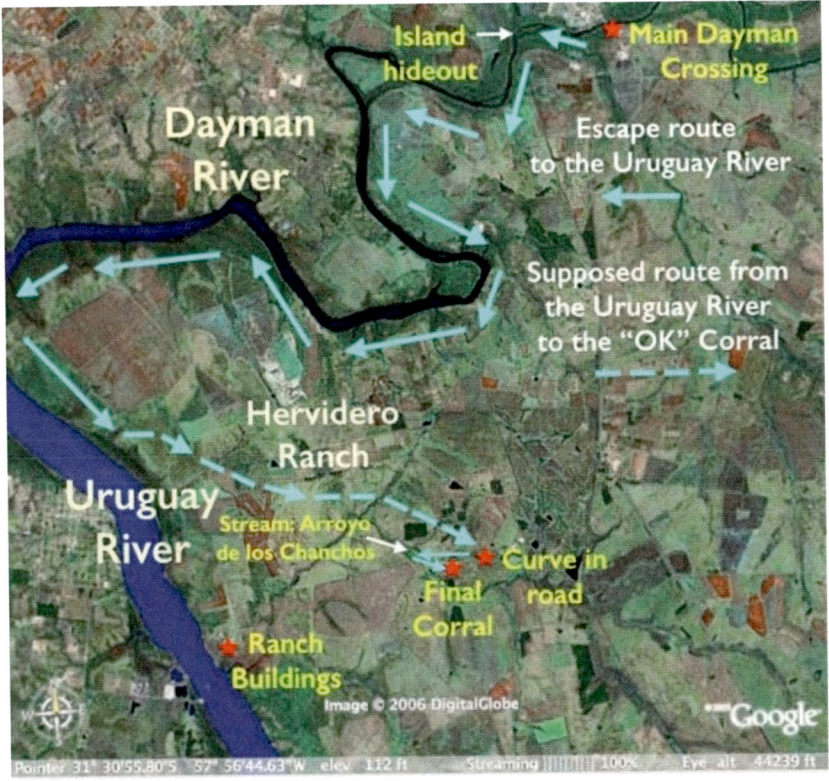

Escape route west to the Uruguay River, then back south

Underlying image from Google Earth, 2006

Long and Weary Road

The map seen here, taken off Google Earth in 2006, shows the area from the Dayman River crossing to the corral where they were discovered on the third day, two days after the killing in Salto. From the river crossing this is only about a 12-13 mile walk if one cuts across country - following the main route south and then the farm road would make that about a 15-mile trek. But going from one area of cover to another, holing up when the police were close, and cutting back from time to time to avoid contact with the officers, made this a two-day, non-stop ordeal. And the incursion into

265

the very center of the ranch, where they tried to stop the rancher's car, added many extra miles to their sojourn. When they were finally *corralled* they were exhausted, hungry, tired beyond hope and at their wits end.

"For I made promises, you know, and miles to sleep before I go, and miles to sleep before I go." (13)

The Hervidero Ranch and the road leading to the main buildings

Underlying image from Google Earth, 2013

References: Chapter 10

1. Miguel Carbajal, "¿Qué pasa en Purificación? - El Hervidero," *El País*, Montevideo, March 10, 2005

2. Luisa Marie Gutierrez Amaro, Interviews on the Hervidero Ranch, Paysandú, August 2005

3. "Como se Efectuó la Captura... Los Bandidos Descubiertos," *El Telégrafo*, October 19, op. cit., p. 1, col. 5

"El Asalto al Banco... Felicitaciones," *El Telégrafo*, October 23, op. cit., p. 1, col. 5

4. *"Es el Hervidero una de las abras más protegidas del Uruguay que mide en esa altura de 15 á 20 cuadras de ancho. El nombre del citado puerto lo justifican unos bajíos que alborotando las aguas causan una especie de ebullición. Este remolino dá lugar á que la corriente se aparte notablemente de la costa argentina quedando la canal sobre la costa oriental. A esta ventaja estratégica agrega el Hervidero la condición de tener muy elevada la margen nuestra que se yergue arrogante sobre el rio de la patria que le sirve de hermosa plataforma. En lo alto de la barranca está el importante edificio de la estancia del señor Amaro."*

Luis Alberto de Herrera, "Por la Patria: la Revolución de 1897 y sus Antecedentes," Montevideo, 1898, p. 248,

5. "Una Banda de Apaches...Repercusión en Paysandú," *La Prensa*, October 17, op. cit., p. 1, col. 6

6. "Captura de los Asaltantes - La Policía Sanducera," *El Telégrafo*, Paysandú, October 18, op. cit., 1917, p. col. 1

7.. *"Corresponde a la policía de Paysandú la gloria de haber capturado a los tres sujetos autores del asalto, después de una acción investigadora seria, perseverante, bien orientada, sin esas exageraciones y exhibicionismos que,* en cuanto a nuestra policía, la dejaron en el más ridículo y vergonzoso fracaso."

"Los celebres apaches....," *La Prensa*, October 19, op. cit., p. 1, col. 1

8. *"...le respondió vanidosamentede que la policía de Salto tenía elementos de sobra para apresurar a los bandolersos!"*

ibid, "Los celebres apaches. La policía de Paysandú," *La Prensa,* October 19, p. 1, col. 1

9. *"Todo, pues, es consecuencia de lo mismo: mal personal y peor organización. El señor Jefe Político, cuyo nombramiento dejó boquiabierto a la población, pues, hasta entonces era un ilustre desconocido, y un buen día de golpe y zumbido surjió de las lejanías de Arapey para ocupar nada menos que el puesto de delegado del Ejecutivo; el señor Jefe Político, repetimos no es persona apta ni indicada para el cargo, puesto que, falta a la verdad quien diga que la policía local ha mejorado durante su actuación."*

"Los apaches en el Salto, La Policía," *Diario Nuevo,* Salto, October 17, 1917, op. cit., p. 1, col. 4

10. "Un Atentado Audaz en Salto," *El Telégrafo,* October 17, op. cit., p.1, cols. 5-6
11. "El Asalto al Banco," *La Prensa,* Salto, October 23, op. cit., p. 1, col. 4

Ecos del asalto...La Cooperación del Teléfono," *Tribuna Salteña,* October 20, op. cit., p.1, col. 2

12. "El asalto al Banco...La policía sanducera," *La Prensa,* October 23, op. cit., p. 1, col. 4

13. Richard Young's dyslexic version of Robert Frost's poem, "Stopping by Woods on a Snowy Evening:"

> "But I have promises to keep,
>
> And miles to go before I sleep,
>
> And miles to go before I sleep."

CHAPTER ELEVEN: THE NOT SO *OK* CORRAL

© Richard Dean Young

**The end of a matter is better than its beginning;
better to be slow to anger than hot-headed.**

Ecclesiastes 7:8 LEB

At 7:00 in the morning on Thursday, October 18th, Comisario Araújo's assistant, Geroncio López, along with another policeman, both dressed in civilian clothes, were walking from the main Salto-Paysandú road to the temporary police headquarters at the Hervidero Ranch. As they were passing near a stream named *Cañada de los Chanchos*, or *Arroyo de los Chanchos*, (1) they noticed the three Apaches all seated by the path. Some reports say that the three tried to then hide in a ditch. (2)

But a more complete report in another newspaper, of which I have photocopies but unfortunately cannot identify, says that the officer and his friend actually greeted the three, and that their greeting was returned. The officers realized that they were dealing with the three fugitives, but did not let on that they were policemen and actually questioned the men if they were on their way to work, to which the Mexican answered in the affirmative. The two officers went on their way towards the main Hervidero ranch buildings, and at a distance López told his companion to hurry on to the ranch and tell Deputy Elías Araújo that they had just spotted the outlaws they were all searching for. López himself stayed in the area at a prudent distance.

The three outlaws then walked on further to a corral seen in the photo at the beginning of this chapter as well as in the Google image below. The corral is located about 200 yards along the farm road to the east of the stream where the two parties had their first encounter. That corral still stands where it was in 1917, and Luisa Amaro informed me that the ranch had put up the barbed wire in 1913, so the reports in the newspapers of the corral being constructed of posts and barbed wire accurately fit the history of the ranch.

Hervidero Posse

When the other officer returned with *Comisario* Elías Araújo he brought another six back-up officers, with at least two mounted on horses. One of the police officers was identified as Ramio Fernandez, and three of the Civil Guards were named in the papers as *Lisandro López, Cecilio Fernández and Mauricio Rivero*. (3) It would have taken López's partner approximately an hour to reach the ranch house and return with the contingent of lawmen. Deputy Araújo told the six assistants to keep some distance while he and Geroncio López approached the three men who were now inside the corral.

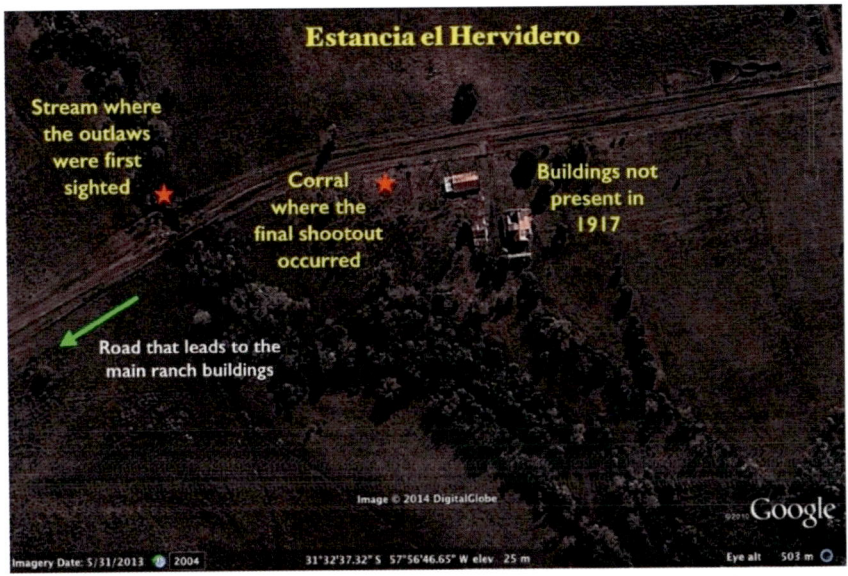

Stream and corral - the final encounters

Underlying image from Google Earth, 2013

All accounts say that the three criminals had placed their rifles up against the barbed wire fence at the rear of the corral. (4) Some say that the three raised their hands in surrender, but the more believable accounts simply say that by placing of the rifles against the fence they were indicating that they were through running and fighting. One account relates that Deputy Araújo approached the group, gun in hand, and demanded their surrender. Another says that he only had his sword drawn when he approached. But we do know the actual words with which Araújo ordered them to surrender, *"¡Dénse presos!"* - translated literally this would not make sense in English; "Give yourselves prisoners!", but in Spanish the phrase clearly means that they were to surrender or give themselves up "as" prisoners. (5)

The "Arroyo de los Chanchos". *The stream along which the Tin Can Gang was first sighted by Officer López*

Untold Story

At this point something happened that only the Amaro family on the ranch knew about; information which was handed down verbally through three generations concerning one of the most momentous happenings ever to intrude on the peace of this idyllic rural setting. (6) When the two officers approached the group of criminals, the Mexican, who had fired the fatal shot into the side of the bank manager, broke and ran towards the two officers, shouting at the top of his voice;

"¿Hay pena de muerte en Uruguay? ¿Hay pena de muerte en Uruguay?" (7)

Twice the Mexican hollered his deeply troubling question... *"Do they have the death penalty in Uruguay?"* Martínez knew that his neck was for the noose if Uruguay shared Argentina's law system.

Luckily for Martínez the death penalty had been abolished in Uruguay in 1907 during the administration of Claudio Williman. This followed the abolition of the death penalty in Venezuela in 1886 and in Costa Rica in 1882. So Uruguay was not the first country in the Americas to take this dramatic step, although in 1907 it was part of a quite small minority club in the Western Hemisphere.

We don't know what answer officer Araújo gave Martínez about the death penalty, but evidently it settled his spirits because he actually sat down on the ground to the Deputy's left as Araújo and López moved even closer to the remaining two gang members. The *Telégrafo* newspaper mentions that Martínez, when he surrendered, turned over to the officers a Colt *revólver*. (8) This was not the same short arm he used when he shot the Bank manager, that had been the Colt semi-automatic .45 which was now again in the possession of Atkins. Rather it was an original Colt revolver, one of two revolvers that Martinez used at different times during the hold-up and the ensuing flight.

Elías E. Araújo, comisario de la 7.a sección rural de Paysandú, que aprehdió a los bandoleros

Deputy Elías Araújo who led the search for the bandits, and who captured them on the Hervidero Ranch. *La República Newspaper, Montevideo, October 23, 1917*

Precision Shootout

Now when Deputy Araújo and López approach the remaining two gang members, with López to Araújo's right, and Martínez seated behind on the ground to Araújo's left, the two officers are just a few steps away when pandemonium is unleashed in the corral. Abbreviating several newspapers: the two officers are very, very close to the remaining two outlaws:

"a pocos pasos, y a boca de jarro..." (9)

The first phrase is literal, *a pocos pasos* means that they are just a "few steps" from the American pair. The second phrase is a metaphor: *a boca de jarro* translated literally says "in the mouth of the jar." Both phrases indicate that they are about as close as they can get without kissing the Americans on the cheek... just a short step or two from the outlaws who are supposedly giving themselves up.

So it is, when the two officers are just about to "look into the mouth of the jar," that John Atkins drops to a knee drawing the Colt 1911 pistol and fires first two shots at Araújo and then two or three shots at López. Frank Lewis simultaneously draws his revolver and fires five shots at the other officers who have stayed some distance back but are now also approaching; (10) one of these five shots strikes and wounds a horse.

Flying Lead, Elusive Targets

One can imagine the chaos that is now breaking out with horses bucking, and with the two Americans who, after firing, are turning to either make a dash to escape or to grab their two rifles that had been placed against the fence. Both of the officers confronting the two Americans also respond by firing their weapons - they are already firing their revolvers before the two Apaches finish firing their guns. The newspaper accounts say that Lewis fired five shots and then his revolver was empty - was this because it was a five-shot piece, or was one cartridge missing from a chamber? Since the Police confiscated MacFarlane's revolver among the captured weapons, it is very likely that Lewis was using just that revolver when he fired five times. (11)

Atkins also fires a total of five shots; we know this because one newspaper reports that the two men fired a total of ten shots. (12) There had been one clip left for the Colt pistol, but only five cartridges remained in it for use. No one appears to now be using the Colt .44-40 revolver, which is likely out of bullets. The imitation Smith & Wesson revolver is not in use and the Colt .38 Revolver has been turned over already by Martínez.

Both Araújo and his assistant fire back six shots each. In all of the crisscrossing hail of lead, one bullet barely nicks Araújo's ear, while another whistles by his head, and one of Araújo's bullets sends Atkins' hat flying. Other than that, with 22 projectiles heading in a variety of directions no one is actually hit except for a horse. That Atkins first fires at Deputy Araújo and then loses his hat to one of Araújo's bullets, places these two facing each other, so the two Americans are standing looking towards the officers with Atkins on the right and Lewis on the left, and Lewis is in fact looking past López and shooting past López at the other officers who are now moving closer because the two Yanquis had previously made their gesture of surrender.

My brother, the expert armorer, who, as a state police officer on the West Coast of the US has trained hundreds of police in the use of short arms, mentions that most shootouts end like this one did, more often than not nobody is hit, even when the shooters are close. It is nothing like what one sees on television or in the movies where the good guys, especially, have an uncanny ability for sharpshooting, and their lethality seems to be even more effective when the bad guys are moving all over the place.

© Richard Dean Young

A house that now stands next to the corral, the buildings were not there in 1917

In the real world a lot of bullets are wasted; even in war it is amazing to see the statistics of the thousands of bullets shot for each enemy actually hit, most of these bullets only displace air. And this is especially true in close-up shootouts when all participants are dancing around, specifically with the purpose of not being hit. This movement compromises one's own shots, and those on other side of the duel have very little possibility of hitting their targets either. What makes for a truly deadly duel is to have a couple of experienced, ice-nerved gunslingers like Wyatt Earp and Doc Holliday who can stand still in the presence of multiple incoming missiles and take their time choosing their targets. Few have that kind of rock-hard nerve along with exceptional shooting ability, and few have those kinds of famous results.

The Uruguayan police and security personnel are distinguished even today for not having any special ability for hitting still targets, let alone moving ones. Uruguay has always been an especially peaceful place, so the need to keep officers up to speed on marksmanship has not been a top priority; after all, ammunition is expensive. While there are exceptions to this, and while Uruguay has always had a few officers who are good shots, most policemen carry a handgun that they realistically never expect to draw with the purpose of harming another human being. (13)

The above-mentioned lack of preparation is something like the state of things when General George Custer led his troops to disaster at Little Big Horn. Most of his conscripts literally didn't know how to shoot, a few had grown up with guns, but most had not, and the wisdom of the army bureaucracy gave each soldier eight bullets a year for target practice. The Indians, on the other hand, actually knew how to make each shot count.

I was with a friend at a shooting range in Montevideo when a trainer brought in a group of new recruits for a local security company, a firm that hauls Bank funds around town. I watched as this group tried to hit a still target with a pistol-gripped shotgun from about ten feet. After the "training" I was convinced that if I were ever close to a shoot-out between security guys and bad guys, I would distance myself as quickly as possible from the good guys.

Slapping Fine Sword Play

The newspapers then say that both Araújo and his assistant moved in to make sure that the two Americans could not make good their attempted move to freedom or, especially, make use of their carbines which were still fully loaded. In the reports on the shootout itself none of the newspapers even mention that the carbines had been placed up against the fence right behind Lewis and Atkins, and that for these long guns they had plenty of ammo left.

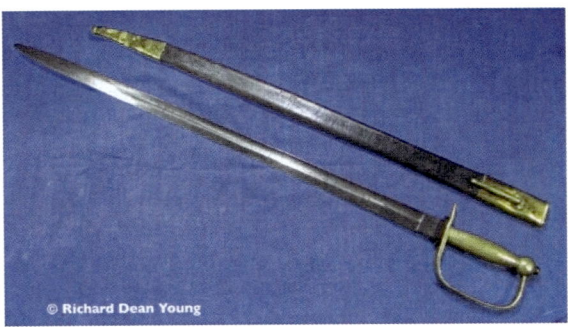

Traditional Uruguayan Police short sword

What Elías Araújo and Geroncio López did next literally hurts; it hurts just reading the news accounts. Both drew their short, narrow police swords and proceeded to beat the two Americans up the side of their heads with the flat of the blades. I have not yet seen one police sword that has a sharp edge, they were made for just this; cold steel applied with alarming efficiency, just as one would use a billy-club. While the police back then received almost no training in firearms use, they did practice the use of their short swords for riot control, and especially for reducing violent criminals.

Both John Atkins and Frank Lewis were beaten to the ground with hard cold steel whacked to their heads. Both would later need medical attention for their wounds. In Spanish these blows are called *palmadas*, a neat euphemism that literally means *slaps*.

Necktie for the Surrender Party

According to *La Prensa*, immediately after the subduing of the gang members and their arrest, Deputy Araújo made a list of the items taken off the Apaches. We have noted previously a few items that did not make it on this list - we surmise that some of these were "requisitioned" by this group of policemen. By recording the items they did put on the list they would avoid any further requisitioning on down the line. This list has been reproduced over and again in different newspapers and historical reports. It includes the weapons we listed in chapter two as well as several personal items of no great interest; shaving supplies, a small mirror, etc. But one item caught our attention and adds some regional color to the Apaches' possessions.

The inner patio of the main Ranch House on the Hervidero Ranch, where the three Apaches were first taken after their arrest.

CAPTURA DE LOS ASALTANTES AL BANCO DE LONDRES

EN EL RINCÓN DEL HERVIDERO

LOS BANDOLEROS SE RESISTEN Á MANO ARMADA

LA POLICÍA LOS REDUCE, ENTREGANDOLOS A LA JEFATURA DE SALTO

"Capture of the Assailants of the Bank of London, At the Rincón del Hervidero, The 'Bandoleros' Resist at Gunpoint, The Police Subdue Them, Turning Them Over to the Salto Headquarters"

Headlines of the El Telégrafo Newspaper of Paysandú, October 19, 1917, announcing the October 18th capture of the three outlaws on the Hervidero Ranch.

This was a necktie that had been purchased in Buenos Aires. Why they would hold on to a necktie during the chase is anyone's guess. The tie carried the brand *Gath & Chavez*. (14) This was a large and exclusive department store on what is now the well-known walking street, Florida, in the heart of downtown Buenos Aires. In 1912 this Company built a large 8-story building in a major expansion, and in 1922 British capital was added to this retail business and it took the name of Harrods. Of course, Harrods of London has long been the gold standard for shopping in Great Britain, and its affiliate in Argentina was the same for South America from that time until a few years after we arrived in Argentina in 1978.

El comisario Araujo y los criminales

Apaches Desplumados

The turnover of the three Apaches at the Dayman River to the Salto Police. Deputy Elías Araújo stands to the left, in the middle is Pablo Martínez with his hands tied behind his back. Between the two is possibly Araújo's Assistant, López.

Silent March, Motorized Caravan

Stripped of their necktie the three outlaws where then marched to the Hervidero Ranch where a journalist noted that the two Americans had "superficial" wounds about their heads. (15) All this happened early enough in the morning on Thursday, October 18th, that the mayor of Salto, Bernardo Gómez, along with the mayor of Paysandú, were able to arrive by automobile and take charge of the prisoners by 10 AM at the Dayman crossing.

As soon as the news reached Salto that the criminals had been apprehended, not only did the mayor and the police chief make their way to the Dayman River, just about every running car in Salto arrived at the crossing. Everyone who had a reason or an excuse wanted to get a close look at the Apaches, now in Police custody. The Salto paper, *La Prensa*, reported that 50 automobiles with "private individuals" arrived for the hand-over. The ride back to Salto must have appeared something like a modern funeral procession for a well-known member of society.

"All of these formed an original caravan, never before seen in this part of the Republic, they followed the car in which the Mayor was carrying the delinquents all the way to Salto." (16)

Postcard showing to the left Salto's Larrañaga Theater, to the right the Police Headquarters where the three prisoners were first taken after their arrest.

Photograph from a special collection of the Museum of the National Library, Montevideo - used with permission

References: Chapter 11

1. Taborda, op. cit., p. 85

2. "Cómo se efectuó la captura...Los bandidos descubiertos," *El Telégrafo*, October 19, op. cit., p. 1, col. 6

3. *ibid.*, "Cómo...Los bandidos descubiertos," *El Telégrafo*, October 19, p. 1, col. 6

4. "Cómo se efectuó la captura...Balas y sablazos," *El Telégrafo*, October 19, op. cit., p. 1, col. 6

5. "La indiada en el Salto, La captura," *El Diario*, Paysandú, October 19, 1917, p. 1, col. 4

6. Historians and anthropologists studying the collective memories of people groups have often noted that shared memories in tribes or even families can be remembered with surprising detail over multiple generations, especially when the memory has to do with a critical event that changed the life of the group. Previous scholarship often "assumed" that oral history was distorted and changed by time and from the passing of the information from one generation to another, and that it would be especially distorted if multiple generations were involved. But more recent studies have shown that the more dramatic and life-changing the event, the more indelibly and accurately were these memories and details stamped into the collective consciousness.

7. Luisa Marie Gutierrez, August 2005, op. cit.

8. "Cómo se efectuó la captura..Los bandidos descubiertos," *El Telégrafo*, October 19, op. cit., p. 1

9. "Cómo se efectuó la captura...Balas y sablazos," *El Telégrafo*, October 19, op. cit., p. 2, col.3

10. *ibid.*, "Cómo..Balas..," *El Telégrafo*, October 19, p. 2, col. 3

11. Most large revolvers chamber 6 shots, although there are 5-shot revolvers, but MacFarlane had fired his revolver once in the Bank office, and if it were the more common 6-shot variety, there would have remained 5 bullets in the chambers.

The only information we have on the MacFarlane revolver was that it had pearl grips and was nickeled, this sounds like a fancy British piece. The penchant of the British, and many more in our own Wild West, to own and carry Bulldog revolvers has often been noted - they were more compact, easy to carry in a pocket, and often quite lethal. Many of the British also used different Webley brand revolvers (some being Bulldogs), and while Webley's could be nickeled, one does not often see factory Webley's with pearl grips.

If MacFarlane's revolver were a Bulldog it could have been chambered for cartridges from the small European .320 right up through the huge .500 Webley, but the published list of captured weapons mentions a .38 revolver without giving any provenance - we assume this was MacFarlane's. Since MacFarlane and the previous Bank manager had discussed the Bank's safety, we can hardly imagine MacFarlane purchasing a small .320 revolver for personal safety only - he would have wanted a side-arm with some stopping power, and the .38 S&W pieces were widely used even by police in that period (today it would be considered a rather light cartridge).

One of the reasons to think that Lewis was using the revolver taken from the wounded MacFarlane was precisely because he shot 5 times. MacFarlane had managed one shot into the floor, so if the MacFarlane revolver was a normal 6-shot piece, and if Lewis then used this same gun, there would have been only 5 shots left. The other .38 caliber revolvers used by Martinez and turned over at the end were most likely chambered for the .38 Special cartridge. No .38 cartridges, either .38 SPL or .38 S&W, were turned in. Although it is quite possible that the two revolvers that Martínez had in use did carry some live rounds at the end. Either there were not enough cartridges to go around and complete the 6 shots in the revolver Lewis ended up using, or more logically, the .38 SPL cartridges could not be inserted into a chamber on MacFarlane's revolver made for the shorter .38 S&W.

Also the gang had done quite a bit of shooting at the Dayman River crossing, so it is logical that they had run out of ammo for the Colt 44-40 and that the stolen banker's revolver was now standing in for the revolver that had previously been used.

None of the weapons turned in were listed as 5-shot pieces; specifically the short guns of the criminals were reported as being the 1911 Colt pistol, a .38 Colt Revolver, and a copy of the Smith & Wesson Revolver, most likely chambered for the same.38 caliber ammo that Martínez was using.

The .38 Colt was a six-shot revolver - probably the 1892 "Army and Navy" Revolver, which after 1905 was chambered for the new .38 SPL cartridges. The press information doesn't give the actual chambering of this revolver, it just says "38" which could even be the earlier .38 Colt cartridge still in use at that time, but that would have meant that Martínez himself was using at least three different cartridges in the three guns we know he employed at one time or another.

There is also a possibility that the .38 Colt revolver was a "New Service", this was the largest-framed revolver ever turned out by Colt and which began to be manufactured in 1898. Some of these larger Colts were in use in the Southern Cone countries, but the Army-Navy revolvers were much more numerous in this period. In fact, one of the newspaper pictures of the "purported" Colt revolver shows the screw settings on the left side that correspond to the larger Colt New Service, - but this cannot be taken as proof positive, rather it could have more to do with a photo the newspaper had on hand of a typical Colt .38 hand gun.

When the guns and ammunition were captured, the only cartridges that were turned in were the .35 Remington bullets, and some small .32 Smith & Wesson cartridges. Our assumption is that the gang shot up most of its ammo - they certainly didn't count on the opposition at the bank, and would not have dreamed of having two later shoot-outs with the police. The nickeled, pearl-handled revolver taken from

MacFarlane did end up in Police custody... no bullets were mentioned for this gun; we assume that when turned in it carried 6 empty cases.

12. "La Indiada en Salto, Últimos Datos," *El Diario*, Paysandú, October 18, 1917, p. 1, col. 4

13. This was why at the turn of the 19th and 20th centuries most police in Uruguay, and especially the police of Montevideo, were armed with Spanish copies of the Smith & Wesson revolvers. Those revolvers, usually Orbea's, were good enough for a few shots, but would never take the year-in and year-out punishment that a Smith & Wesson could be subjected to, both on the shooting range and in real duty.

14. "Los celebres apaches. El arsenal de los apaches," *La Prensa*, October 19, op. cit., p. 1, col. 4

15. "Cómo se efectuó la captura...Indignación pública," *El Telégrafo*, October 19, op. cit., p. 2, col. 4

16. *"Todos estos coches, formaban una caravana original, nunca antes vista en aquella zona de la República, siguieron hasta el Salto, al automóvil donde el jefe político llevara a los delincuentes."*

La Prensa, October 24, op. cit.

CHAPTER TWELVE: GOODBYE COMPAÑERO

Los asaltantes del Banco

**I never meant to be a cheater
But there was blood on the wall
I had to steal from peter
To pay what I owed to paul
I couldn't stay and face the music
So many reasons why
I won't be sending postcards
From Paraguay**

Mark Knopfler, Postcards from Paraguay

On December 18, 1917 the three Apaches were moved from the jail in Salto to the new Penitentiary in Uruguay's capital, Montevideo. They would wait a year and four months for their case to work its way through Uruguay's cumbersome legal system. There was really no speed needed in dealing with these three - the case against them was watertight, they were *extranjeros* from distant lands, and they had committed some quite serious crimes. So they had no natural constituency in Uruguay or local friends who might call for a swift proceeding. A public trial by jury was finally convened in the first months of 1919.

The National Archives and a Dead End

As mentioned in chapter five, our search through the files at *el Archivo de la Nación*, the National Archives, merely turned up the list of prisoners taken into custody on October 18, 1917. (1) We also found the register number of the court case that was initiated in Salto that same year. (2) But the case was then transferred to Montevideo, and the trail runs cold as far as the judicial records go. The numbering system used by the Court in Salto had no relation to the system used in Montevideo, thus, as we wrote earlier, we were unable to find the actual court records of the trial itself. The previous court records from Salto had been sent to Montevideo along with the prisoners and were incorporated into the Montevideo records, so we could not find even the earlier proceedings from the Salto files, although all other Salto files are now stored in the National Archives. We found no public record, either in the Archives or in any newspaper, concerning when the case was reopened in 1919, so looking for a date-related item was also impossible.

**The new Punta Carretas Jail - *at that time some 3 kilómeters from the city of Montevideo.* **Also a view from inside out through the main entrance gate.*

Photograph from a special collection of the Museum of the National Library, Montevideo - used with permission

The file of the Montevideo proceedings has to sit somewhere in the basement or first floor of the archive building, and the good will of the employees there will someday allow us go through multiple stacks of bound records looking for this needle in a haystack.

New Jail for Novel Convicts

The Punta Carretas Jail was a new state-of-the-art prison facility finished in 1915; while somewhat smaller it had the look of Alcatraz. Just two years later three foreign outlaws joined the growing population in this cold, hard hotel for bad guys. While housed in this new efficient slammer they had plenty of time to meditate on their failed project while waiting for the legal system to process their case. The trial by jury was finally held in 1919, and on April 28th the three were found guilty of armed robbery, homicide and resisting law officers. (3)

LÓS ASESINOS EN EL BANCO DE LOS ASCUSADOS

The three Apaches listen as their verdict is announced. *Frank Lewis to the right, with head bowed, and the only good profile of John Atkins, left, from a rather poor newspaper picture.*

"Perched like ghostly birds

Believing in old men's lies,

Then too late unbelieving."

Lyn Hejinian, The water was rising...

The sentence was handed down two weeks later, on May 3, 1919, by the presiding judge, *Dr. Juan Méndez de Marco.* (4) And even though it was a fact that Pablo Martínez had fired the fatal shot that ended the life of George

MacFarlane, he received the simple sentence of 30 years to life for armed robbery. Several reporters mentioned that the three had accused each other of several of the crimes committed during the course of the trial, so at the end no mention of was made of who had fired the fatal shot.

Frank Lewis, with head bowed, listened to the jury arrive at its conclusions, and days later he was given the same "lighter" sentence as Martínez. The investigations and proceedings had abundantly demonstrated that John Atkins was the leader and financier of this *prendimiento*, for which he received the harshest sentence. A lifetime of reclusion was all that Atkins could look forward to from that day on. All three had the benefit of public defenders that simply tried to work for lesser sentences, because they were hard-put to defend the type of crime that these three had committed.

"Going to trial with a lawyer who considers your whole life-style a Crime in Progress is not a happy prospect." Hunter S. Thompson [*white letters set in black backround]

Final Destinies

Because of an already weak constitution, perhaps more from loss of hope, Atkins was not to enjoy even a fourth of the time that nature would normally add to a life-span that already counted "27" years when he entered the Punta Carretas Prison. In 1927, just ten years later, John Atkins was dead from "pneumonia." The prison medical doctor, *Julián Alvarez Cortés*, who served the Punta Carretas prisoners between 1914 and 1925, wrote a brief study on the prison and its conditions, and while carefully recording the difficulties suffered by the prison population, Alvarez also made a logical plea for the prison authorities to separate from the general prison population a group of inmates who suffered from tuberculosis. (5) That wise move was never carried out, and one wonders if Atkins' "pneumonia" was in reality a case of tuberculosis he picked up in prison, which was, at the end, disguised by a more acceptable diagnosis.

Article in the Montevideo newspaper, La Razón, on April 29, 1919, announcing the decision of the Jury finding the three prisoners guilty; on the top left is a picture of the two Attorney's who defended the accused: Dr. Eduardo Robaud and Dr. Hugo Antuña, at the bottom is a picture of the jury - no names give -, and in the middle the photo of the three accused listening to the decision of the jury.

Prison Mechanics

What has been noted by several Uruguayan sources is the useful skill that both Frank Lewis and John Atkins, as long as he lived, applied within the prison walls. They were both appreciated for their maintenance of the prison and police vehicles. Frank Lewis had brought that skill with him from Argentina, or wherever he had previously resided and worked, and he taught Atkins the rudiments of the upkeep needed for the early automobiles and prison trucks that would have been used in those days.

It is doubtful that Lewis and Atkins integrated totally into the prison population, the majority of whom were of the lower criminal classes of Uruguay. While Lewis could speak Spanish very well, and Atkins hardly at all, they would both be known as *gringos* or outlanders among most of the prison population. In Doctor Alvarez Cortés' study there are notes on difficulties among the prison population; fights, attacks and disciplinary matters centered especially on one or two intransigent prisoners. One of these who was jailed for homicide, and only referred to by his prison number, who incidentally had recently started his own jail stay just 37 days earlier on November 11th, ended up working in the same mechanical workshop and provoked fights with several there over a long period of time. This troublesome fellow with the number 13 was Uruguayan, and nothing is said about the objects of his wrath other than their numbers. It would not be surprising to find out that this criminal with a bent towards *conflicto* had a special problem with the two gringos; at least two of the fights he provoked were with the same prisoner, N° 53. (6)

Abandoned Punta Carretas Prison in the 1980's

The continuing stories of the two *pandilleros* who survived their prison experience are punctuated by question marks. First, it is known, but not documented, that the Mexican, Pablo Garcia or Martínez, was let out of the prison at a somewhat early date. It is possible that Mexico had a treaty with Uruguay by which Garcia could serve out his sentence in his own country.

The most curious bit of information that I picked up in Salto from descendants of those affected by the attempted robbery, was that Pablo Martínez appeared in Salto some years later and was seen standing across from the Bank of London. The testimonies were insistent that it was Martínez himself, and they say that he stood staring at the Bank for the longest time. (7)

Another version of Martínez's fate was mentioned briefly in a Montevideo Newspaper's online magazine in 2012. According to this account Martínez, using a ruse, got one of the guards to approach his cell, and then he attempted to take the officer's firearm. This account says that Martínez died in prison, most likely from wounds received during this failed attempt at freedom. This story lacks details and the more certain word of witnesses, and appears to us as the product of rumors concerning Martinez's later fate. (8)

Headline announcing the 1971 Prison Escape of 100 prisoners from the Punta Carretas Prison

In 1945, after appealing to the Uruguayan Penal Code of 1934 concerning the length of prison sentences, Frank Lewis was released from the Punta Carretas Prison. The only reference we have concerning Frank Lewis' later sojourns is that he was found residing in the State of Missouri. (9) But this is information that comes from Uruguay, not from the US, and it comes from later stories which also give no corroborating evidence. It is quite possible that Lewis *said* he was returning to Missouri, the state that he gave as his birthplace before the presiding Judge in Salto. We have good reason to doubt that earlier testimony, thus we must question the later information as to where he planned to travel. It is just as likely that Lewis returned to Argentina as to the United States.

Our last task before leaving Uruguay had been to inquire into the consular records of the US Embassy from that time - which are almost surely found now in Washington D. C. Our time in Uruguay ran out and our guess is that a Frank Lewis will not be found applying for a US passport towards the end of WWII.

The New Punta Carretas

In the early 1990's my wife and I rented an apartment in the Montevideo neighborhood of Punta Carretas called *Villa Biarritz*; this neighborhood is part of the Punta Carretas Barrio whose southern border is the road along the Uruguay River called *La Rambla*. It includes a quite large park surrounded by tall apartment buildings and is home to one of the larger private clubs of Montevideo, which has its own basketball team, large swimming pools and well-kept clay tennis courts. Just two blocks to the west of this park, as well as from our home, was located the former Punta Carretas Prison. It had closed in the 1980's after becoming famous, not for the residence of the Tin Can Gang, rather for the 1971 mass tunnel breakout of 100 urban guerrillas, most of them members of the famous Tupumaro organization. In an uniquely *uruguayo* twist of fate, two of the prisoners who escaped that day are today President of the Republic of Uruguay, *José Mujica*, and the present Minister of Defense, *Eleuterio Fernández Huidobro*. The contradictions and mysteries surrounding both Uruguay's political life as well as its penal history still prick the curiosity of historians and simple writers like myself.

The new "prison facility": now the Punta Carretas Shopping Center

In the early 1990's the old Punta Carretas Prison was turned into one of the most modern and architecturally interesting shopping centers in all of South America. This project was designed by Argentine architect Juan Carlos López and Uruguayan architect Casildo Rodríguez, and it contains at least 200 businesses on three floors as well as a Sheraton Hotel attached. We have toured this medium-sized shopping center with architects from the United States whose careers were made re-outfitting buildings and industrial sites, these professionals commented to us that this is one of the most unique projects they have ever seen.

Much of the older structure of the Prison was incorporated into the new shopping center, including some of the outer walls that now look something like the Hanging Gardens of Babylon; and right inside the main entrance, totally within the roofed area of the shopping center, stands the old main arch that was the final entrance point into the central area of prison cells. The architects called this the "Arch of Triumph." Who eventually triumphed after the prison's rather checkered history is still the talk of many Uruguayans.

The huge arch incorporated into the modern shopping center

"...but this is the real objection to that torrent of modern talk about treating crime as disease, about making prison merely a hygienic environment like a hospital, of healing sin by slow scientific methods. The fallacy of the whole thing is that evil is a matter of active choice whereas disease is not." - G. K. Chesterton

References: Chapter 12

1. "Año 1917, Estado de presos a disposición de este Juzgado," Juzgado Letrado Departamento

Salto, Archivo Nº 135, signed by a court representative, October 31, 1917

2. "Salto, Libro 6º de Conocimiento," Index of Arraignments 1914 through 1926, Book #635, Page #72, Note: a fuller translation of the relevant portion of this document is found in chapter 3, pp. 64-65

3. "Ecos del Asalto al Banco de Londres," *Tribuna Salteña*, Salto, April 29, 1919, p. 4, columns 4-6

4. "El Proceso a los asaltantes al B. de Londres - La sentencia del juez Dr. Méndez de Marco,"

Tribuna Salteña, Salto, May 4, 1919, p. 4, columns 5-6

5. Julián Alvarez Cortés, "Recopilación de Informes Médicos del Cárcel Penitenciario, 1914-1925," Peña Hnos, Montevideo, 1925, pp. 219-222

6. *ibid.*, pp. 159-160

7. Elena Miguens Meloni - interview, Salto, May 2009, op. cit.

8. Alberto Moroy, "Cuando Uruguay importaba asesinos de EEUU," *El País Viajes*, Montevideo, May 18, 2012, op. cit.

http://viajes.elpais.com.uy/2012/05/18/cuando-uruguay-importaba-asesinos-de-eeuu/

9. *ibid.*, Alberto Moroy, elpais.com.uy, May 18, 2012

CHAPTER THIRTEEN: THE PHANTOM OF THE REPAIR SHOP

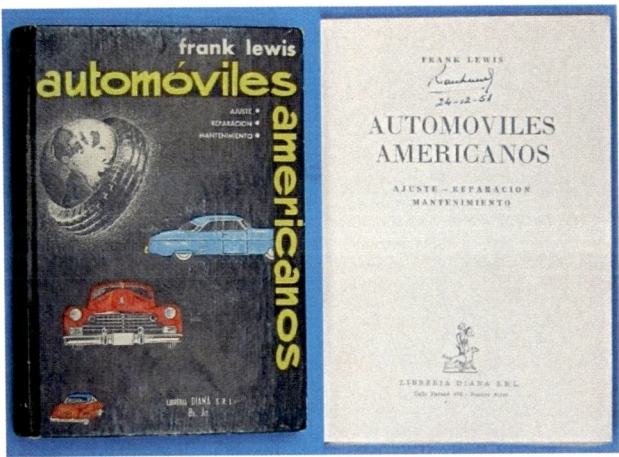

In plain sight, but out of sight. *Frank Lewis in his classic book on repair and maintenance of American cars.*

As this investigation neared its completion, and finding myself in California going through *trámites* for my retirement as well as putting a few finishing touches on this book before its publication, I decided to make one more attempt at encountering a second Frank Lewis in Argentina. I was convinced that our *Uruguayan* Frank Lewis had returned to Argentina in 1945 after his release from prison. All the signs, circumstantial as they were, pointed to Lewis having a significant previous involvement in Argentina. And although both British and American persons who had lengthy conversations and contacts with him, especially in Salto, Uruguay, distinctly identified him as a North American, a North American without a southern accent, his secret Spanish speaking ability and other multiple and bedeviling hints, pointed him south towards a long sojourn in the Southern Cone as well as the possible link to the Cassidy gang.

Well, as they say, some of us cannot see the forest for the trees. All of my searches for another Frank Lewis in Argentina had consistently turned up a book on American cars written by a Frank Lewis. I had even noticed this book appearing in searches I made years back, which I had also *consistently* dismissed out of hand, thinking that it was surely a book translated from English to Spanish and authored by another Frank Lewis in the United States. Any Google search for authors with this name turns up a good number of American Frank Lewis', some are simply "Frank Lewis" as with our subject in South America, and there are a variety of Frank L's, Frank W's and Frank D's populating the literary realms of cyberspace. Thus a Frank Lewis writing a book about American Cars just didn't stand out to me as particularly relevant.

Another Look

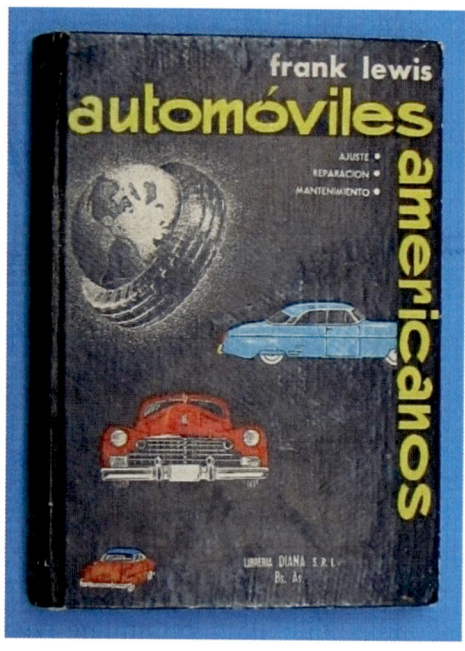

Abundant details on the mechanics of American vehicles, meager details about the author

This recent empty-handed search had also brought up this same book, titled *"Automóviles Americanos, Ajuste, Reparación, Mantenimiento,"* (1) "American Cars, Adjustments, Repairs, Maintenance" - but this time I was much more familiar with our previous driver and later expert vehicle mechanic. In a sense I was now noticing out of the corner of my eye a piece of evidence that had always been there in plain sight, and it suddenly occurred to me that our *uruguayo* Frank Lewis may well have written this book. He started out in our story as an expert mechanic, he was familiar with the first motorized vehicles manufactured in the Western Hemisphere, and he spent almost 30 years repairing the Prison vehicles in Montevideo honing his skills, so why not write a book?

Uruguay, like Argentina, in those first decades of the 20th century had no local manufacturers of cars. And while Argentina began some of its own design and manufacturing in the 1930's, Uruguay was just a small market that could not justify the kind of investment and industrial outlay that was required for turning out modern automobiles.

"Automóviles Americanos" - *Frank Lewis' guide to maintenance and repair.*

We understand that many of these books were literally worn out from use in repair shops, and that some can be found almost totally darkened by grease marks.

While today Uruguay does have a few shops that assemble limited lines of a few European cars (like my Peugot 205), and while Argentina and Brazil have brought in their own Ford, Volkswagon, Chevrolet, Fiat and other manufacturing factories, Uruguay has basically been an importer of automobiles since these machines first appeared on the world scene. And up until at least the 1960's the predominant vehicles imported into Uruguay were almost exclusively American. The national police of Uruguay only experimented with patrol cars of European origin in the 1970's. Thus all mechanical repairs and maintenance that Lewis did with the prison and police vehicles in Punta Carretas were done on American cars and trucks.

What really caught my attention, once I stopped to look over the information available, was that the Lewis book was *only* published in Buenos Aires, Argentina, and *only* in Spanish. Therefore, it was not a translation of a North American publication to Spanish; rather it had originated in South America, right across the river from Uruguay.

We know almost nothing of the circumstances surrounding the book that appeared in Buenos Aires in 1956, eleven years after Frank Lewis was released from the Punta Carretas Prison. But a book was published, and there were only two Frank Lewis' in Argentina; the real, original Frank in Patagonia and the outlaw Frank who showed up in Uruguay in 1917. But our outlaw's mechanical skills were apparent to us right from the moment he emerged on our radar screens.

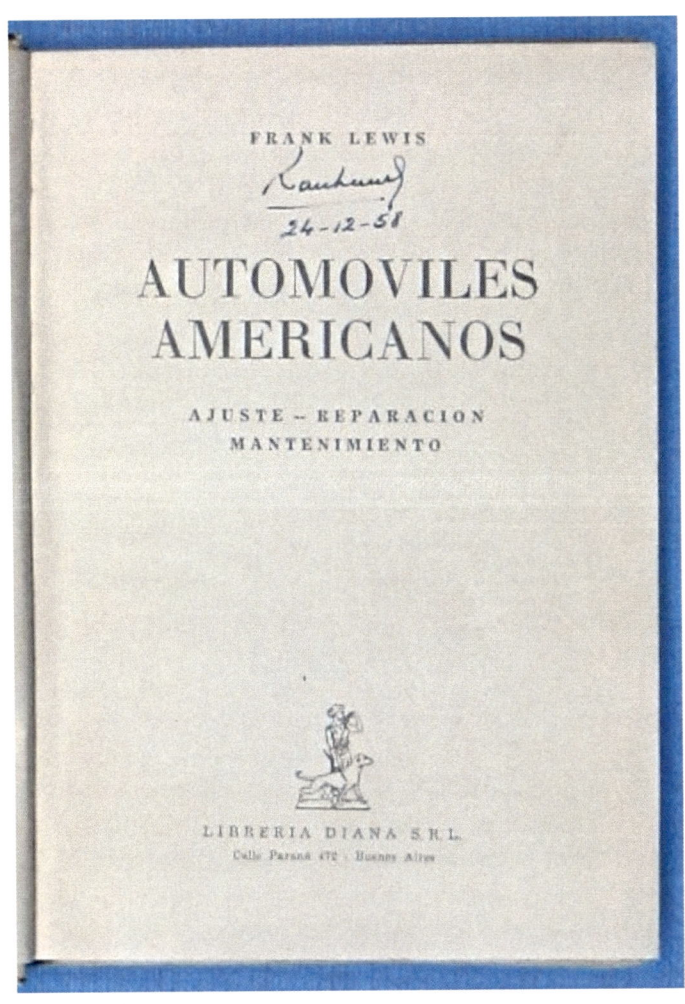

FRANK LEWIS

24-12-58

AUTOMOVILES
AMERICANOS

AJUSTE – REPARACION
MANTENIMIENTO

LIBRERIA DIANA S.R.L.
Calle Paraná 472 · Buenos Aires

The title page of Frank's book. *One of two places where his name appears. Also showing a hand written signature of an individual who obtained this book in December of 1958.*

Lewis' book was printed by *Talleres Gráficos Lumen Noseda y Cia.*, an established print shop that turned out many well-known Argentine titles up until 1970. The book became not only a standard on repairing American cars built between 1936 and 1949; De Sotos, Dodges, Fords, Lafayettes, Hudsons and more, but it has since turned into an Argentine classic on cars which will now bite you for at least $150, if you can find one. While the tables at the end of the book for adjustments on distribution, spark plug settings, etc., only go through the year of 1949, there are references in the text itself to mechanical details on some cars up through the year of 1952. So the preparation of the book itself was begun in or after 1952, and, of course, its publication is dated in 1956.

I anxiously awaited for my bargain $125 copy to show up in Los Angeles through the good services of DHL Express, both because I was finally getting the "Apache" book ready for publishing, but also, and more importantly, because I sensed that this "Lewis" book would be a concrete piece of evidence from the life of a person for which we have some huge yawning holes.

In the book itself the descriptions concerning the repair of these now classic American cars are wonderfully detailed and organized, the Spanish is clear and educational, and the professional drawings, which had to have been arranged through a skilled graphic artist, are surprisingly explicit.

The Elusive Lewis

But there is a paucity of details on Frank Lewis himself. In fact there are none, other than his name. The author's name appears on the cover and on the title page, and after that... nothing, zip, *nada*; not one word about the expert mechanic himself anywhere in the book.

This is the most telling aspect of the book; Frank Lewis did not want the world to know even the slightest detail about his person or his life. Quite simply he was sharing his expertise in the repair of automobiles, but definitely was *not* sharing anything about himself.

So we add one more piece to the puzzle. And while our evidence might not hold up in a court of law, we are convinced that Frank Lewis spent the rest of his life in Argentina.

And that leaves a whole period of Lewis' later life that we know almost nothing about. From the book itself we can deduce that he continued to work as a mechanic. And the clear, educational tone of the book makes us wonder if somewhere in the huge metropolis of Buenos Aires Frank

Lewis may have spent all or part of his time training young mechanics as he had done with his partner in the Punta Carretas prison. He lived somewhere in "BA" as we call the big city down south, he met people and certainly made friends or acquaintances during his later years. It is quite possible that in Buenos Aires some of those persons who knew Frank may still be alive.

Published by "Librería Diana", and printed by "Talleres Gráficos Lumen…" two businesses that no longer exist in Buenos Aires

So we now have another *cometido*; a serious investigation in Buenos Aires to see if we can locate anyone still living who might have known Frank Lewis, or any source which has specific data from the post-WWII period concerning the author of this classic book. At the very least, we should be able to turn up a public record as to the year of his demise in the southern climes.

Already we have made contact with friends and writers in Buenos Aires who were into their adult years during this post-war period. Like us they were surprised to learn about this elusive person, and while some knew about the book itself, no one has yet turned up any specific information about Lewis and his life in Buenos Aires after his release from the Montevideo prison. Time is part of our problem because living witnesses to the *porteño* Frank Lewis's later life and work are right now in the process of moving on to the big repair shop in the sky. And it also appears, with our first inquiries, that Frank Lewis did a pretty good job of keeping in the shadows, especially in this later period of his life.

Since there was only one legitimate "Frank Lewis" in Argentina in the first half of the 20th century, our "Uruguayan" Lewis came late to his name. Upon release from prison he would have found himself stuck with an official history, at least in Uruguay, as well as with the name he had reported as his own decades earlier. Whether he got attached to his new name during his 28-year prison stay, or whether he now had a legal title he could not easily shake, Frank Lewis did pass the rest of his life using what we consider a borrowed name.

And it now appears quite distinctly that his later life was spent in much more honest and useful endeavors than were his early years.

References: Chapter 13

1. Frank Lewis, "Automóviles Americanos, Ajuste, Reparación, Mantenimiento," Librería Diana S.R.L., Buenos Aires, 1956

Detailed instructions for repairs

MOTORES EN LINEA

LUBRICACION DE LAS BIELAS

El sistema conocido para la lubricación de las bielas es el de chorro a presión y salpicadura. Una lubricación correcta depende de un ajuste preciso de las cucharillas de aquéllas, profundidad de las canaletas del cárter y, además, que los surtidores del cárter estén apuntados en la dirección correcta.

El cárter de los motores es igual; sin embargo, existe una diferencia en la longitud de la carrera de los cilindros. Cuando se comprueben las alturas de las canaletas de cárter y las cucharillas, deben usarse herramientas calibradoras.

Altura de las cucharillas

Con el cárter desmontado, dé vuelta el cigüeñal hasta que la biela esté en su punto muerto inferior; instale las dos varillas la-

Fig. 8.— Comprobando la altura de las cucharas de las bielas

terales de la herramienta calibradora apropiada en los costados del bloque del motor, adyacentes a la cucharilla que se desee verificar, fig. 8.

Al correr el calibrador sobre la cucharilla, la sección baja "GO" (Pasa) de aquel debe pasar sobre la cucharilla; en cambio, la sección alta "NO GO", no deberá pasar. Si la primera no pasa sobre la cucharilla, golpee ésta suavemente con un martillo para bajarla hasta que el calibrador pase libremente sobre ella. En caso que la sección alta pase, deberá instalarse una nueva cucharilla.

Professional mechanical drawing in Frank Lewis' book

MOTORES EN LINEA

LUBRICACION DE LAS BIELAS

El sistema conocido para la lubricación de las bielas es el de chorro a presión y salpicadura. Una lubricación correcta depende de un ajuste preciso de las cucharillas de aquéllas, profundidad de las canaletas del cárter y, además, que los surtidores del cárter estén apuntados en la dirección correcta.

El cárter de los motores es igual; sin embargo, existe una diferencia en la longitud de la carrera de los cilindros. Cuando se comprueben las alturas de las canaletas de cárter y las cucharillas, deben usarse herramientas calibradoras.

Altura de las cucharillas

Con el cárter desmontado, dé vuelta el cigüeñal hasta que la biela esté en su punto muerto inferior; instale las dos varillas laterales de la herramienta calibradora apropiada en los costados del bloque del motor, adyacentes a la cucharilla que se desea verificar, fig. 8.

Al correr el calibrador sobre la cucharilla, la sección baja "GO" (Pasar) de aquel de pasar sobre la cucharilla; en cambio, la sección alta "NO GO", no deberá pasar. Si la primera no pasa sobre la cucharilla golpee ésta suavemente con

Fig. 8. — Comprobando la altura de las cucharas de las bielas

un martillo para bajarla hasta que el calibrador pase libremente sobre ella. En caso que la sección alta pase, deberá instalarse una nueva cucharilla.

Cutaway pictures of essential car parts

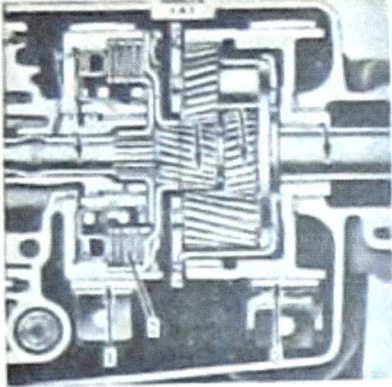

Fig. 71. — Transmisión de la fuerza en directa.

Directa. En esta posición el eje impulsor y el eje transmisor tienen que girar a la misma velocidad y en la misma dirección. Para obtener la marcha directa, el sistema planetario queda trabado y gira como una sola unidad. (fig. 71).

Baja de emergencia. Aquí el portaplanetario tiene que girar en la misma dirección que el eje impulsor, pero a menos velocidad. (fig. 72).

Con la palanca en esta posición, se suelta el embrague y se aplica el collar sobre la superficie exterior del tambor de embrague. Esto inmoviliza el tambor; éste a su vez, inmoviliza la pestaña y esta última el engranaje central de baja, el que está fijado a la pestaña por medio de ranuras.

La fuerza es entonces transmitida del eje impulsor al engranaje central de marcha atrás, luego a los satélites largos y de ellos a los satélites cortos, los cuales endientan con el engranaje central de baja. Como éste está inmovilizado por la aplicación del collar, los satélites cortos giran a su alrededor llevando consi-

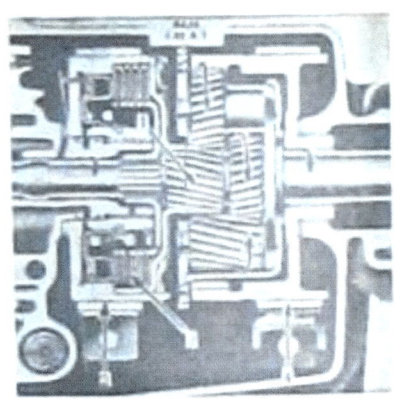

Fig. 72. — Transmisión de la fuerza en baja.

Distribution Drawings

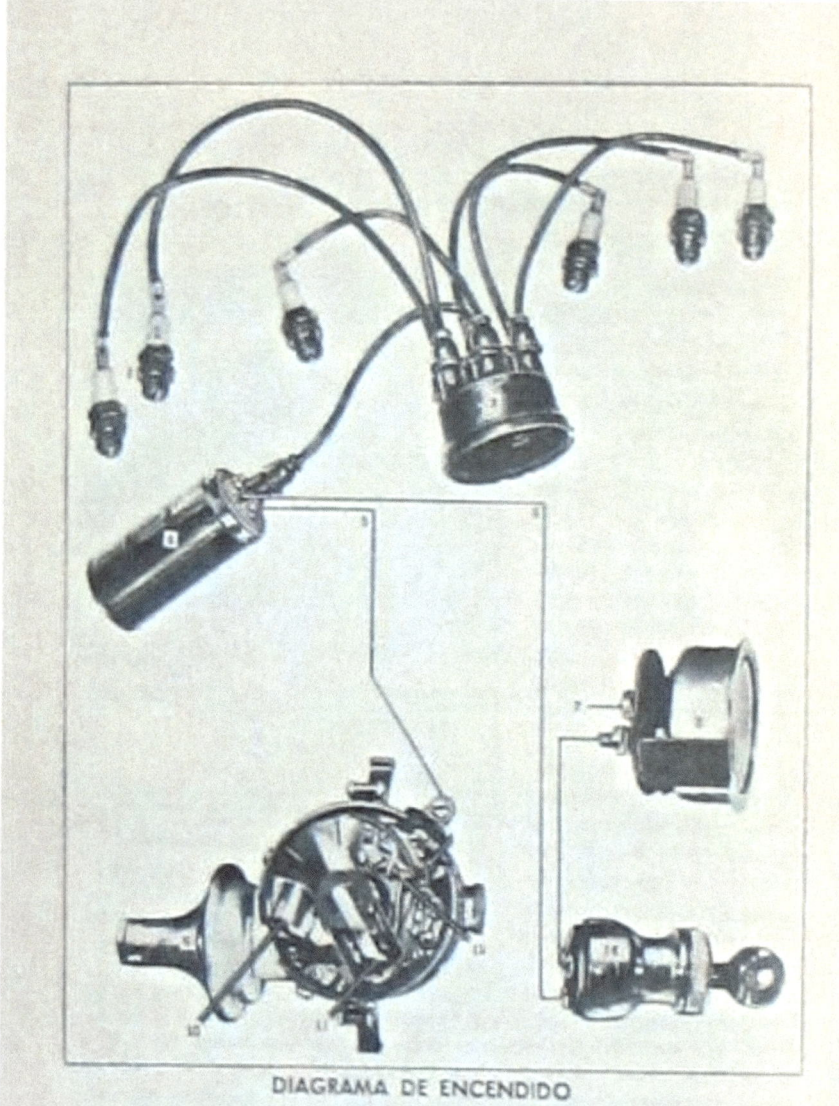

DIAGRAMA DE ENCENDIDO

1. Bujía. — 2. Porcelana. — 3. Tapa distribuidor. — 4. Bobina. — 5. Conexión bobina-magneto. — 6. Conexión bobina-llave de contacto. — 7. Borne del amperímetro. — 8. Amperímetro. — 9. Control de avance de vacío. — 10. Condensador. — 11. Distribuidor de encendido. — 12. Platinos. — 13. — 14. Llave de contacto.

Tables of settings for tune-ups

	A	B	C	D	E	F	G
1936 6, después del No. 217746	22	0,020	36	119	0,030	0,008	0,010
1936 8	22	0,015	31	124	0,030	0,008	0,010
1937 6	30	0,020	35	121	0,040	0,008	0,011
1937 8	30	0,015	31	124	0,030	0,008	0,011
1938 6	28	0,020	35	119	0,040	0,008	0,011
1938 8	28	0,015	31	121	0,030	0,008	0,011
1939 6	29	0,020	35	134	0,040	0,008	0,011
1939 8	29	0,015	31	134	0,030	0,008	0,011
1940 6	33	0,020	35	146	0,040	0,008	0,011
1940 8	33	0,015	31	152	0,030	0,008	0,011
1941-42 6	34	0,020	35	115	0,040	0,008	0,011
1941-42 8	34	0,015	31	105	0,030	0,008	0,011
1946-48 6	35	0,021	35	115	0,040	0,008	0,011
1946-48 8	35	0,015	31	107	0,032	0,008	0,011
1949 6	40	0,020	35	125	0,040	0,008	0,011
1949 V-8	40	0,015	22	136	0,030	A	A

DE SOTO

	A	B	C	D	E	F	G
1936 Airstream 6	21	0,020	38	119	0,025	0,006	0,008
1936 Airflow 6	21	0,020	40	132	0,025	0,006	0,008
1937 6	20	0,020	40	132	0,025	0,008	0,010
1938 6, S-5	28	0,020	38	126	0,025	0,008	0,010
1939 6, S-6	28	0,020	38	139	0,025	0,008	0,010
1940 6, S-7	35	0,020	38	145	0,025	0,008	0,010
1941 6	35	0,020	38	130	0,025	0,008	0,010
1942 6	35	0,020	38	130	0,025	0,008	0,010
1946-48 6	35	0,020	38	115	0,025	0,008	0,010
1949	40	0,020	38	118	0,040	0,008	0,010

DODGE

	A	B	C	D	E	F	G
1936 6	21	0,020	40	132	0,025	0,006	0,008
1937 6	20	0,020	28	132	0,025	0,006	0,008
1938 8-D8	28	0,020	38	126	0,025	0,006	0,008
1938 8-D9	18	0,020	38	126	0,025	0,006	0,008
1939 8-D11	28	0,020	38	136	0,025	0,006	0,008
1940 6-D14, D17	35	0,020	38	140	0,025	0,008	0,008
1941 6	35	0,020	38	113	0,025	0,008	0,010
1942 6	35	0,020	38	130	0,025	0,008	0,010
1946-48 6	35	0,020	38	115	0,025	0,008	0,010
1949 6	35	0,020	38	118	0,040	0,008	0,010

FORD

	A	B	C	D	E	F	G
1936 V-8	15	0,012	*24	127	0,025	0,013	0,013
1937 V-8—60	18	0,014	*22	135	0,025	0,014	0,014
1937 V-8—85	16	0,014	*22	125	0,025	0,014	0,014
1938 V-8—60	18	0,014	*22	129	0,025	0,013	0,013
1938 V-8—85	30	0,014	*22	120	0,025	0,013	0,013
1939 V-8, 922A	18	0,014	*22	130	0,025	0,013	0,013

CHAPTER FOURTEEN: THE SINS OF THE CRIMINALS

The mystery of the "missing" wife was resolved recently in 2007. *When Daisy's tomb was found in the Montevideo British Cemetery. Friends in Salto thought the MacFarlane's should be buried together, but no death certificate, nor body, was found until a few years back - and that by Daisy's own grandson.*

"He will by no means leave the guilty unpunished, visiting the iniquity of fathers on the children and on the grandchildren to the third and fourth generations."

Exodus 34:7 NASB

"The sins of the fathers": an enigma and a reality that has been discussed for *millennia*. Is there something in the DNA of the wicked that is passed on down to their children? Or is it more like those patterns which Oscar Lewis discovered in his anthropological studies in Mexico, and later with Puerto Ricans who immigrated to New York; (1)

where the culture and values, or lack of them, handed down to children in any family are extremely hard to escape or change in just a generation or two. Thus we have a "culture of poverty," a "culture of crime," and various other subcultures that obstinately stick around and damn the following generations, quite often whether they like it or not. Of course, we do believe in free will and the ability of just about anyone to pull themselves up by their bootstraps; it's just that the examples of such liberating bootstrap liftings' are so few and far between.

Even more intractable and so unjust are the results we see in the lives of victims. And in studying the tragedy of the individual victims of this gang of Apaches, with both the physical and emotional fallout in this saga of death and destruction, I am tempted to paraphrase the Biblical saying as follows, which in its concise cruelness sums up the bad luck of victims around the world:

"He will by no means leave the victims unpunished, visiting the iniquity of the criminals on the victims' children and grandchildren to the third and fourth generations." (2)

After such a cruelly heartless statement that appears to leave no room for hope, I should clarify my views as a Christian pastor; I personally do not believe that *God himself* is anything like this. However this misquote of a Scriptural passage does accent the grim reality that afflicts so many victims in every society of our broken world. I could go on to state what are my beliefs as well as my experiences as a pastor who worked with individuals and families crushed by both state and left-wing terrorism in Argentina; I could bear witness to the amazing grace of God that we saw bring healing and redemption in cases quite similar to those in the story we are drawing out in these pages. But I did not set out to write a theological or pastoral treatise in these pages, so I will limit my spiritual views to this one paragraph.

Young George

George MacFarlane's oldest son, George Robert MacFarlane, eight at the time of the shooting, was just old enough to know what happened, but not old enough to *understand*. What we know of his life doesn't reveal to us even a hint of serenity. While he did enjoy sports, as had his father, he did not always do well in school. He married a schoolteacher in Argentina in 1938, and they had a son a year later, Jorge Enrique MacFarlane. Then in 1941 George Robert went off to England to join the RAF for WWII. He was discharged in 1943 after a training accident left him with multiple fractures of one of his legs. He then returned to Argentina where alcoholism and increasing mental instability left his family in dire economic straits. His marriage fell apart and he moved back to England where he died at St. John's Hospital in London, this in his middle years at the age of 55.

Grandson "Jorge" MacFarlane

In 2007 I discovered the MacFarlane online web site. (3) Through the site I began a lively correspondence with Jorge Enrique MacFarlane, grandson of George and Daisy MacFarlane, the only son of George Robert MacFarlane and Dora Valsecchi. From Jorge I learned about the fate of the five children who were left orphans when both of their parents died within 50 days of each other. The four children were sent to a ranch in Buenos Aires Province, where George MacFarlane's sister, Margaret Runnacles, took them in. The children were never told what happened to their parents, although young George did in fact know the basic facts of the tragic time in Salto, and we cannot even begin to fathom the drama this little kid went through when he lost his mom so soon after losing his dad.

George L. MacFarlane with young George about 2-3 years old. c1912

Jorge informed me that he began searching for answers about his grandfather and grandmother's past, a seemingly taboo subject among the extended family in Argentina. One has to remember that almost 100 years back, even well educated people would not be familiar with the findings of modern psychological studies and the more healthy ways of dealing with loss that we know today. Most of us have simply to think back to our own grandparents, and even our parents, and their reticence to bring out in the open the more tragic sides of their own family histories. For them, often the renewed pain of reliving tragic situations simply seemed too difficult to handle, so silence was the ready, but even more tragic, answer to the questions of why.

Added to this is the tremendous uprooting caused by the immigrant experience; the adaptation to a new world, a new culture and a new language - a process in which only the mentally tough get through with any kind of stability and sanity. And all larger immigrant experiences are ridden with those sad stories of loss, lunacy, suicide and desperation.

It would have surprised the socks off me to discover that the loving aunt, which we are sure she was since she took in the five kids, had sat the poor little folk down and explained to them exactly why their lives had fallen apart.

The Other Children

George and Daisy's eldest daughter, Renee Iris, born in Salto in 1910, tragically died of typhoid in Argentina at the age of ten – this just three years after the loss of her two parents. I myself was assailed by a case of typhoid in North Argentina in the 1980's, this at a time of stress and travel and having had brushes with other somewhat rare diseases - it was a most unpleasant experience and modern medications were what surely kept me in the land of the living. I have wondered if little Renee spent those last three years of her earthly life in such a wistful, joyless existence, that when this vicious affliction struck she had no resistance to offer. For the siblings the tragic loss of their sister, just a few years after the death of both parents, had to have been an emotionally bitter time.

Anglican or "British" Cemetery of Salto

Another daughter, Jean Edith, lived until the WWII era in Buenos Aires, and later died in England in 1974. We have almost no information on Jean Edith's life or whether she was able to find some measure of happiness and fulfillment in the cross-cultural settings she had to navigate from the Southern Cone to the British Isles. The third child born to George and Daisy, and second son, was Frederick Lauderdale, who was five years old when he lost his two parents. His life at least looks to have been somewhat more purposeful. He turned out to be quite the athlete, much like his father; rugby, cricket and boxing, and he later worked in a popular radio station in Buenos Aires. At the end of WWII Fred was contracted by the BBC in London, and for many years was the main speaker on Spanish programs broadcast to South America. Fred passed away in 1966 in Westminster, London.

The youngest of the children, Martha Alice, was only three years old when tragedy stuck. She also grew up on the ranch in Buenos Aires Province, and in 1939 she both married Richard Lewis and moved to London. A few years later she was found working in the BBC, alongside her older brother Fred. These two seem to be the ones who led a more stable and happy life, and it certainly appears that there was an ongoing care and concern, especially of the older brother for his younger sister.

Jorge Enrique MacFarlane, December 2007

318

When I first made contact with Jorge MacFarlane, I was able to fill in for him some of the details of the MacFarlane tragedy from the Uruguay side of the *Río de la Plata*, and Jorge was able to give me first-hand information of the MacFarlane children. This was the first time anyone in Uruguay, modern Uruguay at least, found out what had happened to the five little ones. I had heard stories that they had returned to Great Britain, and that the children had been split up and sent to different British families in Argentina, etc. It was comforting to know that an aunt took in all five of the children and that they were able to spend at least the rest of their childhood together.

Daisy's Remains?

Jorge told me of a recent trip he had made to Salto, where for the first time he had discovered the elements and setting of the murder of his grandfather as well as a few details about the ensuing demise of his grandmother. With the help of the local Anglican Church he was able to procure a copy of his grandfather's death certificate. But the story of what happened to his grandmother, Daisy, remained a mystery. All Jorge knew was that she died soon after the killing of his grandfather.

"What happened to Daisy up until the December 5, 1917, and where she died continues to be a mystery for us." (4)

At that time I conversed with Jorge about some of the theories concerning Daisy's death and where she might be buried - these stories I had heard especially from people in the Salto area who still had varied memories passed down through their families about the incident and its fallout. Some commented that Daisy had returned to England where she then passed away. Jorge himself talked to me about the mystery of the tombstone in Salto being inscribed with the names of both George and Daisy, but that since there was no local death certificate for Daisy, technically there could be no body.

Others said that Daisy had gone to Buenos Aires, where the family did have relatives, and there her life sadly ended. The only fact in common among the different theories was that Daisy had passed away soon after her husband, and that the five children were orphaned by the two grievous losses.

In early November of 2007 Jorge MacFarlane wrote to me from Buenos Aires telling of the trip he had made to Salto some two or three years earlier. He mentioned that the caretaker of the Salto British Cemetery told him that Daisy had not died in Salto, but that her body had later been taken there. This coincided with Daisy's death certificate not appearing in Salto and with the fact the both George and Daisy's names were inscribed on the gravestone. Right up until a trip that the MacFarlane's made to Uruguay a month later, Jorge believed that his grandmother was buried in Salto, and he thought that the mystery only had to do with where she had passed away.

All of my contact with Jorge MacFarlane in Buenos Aires was either by email or by telephone - we had some lively conversations, sharing different theories about several aspects of the Salto tragedy. For me it was a wonderful privilege to be in touch with a living link to the stories I was investigating, and I couldn't shake off the sense that even though I was communicating in Spanish with Mr. Jorge MacFarlane that I was actually getting to know a classic British gentleman.

An Emotional Discovery

In December of that same year, which is summer season in the southern latitudes, Jorge let me know that he and his wife Nilsa were taking a short vacation on the beaches of Uruguay to pass the Christmas holiday with their grandchildren. He said that in January, when returning by car through Montevideo on their way home to Buenos Aires, they wanted to stop and get to know us as well as exchange more information.

But Jorge and Nilsa never showed up, they didn't call... and several days passed with me wondering what might have happened. That was when Jorge wrote to me from Buenos

Aires, sincerely apologizing for not looking us up. He then told me of the discovery they made when they drove into Montevideo along the *Rambla*, the road running beside the river that flows along the southern coast of the country; the same Uruguay River which passes both Salto and Paysandú, and which at the level of Montevideo is mixing with saltwater somewhere out near the horizon.

Daisy's Tombstone in the Buceo British Cemetery

"IN LOVING MEMORY OF

DAISY MACFARLANE

WIFE OF GEORGE L. MACFARLANE

YOUNGEST DAUGHTER OF

ROBERT McVICAR

OF MAIDSTONE KENT ENGLAND

THE LORD COMFORT THEE"

Right there along the coast, in the *Buceo* neighborhood, is located the old *Cementerio Británico*, the Montevideo

British Cemetery. The MacFarlanes decided to stop, and Jorge questioned the manager, who happened to be there, if he had ever heard of Daisy McVicar MacFarlane. To his great surprise the caretaker said "Yes, she is buried right here."

Jorge told me that along with the shock of this discovery he also realized that he needed to ask for a copy of Daisy's death certificate. After taking pictures and going downtown to request the certificate, he said that he was just too emotionally distraught to look up some new friends, so he and his wife got back in their car and drove straight to Buenos Aires. Here is part of what Jorge wrote to me about the experience:

"I felt very emotional and fell in a pit when we learned that she had died of 'psychopathic cachexia', which in plain language means that she let herself die of starvation (my father told me that she had died of sadness)." (5)

And that was how we were able to put together one more important piece of this complex puzzle. I later found press articles that told of how Daisy's health became increasingly worse in the hospital in Salto, and that finally the medical personnel there felt it necessary to send her to Montevideo with the hope that she might receive more effective care. But she passed away within two days of arriving in the capital city.

It is clear now that the friends in Salto, who would have found out about Daisy's passing in Montevideo, assumed that her remains would be sent back to Salto. So when they had the tombstone made for Jorge MacFarlane they added Daisy's name. But by that time she had already been buried in Montevideo. The MacFarlane's had already lived in Montevideo for at least two years before moving to Salto. Montevideo had a significantly larger British community than Salto, thus it is certain that donations were raised to cover Daisy's funeral expenses as well as to put up a quite elegant tombstone.

The MacFarlane Legacy

The only regret I have is that Jorge never found out about his grandfather beginning the Salto Soccer League, although Jorge did know about the family starting the soccer club in Buenos Aires. Nor did Jorge know about his grandfather's multiple contributions to the civic life of his adopted city. The further information, especially about the Salto Soccer League, I ran across later in another of my journeys to Salto, this about a year after Jorge passed away. I have stayed in contact with his widow Nilsa, who will get copies of this book in Spanish. But even now Jorge's children, the great-grandchildren of George and Daisy, are much better informed about the all-around sportsman, philanthropist and gentleman who was their forebear.

In my reading of the many newspaper accounts printed during the days following the death of George MacFarlane, I discovered among the telegrams sent and expressions of sympathy to the family one special communication from MacFarlane's former boss and close friend, Theodore Bourse, whom George had replaced as manager of the bank just seven months previously. Mr. Bourse was now in Buenos Aires, perhaps still employed by the Bank of London, when he wrote the following.

"Buenos Aires, Oct. 17. 10:26 a.m. [1917]
Jorge Armstrong;
Telegrams this morning announcing the death of my dear friend MacFarlane, my good companion in work and sport. Poor Mac!
How many times we commented on the possibility of an attack on the bank and how could we prepare the best defense! I knew very well that my accountant would always confront any attack!
I request, that in the act of the burial of his remains, that my great sorrow be made known as well as my inability to be there for reasons of the strike. Do not forget to add my name to the flower arrangement or some other memorial! - Bourse." (6)

Close Encounters

One afternoon in August of 2005, Luisa Maria of the Hervidero Ranch, where the Apaches were caught and the final shootout went down, told me of an encounter that had happened to her back in the 1950's. As a young woman she was on a trip to Buenos Aires, and like so many who visited the big city in those days, she went to the large Harrods Department Store on Florida Avenue. She was in the cosmetic section when the lady who was assisting her asked where she was from. Luisa answered that she was from near Salto in Uruguay. Immediately the face of the employee clouded over and her eyes turned sad. "What happened?" asked Luisa, mystified by the reaction. The woman answered, "Oh, it's just that my uncle was murdered there at the Bank of London back during the First World War." Luisa went on to tell her that the coincidence of their encounter was even greater, because the perpetrators had been apprehended right on her ranch, *El Hervidero*. (7)

Luisa Maria Gutierrez Amaro - stories of another time.

"We want to be saved from our misery, but not from our sin. We want to sin without misery, just as the prodigal son wanted inheritance without the father. The foremost spiritual law of the physical universe is that this hope can never be realized. Sin always accompanies misery. There is no victimless crime, and all creation is subject to decay because of humanity's rebellion from God.
— R.C. Sproul, Choosing My Religion

References: Chapter 14

1. Oscar Lewis, "The Sons of Sanchez," Random House, New York, 1961

Lewis, "The Culture of Poverty," Scientific American, N°4, Vol. 215, October 1966, pp.19-25

2. My poor paraphrase of Exodus 34:7, and, of course, as mentioned I do not personally believe this about God himself, rather I am underlining the sad reality that so often seems to plague the lives of those who suffer at the hands of others.

3. http://www.clanmacfarlane.com.ar/index4.php?IDM=13&IDSM=20&IDN=3

4. *"Que hizo Daisy hasta el 5 de diciembre de 1917 y donde falleció sigue siendo un misterio para nosotros."*

Jorge MacFarlane, email, November 5, 2007

5. *"Yo estaba muy sentido emocionalmente y terminé de caerme cuando supimos que había fallecido por caquexia psicopática que, en buen romance, significa que se dejó morir de inanicion (mi padre me decía que había muerto de tristeza)."*

Jorge MacFarlane, email, January 7, 2008

6. "Buenos Aires, Oct. 17, 10 y 26 a.m.

a Jorge Armstrong;

Telegramas de esta mañana anuncian el fallecimiento de mi querido amigo

MacFarlane, mi buen compañero de tareas y sport. ¡Pobre Mac! ¡Cuántas veces hacíamos comentarios sobre la posibilidad de un atropello al Banco y la manera como mejor podría hacerse la defensa! ¡Bien sabía yo que mi contador haría siempre frente a cualquier atentado! Ruégote que, en el acto de la inhuminación de sus restos, hagas presente mi gran pesar y mi imposibilidad de ir allí por motivos de la huelga. No olvides agregar mi nombre a la corona u otro recuerdo! - Bourse.

"El Asalto al Banco...Telegramas de pésame," *Tribuna Salteña*, October 19, op. cit., p. 4, col. 1

7. Luisa Marie Gutierrez, August 2005, op. cit.

ABOUT THE AUTHOR

Richard Young was raised in Washington State, the second of nine kids in the family of a poor Minister - in today's world having nine kids just about guarantees relative poverty. With his younger brother, Dave, Richard hunted and fished on the east side of the Cascade Range, mostly with the purpose of putting rabbit, venison, trout and pheasant on the table.

Richard followed his Dad into the ministry, studied in Canada and Texas, and in Dallas married his wife, now of 47 years, Beverly Tolson. In 1971 they went to India as missionaries. Their three children were born in India and Nepal, and then raised in Argentina, South America. The last 22 years Richard and Beverly have lived in Uruguay. Richard pastored congregations in these countries and taught Church History at two Seminaries.

Richard's love for history and for Old West stories came honestly. Back during the Great Depression his maternal

Grandfather had a successful gold-mining operation on the big bend of the Columbia River in Washington State, and he packed a Colt.

A wide interest in just about any kind of history led Richard to delve into the most famous attempted bank heist in Uruguay's history. For the past 10 years this investigation has been his pastime, and trips to the north of Uruguay, interviews with persons whose families were affected by the tragedy, as well as studies in literary sources have finally been put together in Richard's new book, "The Last of the Apaches."

http://apacheuruguayo.wix.com/apaches-down-south

Made in the USA
Columbia, SC
17 June 2023

17911746R00184